Rethinking the Relation between Women and Psychoanalysis

Psychoanalytic Studies: Clinical, Social, and Cultural Contexts

Series Editor:

Michael O'Loughlin, Adelphi University

Psychoanalytic Studies seeks psychoanalytically informed works addressing the implications of the location of the individual in clinical, social, cultural, historical, and ideological contexts. Innovative theoretical and clinical works within psychoanalytic theory and in fields such as anthropology, education, and history are welcome. Projects addressing conflict, migrations, difference, ideology, subjectivity, memory, psychiatric suffering, physical and symbolic violence, power, and the future of psychoanalysis itself are welcome, as are works illustrating critical and activist applications of clinical work.

See https://rowman.com/Action/SERIES/LEX/LEXPS for a list of advisory board members.

Recent titles in the series:

Rethinking the Relation between Women and Psychoanalysis: Loss, Mourning, and the Feminine, edited by Hada Soria Escalante

Lives Interrupted: Psychiatric Narratives of Struggle and Resilience, edited by Michael O'Loughlin, Secil Arac-Orhun, and Montana Queler

Women and the Psychosocial Construction of Madness, edited by Marie Brown and Marilyn Charles

Revisioning War Trauma in Cinema: Uncoming Communities, by Jessica Datema and Manya Steinkoler

Women & Psychosis: Multidisciplinary Perspectives, edited by Marie Brown and Marilyn Charles

Psychoanalysis from the Indian Terroir: Emerging Themes in Culture, Family, and Childhood in India, edited by Manasi Kumar, Anup Dhar, and Anurag Mishra

A Three-Factor Model of Couples Psychotherapy: Projective Identification, Level of Couple Object Relations, And Omnipotent Control, by Robert Mendelsohn

Rethinking the Relation between Women and Psychoanalysis

Loss, Mourning, and the Feminine

Edited by Hada Soria Escalante

LEXINGTON BOOKS
Lanham • Boulder • New York • London

Published by Lexington Books
An imprint of The Rowman & Littlefield Publishing Group, Inc.
4501 Forbes Boulevard, Suite 200, Lanham, Maryland 20706
www.rowman.com

6 Tinworth Street, London SE11 5AL

British Library Cataloguing in Publication Information Available

Library of Congress Cataloging-in-Publication Data

ISBN: 978-1-7936-0579-5 (cloth)
ISBN: 978-1-7936-0581-8 (pbk)
ISBN: 978-1-7936-0580-1 (electronic)

Contents

Acknowledgments

First of all, I would like to thank the authors of the book. Some friends and fellow professors, all united by psychoanalysis, in spite of geographical distances. Drs. Mario Orozco, Marilyn Charles, Shalini Masih, Paola González, Angélica Toro, Carolina Koretzky, and David Hafner. Your contributions have brought variety and innovation to the subject of loss and the feminine. Under all your singular perspectives, we have created a community interested in a contemporary psychoanalysis, one that questions the subject in context.

I would like to thank University of Monterrey, particularly Dr. Alejando Moreno Martínez, Dean of the School of Psychology, who, as director, but also as a psychoanalyst and professor, showed interest in the main topic of the book. I also thank Dr. Eduardo García Luna, Health Sciences Vice Chancellor, who, along with Dr. Moreno, supported this ambitious project until it became a tangible reality.

A special thanks to the team constituted by Karla Gómez, Juan Jaime de la Fuente, and Luis Carlos Ramos for the editing work, and the detailed revision of translations from Spanish to English. Thanks to Miriam Castellanos and Claudia Quintero for their revision of style and formatting.

I would like to thank Lexington Books and the Rowman & Littlefield Publishing Group, especially to Michael O'Loughlin, Kasey Beduhn, and Alison Keefner for their time and interest in this book. Their precise and pertinent comments contributed significantly to the development of the final manuscript.

Finally, I would like to thank personally to all who have contributed by nourishing my interest and liking for the research in and from psychoanalysis. It is from this genuine joy that the book proposal emerged.

Introduction

The Debt of Psychoanalysis to Women

Hada Soria Escalante

Rethinking the Relation between Women and Psychoanalysis: Loss, Mourning, and the Feminine is a book assembled of psychoanalytic research. It is an effort of eight authors to account the complexity of the loss in its relationship with femininity in the contemporary era. Psychoanalysis, in its dialogue with the sociocultural context, will be the conductive line set in each of the chapters. From this perspective, there is no possible contemporary psychoanalysis without appealing to the context, just as there is no possible social context, without questioning the singularity of desire. This is the psychosocial perspective of the conjuncture proposed throughout the book.

We do not speak of a mourning "of women," nor of a loss by feminine definition, because that would make us fall into one of the many barren efforts to capture that which could not be grasped of the woman, some of them suggested by psychoanalysis itself. Instead, we raise the question about the position of women in the face of their losses currently and today in different contexts.[1] Women are defined from themselves, from their desire, declaration/declaring of announcement from the lack and loss. To speak of loss is then to speak of desire, to think of women beyond the terms inaugurated by the original castration outlined by Freud. Therefore, psychoanalysis has a debt with women, particularly with the recognition of a function of the women's desire once it has been released and sometimes even liberated from the phallic norm. Apart from the many discussions and attempts to conceptualize, apprehend the woman and the feminine, and make it into a category, in this book we seek a different position, one that goes beyond any possible capture, it does not intend to respond to this impossible task that has been dealt with beforehand. We appeal to the subjective positions of women in the presence of their own desire and the desire of others, the opening of desire takes place from the encounter with loss.

The text is constituted in this way as an invitation to interrogate about the loss and what the female subject does in function of it. This suggestion arises in the Laboratory of Psychoanalytic Theory and Clinical Studies of the Subject and the Culture, of the School of Psychology of the University of Monterrey (Mexico), as an opening to the research line of Hada Soria Escalante, about loss and sociocultural contexts. That is why we called upon a wide diversity of voices in the field of psychoanalysis. Those who responded: Marilyn Charles (Austen Riggs Center), Shalini Masih (Universtiy of Delhi), Carolina Koretzky (University of Paris VIII), Angélica Toro (University of Rennes II), Mario Orozco (Universidad Michoacana de San Nicolás de Hidalgo), as well as Paola González and David Hafner (University of Monterrey); all speaking from the ethics of psychoanalysis that unites us, as a clinical and investigative practice.

From the singularity of each author's vision and understanding, fundamental themes are broadly presented, which invite to a rethinking regarding women and loss from a contemporary psychoanalytic point of view that does not seek to disavow its past. This supposes, on first instance, an appeal toward the particularity of each theoretical perspective presented in each of this book's eight chapters. As a whole, these chapters attempt to point toward a precise issue, which constitutes a debt owed to women by psychoanalysis: to restitute their right place as desiring subjects, not as objects of desire or subjects of the other's desire (as subjects inhabited by the other's desire). To question this, we recur to the subjective positions that are generated by lack, the loss which puts into question the nucleus of desire, as well as subjectivity itself.

In this way, the journey through this chapters highlights a freedom of writing that manages to hold a common thread, which takes us from one elaboration toward the other, just as the sliding of signifiers in the subject of language. Each chapter goes from a position on women and loss to derive associatively toward another, establishing connections between chapters, as well as tensions and resolutions. This work is supported by the pillars of psychoanalytic ethics, and through them it speaks about various ways in which women position themselves in relation to their losses, going beyond a mere reprint of the Freudian reading that postulates an original/originary lack.

In chapter 1, Hada Soria Escalante inquiries into the intolerable revelation of many women's place in the world, on the basis of an unbearable loss, that of the father, specifically the father's love that drags away the narcissistic remains of a grief begun but unfinished. The death of the father reveals the dual woman-daughter position subjected to the designs of interior voices in stalemate with the external demands of what it means to be a woman. The mourning undertaken for the loss of a beloved entails a fundamental questioning on the female subjects' worldly place, such that its interruption discloses the unacceptable eruption of the Other's desire in opposition with one's own. As this non-mourning, or the interruption of mourning, implies an unconscious evaluation of the beloved, a woman faced with loss may choose to detach from her ideal self. The father's death and accompanying loss of mourning illustrate an authentic occurrence.

In chapter 2, Marilyn Charles questions how women can get caught at the crossroads of very different cultural expectations; to be subservient to the needs and desires of men versus the more difficult challenge of discovering and fulfilling her own. The latter is complicated by cultural messages that make the latter course dangerous. In spite of changing ideas about women's sexuality, cultural pressures still invite a sense of guilt that can make it difficult to find one's own desire, which also makes it more difficult to say no to the desire of the other. Those oppressive injunctions can be seen as one means for managing the power of the maternal imago. By using illustrations from film and from literature, the author explores ways in which the enigmatic message of maternal abjection has invited women to subjugate themselves in relation to grieving processes that too easily become perverse rather than transformative.

In chapter 3, Shalini Masih inquires, through the life story of a young married woman observed over a long period of time, how seemingly ordinary difficulties for her, in Indian context, slowly begin to give way to the "extra" in this "ordinariness," thus sharpening her image as helplessly "possessed" by a dark devilish force from within. Sometimes this internal demon appears stronger, sucking from her peculiar familial matrix, uncannily invoking the grotesque images from strangely familiar labyrinths of past. While tossing and turning in her nightmarish life characters like the mother, father, mother-in-law, creative work and muse at times appear misty like ghosts, and at other times they seem relatively well bounded. In surreptitious affair with an internal devil, she struggles to live creatively. The author is positioned here as a researcher, a listener, merely receiving the narrative of a struggling life and witnessing how peculiar psychosocial matrix shapes an inner life, how shadows of this inner life fall in the space of a coupledom where these shadows, once cast beg to be rescued through some transformation.

In chapter 4, Angélica Toro addresses the question of the feminine and loss from testimonies of women involved in the armed conflict in Colombia. The author studies the theme of mourning and loss from two contemporary feminine figures that belong to a period following the signing of the peace treaty with the FARC, denominated as "post-agreement": the old combatants and the victims. Obliged for years to put aside their lives as women, wives, mothers—considered incompatible with the life of the guerrillas—the signing of the agreement confronted us with the appearance of these "femininities in suspense," which implied for many of them the dimension of a renunciation, even of a loss.

In chapter 5, Paola González interrogates how something of the feminine is lost with a child's birth, so that a mother may also be born. The sociocultural conditions in which the puerperal moment is inscribed provide support during this moment of subjective mutation. Although these symbolic underpinnings cannot completely insulate from the vicissitudes of the postpartum, they at least constitute pillars protecting women during this redefinition. Prior to the various waves of feminism, popular culture often equates femininity with maternity, as though the reproductive capacity possessed by female subjects were a clear, univocal path toward self-fulfillment; such thought supposes that the nature of the feminine culminates in motherhood. One speaks of maternal instinct, the mother archetype, of Mother Nature, with the primary function of veiling our eyes from the calamitous possibilities of the reclamation of the newborn in perverse or infanticidal versions. Psychoanalysis has broken with this ideal and demonstrated that wherever language reigns, natural instinct alone doesn't suffice to sustain the function of the mother in interpersonal relations.

In chapter 6, Mario Orozco addresses the configuration and scope of violence of the passion of jealousy in three moments, involving the narcissistic dimension of loss and its double constituents of pain and grief. The author explores three surges of jealous rage in the figures of Oedipal death vows, the projection of desire-responsibility, and a demolishing certainty. During a second moment, he focuses on amorous preference from the viewpoint of the Other's discourse, overflowing with myths and dreams, as an inciting factor in jealousy. Thirdly, the author opens the way for the insertion of jealous certainty dependent on the function of the ardent jealousy of fidelity. The quintessential case of the alleged serial killer, Vera Renczi, illustrates the entwined knot of a devouring, jealous love and a zeal for an ideal which dredges up a pleasure beyond the phallic coupling.

In chapter 7, Carolina Kotezky takes as a starting point a dream analyzed by Freud: "the dream of the dead father." The place of the father loses value in the structuration and normalization of desire, thus opening a path toward a conceptualization of desire that goes beyond the father. This reading allows readers to orient in the analytic endeavor with a subject that has traversed through a mourning process. The author shows how, in the course of Lacan's teaching, he shows that the analytic work in regards to mourning allows us to go from a type of love that was sustained by the narcissistic image toward an object that he defined with the term of "a," designating with this a function: being the cause of desire. The theory of mourning is strictly linked to advances and conceptualizations about the object in Lacan's teachings: the pain of losing a loved one, passing through that which the subject lost as a result of the other's disappearance, until reaching the question of which object have

I been to the other that I lost. This last finding orients the analytic cure in search of distinction between the narcissistic image and the object-cause of the other. The emergence of this irreducible remainder appears as the condition and the necessary way to elaborate mourning and to reactivate desire.

In chapter 8, David Hafner addresses how dreams are fragmented and fragmenting; we find in them the most blatant paradoxes, where impossible is nothing. Resisting realist knowledge in favor of elaborating our truer motivations, they reveal us as moral relativists, showing the idiosyncratic fundamentalism grounding our ethics. Freudian psychoanalysis rests on a few fundamental discoveries. Dreams include but are not limited to the notion that life is fundamentally suffering, and many humans choose partial blindness over conflictual truth, that the human condition involves unresolvable otherness, that though language distorts thought it rarely if ever depicts with precision a given qualia (a dreaming experience), and that the endless variety of symptoms found in the psychoanalysis are singular responses to underlying painful conditions of humanity. Though we typically understand dreams as unconscious formations, toward the end of analysis we come across another style of dream. Simply put, dreams at the end of analysis are not encrypted formations of the unconscious to be recounted in stream of consciousness; they are the paradoxical statements of how partial objects relate. As they become denser and more compact they reduce down to the grammar of unconscious fantasy. One dreamer sees a piece of meat in a frying pan moving and asks, "but how could it move, c'est cuite?" Or another, whose life was saved by analysis, dreams of walking through the valley of death with vultures circling overhead. Or another, dozing, waiting alone for the next session, sees a woman abruptly swoop down in front, grabbing his throat with her hand while commanding, "come." These dreams are not dreams for interpretation, they are transparent. They are without the anxiety of the refusal of subjective division.

The ensemble of these eight chapters, in accordance with the ethics of psychoanalysis, seeks to give voice to desire from the losses of women, painful and amorous losses, in the course of their lives. The reader will find the theoretical rigor expected from the chapters derived from research, but at the same time these chapters contain the possibility of being read and consulted by professionals outside of the psychoanalytic field. The themes intertwine with the purpose of not rushing into conclusions, but rather invite exploration of the contemporary conditions of mourning. This book speaks through multiple voices and seeks to restore the women's voice in facing their losses, it presents itself as unique in its type, seeking to reconcile psychoanalysis with the voice of women. The pain of mourning is also the pain of openness and creation, of (re)positioning oneself toward one's own desire, we attempt to show this theme throughout the whole text, showing women in movement, women dancing around the void.

NOTE

1. Some of the chapters include interviews or discourse from patients or research participants. All these chapters have changed or removed identifying factors from the people interviewed. Also, names and other private information have been modified to ensure confidentiality.

Chapter One

On Mourning's End

Sacrificial Feminine Positions and Their Intolerable Revelation Before the Death of the Father

Hada Soria Escalante

We pose the question about the intolerable revelation of women's place in the world, from the starting point of a loss that is also intolerable: that of the father. More precisely, that of a father's love which drags with his death the narcissistic remains recovered after mourning began; but through its abrupt ending, remained nothing more than an interruption. The opening that a father's passing brings unveils the subjective role of *women-daughters* who are subject to the intentions of internalized voices that quarrel with the external voices that dictate what being-woman involves. Mourning after the death of a loved one involves a fundamental questioning about the position of the female subject in the world; thereafter, the interruption or ending of mourning reveals itself as a subjective repositioning, summoned by the intolerable emergence of the Other's desire, in opposition with one's own desire. The absence of mourning, or its ending, would imply an unconscious assessment of the loved object; therefore, to detach the object from its being-idealized is also what the woman is summoned to do upon facing the loss. The father's death and the switch from mourning to the absence thereof is the authentic event in which sacrificing the father as object is necessary for salvaging the ego. One must die for the other one to live.

These "mournings," ended upon facing the intolerable truths revealed through the analytic dialogue, portray different forms of grief that many women experience upon the loss of their father, thus putting in evidence not only the singularity of an impossible and idealized relationship, but also the position of women in a world determined by the Father, by their fathers, by men. We could also state that while reviewing loss and mourning from an analytical framework, we also review something else, something that transcends the clinical field. Thus, we move from the clinical to the macrosocial context, from the singularity of women to questioning the feminine position. From the father to the patriarchal heritage and the still very palpable submission of the feminine desire to the desire of the other-men.

ON DEATH AND WHAT REMAINS

Psychoanalysis has tackled the issue of mourning from different sides. From a Freudian perspective, it bears the enigmatic character described by him: its ubiquity, malleability, and closeness to other affections that tend to go hand in hand with the topic of loss. While Freud highlights the issue of the closeness and, at the same time, distance that mourning has with melancholia, as well as the problem of the supposedly replaceable object, and the ambivalent features that make mourning pathological, Lacan addresses the issue from the starting point of the lost, blurry, and dazed desire. At the same time, he retrieves the basic issue of the lost object; the state of the object as the pivotal element in the dialectics of mourning and the traumatic nature of the abrupt disappearance of the other.

Freud (1917) depicts the classic manifestations of mourning: a painful uneasiness, the loss of the ability to love, the inhibition of psychic capabilities, and the perception of the world as a shallow and empty place. The subject, in the most painful and heartrending way possible, acknowledges his or her desire, placed upon another being who has left, sometimes in an abrupt and real manner. This traumatic rupture of the being is revealed through its typical manifestations. More than anything else, the subject experiences grief, which—aided by the function of language and the socialization of the loss—turns into something else, something different. It is a "bonding" pain (Nasio, 1996) that, although many times reveals itself as authentically physical, also has sadness as its core and distinctive (although not exclusive) feature. Sadness as "a sign of a primitive ego that is hurt, uncomplete, empty"[1] (Kristeva, 1987, p. 21). A narcissistic wound is revealed through the grief of the mourner. It is the ego wounded in its narcissism, in its position in life, which stumbles, oscillates, and becomes ambivalent.

Kristeva (1987) relates the issue of sadness, a characteristic of loss, with trauma: "Irreducible to its verbal or semiotic expressions, sadness (as all affects) is a psychic representation of the energetic shifts provoked by some internal or external trauma"[2] (p. 31). Indeed, the suffering subject who grieves over the abrupt absence of a loved one seems to show, both through symptoms and through words, the trauma of loss. Therefore, it is not surprising that death or the definitive departure of a loved one involves a traumatic shock. What is surprising is the seal of sadness as telltale of the traumatic that has been displaced, especially from the perspective of libidinal economy. We can state that the progression from pain to sadness also entails a progression from the trauma to the dialectics of loss. From the real to its translation into the symbolic world. From grief to suffering.

The death the other, the permanent loss, necessarily entails a narcissistic affront that is exceptionally dangerous, since it reveals a fundamental aspect of oneself. Mourning comes after loss, but paradoxically, the end of mourning involves another loss. Mourning involves a sacrifice, as it was described by Allouch (1998), who locates the function of the phallus in the core of the dreadful suffering that comes with mourning. According to Allouch, mourning involves supplementing the loss with a piece of oneself. An overwhelming statement, since a piece of "oneself" lacks any subject of enunciation, turning imprecise the dialectical order it supposes. There is no subject to claim this "piece"; it is neither yours nor mine. No one claims something that refers to "oneself," since it seems to belong to another person or people, who remain undetermined. A "piece of oneself" remains in a space that is also undetermined, that is property of both and none. Something is lost, there is no doubt about it. But what is lost belonged to both; it existed as long as an "us" existed, and, now, with one gone, this piece also disappears, and the only thing that remains is an undeniable feeling of having been robbed, since the object has taken something of oneself. There is a theft, according to Allouch (1998). But nobody knows who the real thief is, since death, as psychoanalytic work has evidenced in every critical moment, is not a matter of two. Therefore, something becomes lost along with the object, and that is the sacrifice. One loss brings about another loss.

Naturally, this makes us think about a succession of losses throughout life. We could think of a primary element that was lost and was continuously supplemented by another piece, assigned to the object that is now also lost. In a certain way, we are all a combination of losses and replacements that alternate throughout life. After all, considering the ego as a set of identifications, these entail preceding losses. Like the child who, having gone through the Oedipus, has identified with his objects of love and hate, insofar as they have been constituted into something else. From this perspective, Allouch's statement on thinking about the clinical work as mourning acquires meaning, since both consist of replacing what has been lost with words. To recover the object through language, jokes, dreams, and writing. To recapture it somehow.

Therefore, mourning does not end with the problematic concept of "letting go," since, as Freud warned, we do not let go the objects-guardians of our desires. Mourning ends by acquiring a new stance toward the world. It ends, to a great extent, once the subject delivers to the object that left the unique component of oneself which used to be shared among the two.

> Signs are arbitrary because language begins through a denial of loss, at the same time as depression caused by mourning. I lost an indispensable object that is, ultimately, my mother, seems to be what the speaking being utters. But no, I found it in the signs, or, more likely, since I accept that I lost her, I did not lose her, I can recover her through language. (Kristeva, 1987, p. 55)[3]

If there is at least a minimal part of oneself that dies together with the deceased (and, thus, there is a narcissistic affront), then we must agree with the statement that death calls upon death. Mourning is not only about losing someone (a hole in the real) but also about summoning, in that place, a phallic being, in order to sacrifice it. There's mourning if, and only if, that sacrifice has been effective. The subject will then have lost, not only someone, but, also, as a supplement, a tiny piece of oneself (Allouch, 1998). Thus, the death of oneself implies a mourning in which the person seems to reabsorb himself in that piece of oneself, to become realized as piece of oneself; he prefers becoming it rather than losing it, in the sense of being deprived of it. At a clinical level, it is not unusual to hear those who wish they would have died with the other in order to avoid the grief that seems to be unbearable.

In strict sense, there is a kind of death with the other's departure. When there is a loss, a part of oneself dies, bringing grief and sadness as a result. The subject, in mourning, can never be the same again. Therefore, there is not a single mourning process; there is no set of rules or norms. There are no fixed stages to it, although the deceiving nature of psychiatric and psychological jargon tries to prove us otherwise, as well as psychoanalysis itself.

Allouch (1998) recalls that Freud offers us, as an addition, the well-thought benefit of trying to incite us to problematize each case as mourning. To achieve this, it would be better to admit that we do not know what mourning is, nor if there is only one or many. The issue of mourning is therefore a mystery, an X, whose value depends on what each singular case brings.

We still do not know what mourning is! Or how long it lasts, or under which circumstances it occurs. But remitting ourselves to cases is a good way of shedding some light on the issue. Lacan (2009) refers to mourning as a function, not as a work or even as a process. Mourning is, above everything, a function. Considering it from this perspective, the function of mourning is related to turning a real loss into a symbolic one. The issue with mourning is the issue of the object, and this is clearly stated. Therefore, to talk about an object that is gone, it is first necessary to admit that an object was once here. The death of the other, of a loved one, is a loss, in its most real conception possible.

For Lacan (2014),

> "the hole in the real provoked by loss, by a true loss, that sort of intolerable loss for a human being that brings about mourning, that hole in the real founds itself, by that same function, in a relationship that is the complete opposite of the one I introduced to you by the name of Verwerfung. In the same sense in which what is rejected from the symbolic reappears in the real, the hole left by loss in the real of something that is, properly speaking, the intolerable dimension offered to human experience (which is, not the experience of one's own death, which no one experiences, but the death of the other, which is for us an essential being); that is a hole in the real, it finds itself in the real, and it in fact finds itself, and with the same correspondence which I articulate in the *Verwerfung*, which offers the place where the missing signifier is projected, that essential signifier to the Other's structure, that signifier whose absence turns the other incapable of giving you answers, that signifier for which you can't pay but with your flesh and blood, that signifier is, essentially, the phallus under the veil" (p. 371).

This passage from the real of loss to the symbolic is once again articulated in the notion of sacrifice of oneself expressed by Allouch (1998.) If what is sacrificed is, indeed, as was stated, the phallus, Allouch positions mourning as an *erotic experience*. Sacrificing the phallus as the end of mourning. Therefore, we face a position of castration. The end of mourning would be, as in that first great Oedipal loss, to assume oneself as castrated, to relinquish one's narcissism, to reassume the violent shake of libidinal energy. Turning the traumatic into something else.

Still, a fundamental question remains unaddressed by Freud: what happens to the deceased? The object is not simply erased from the psyche, like it is from the world, but also changes its constitution, necessarily. Following the perspective of physics, something that once existed cannot simply disappear: it can only change its quality and spatiality. Maybe that is what Freud meant when he stated that in mourning, there is a detachment "ideal by ideal." The object leaves my exteriority: that is an undeniable reality. But a part of it stays preserved inside the mourner, via identification, but—possibly—also due to other psychic operations.

As far as psychoanalysis is concerned, the object's existence does not depend on a not-psychic reality, insofar as, while it is an object of desire, it is of little importance if the object is physically present or not. If it is an object of desire, it is there, it exists for me, in an absolute way. Thus, it is an object without correspondence (Allouch, 1998). The subject that is going through mourning can pour over this object all kinds of things; symbolic things (signifiers), but also imaginary things (ideals) and a mixture of both, scenic fantasies of what could or could not have happened if the death had not occurred. Therefore, mourning displays the three registers: the symbolic, the real, and the imaginary. The three work in full capacity, since the psychic integrity of the subject is at risk.

Thus, the object stays alive, but in a different way. The legacy of the deceased is the living testimony of his presence. "While the body rots, the other body, incorruptible, immortal, will continue living, separated from it" (Morin, 2011, p. 145). It is not forgotten, it is not fully replaced; it is not erased from space, time, or the psyche. It is impossible to forget everything and erase its trace. Therefore, it is not a *mort seche*[4] (Allouch, 1998), nor a way of thinking the lacanian precept of second death. Perhaps it is after the second death that the object could be effectively considered dead; in this scenario, no mourning would be possible. This is somehow illustrated in the two clinical vignettes presented. The fact that a remnant of the deceased still remains is not necessarily pleasant for the surviving subject. This posits the starting point of the basic issue that we are trying to demonstrate, that the remains of the deceased make the subject question the relationship he thought he had with the object, or the idealized version of this relationship, and many other elements that are also put into play in mourning. Allouch (1998) recalls, due to metonymic contiguity, the objects of the deceased, starting with his body and his grave, are also the deceased, or more precisely, they are his second life, and death is then considered a progression from a mobile state to an immobile state. To give life to those signs means to keep the deceased's a second life.

In an inverse movement, the signs that somehow keep the deceased alive also acquire other nuances. In some cases, they can be tempestuous. The deceased can also become a ghostly and terrifying persecutor, rendering impossible the advent of the new or the different, as is revealed through a fear of ghosts and specters, which has existed in all cultures and throughout history. From a position of "not letting go" the other, to a position of "(he) does not let me go." This is why, for Allouch (1998), the deceased takes the character of the disappeared, since, as he stated, to acknowledge the inexistence of another world does not drag us to believe, ipso facto, that the deceased are nowhere to be found (p. 353). In that case, where are the deceased? Maybe they are not as far away as the word "death" may lead us to believe. After all, they are buried, cremated, or far away, but they are still here, in this world. There is no other world. And, if there is another world, I know that they are not there, because I buried them in this one. To a great extent, they are still here. Allouch's formula to solve this issue is claiming that the deceased for which the subject is in mourning belongs to a world that does not exist, as neither does the living world, since it depends on the same intrinsic reality. The imaginary movements summoned by the disappearance of the other show this idealized construction of what could be or could have been.

Even if the deceased is not dead, and we consider him disappeared, the danger resides in their possible return, as evidenced in many typical grief expressions throughout mourning. We know that there is no "nonexistence"; the characteristics of the unconscious, revealed by Freud, showcase this. Therefore, mourning, far from being based on reality, reveals the falling apart of reality, by awarding the deceased with the status, not of nonexistence, but of disappeared (Allouch, 1998). This leads Freud (1913) to think of the permanence of the deceased in life, as someone who stays with the living during a period of time immediately after the death. This period of time could overlap with the period that is generally known as mourning. In that case, mourning would be a situation of distancing ourselves from the deceased, to protect the living. This way of thinking is similar to the rituals of absolute disappearance of the body of the deceased that were portrayed in Homeric poems (Rohde, 2006).

Addressing mourning within these characteristics and possibilities leads us to the topic of melancholia in Freud, who stated the shadow of the object falls upon the ego; the identification with the deceased as a trait of calling upon death. But for Allouch (1998), and this is of utmost importance, during mourning, there is also an identifying function, as was already mentioned. In cases of mourning, we might consider this identification, not as a way of not letting go of the object through an absolute incorporation that leads the subject to death, but possibly as a way of acknowledging that between the subject and the deceased there was an undeniable shared bond that cannot be abandoned.

Features of the other, whether they are acknowledged as such or not as being part of me, and which in some way are already part of me, but suddenly they become obvious, evident, sometimes even shameless and transparent, like the subject that starts using expressions that were typical of the deceased, or starts liking what the deceased used to enjoy. It might also be a way of honoring the memory of the person who is gone. It is a different way of admitting that it is impossible to fully erase someone. Not even death can achieve that.

OPHELIA MUST DIE FOR HAMLET TO LIVE

Lacan (2014) states decidedly that at the core of the theme of mourning, there is desire and the object. Freud does not explicitly address the question about the destiny of the lost object (as if it just faded away) or what happens to the missing object. However, he sheds some light upon a change of quality that the object undergoes, therefore, it somehow abandons its privileged state, *piece by piece, ideal by ideal.*

Ophelia must die for Hamlet to live. She must die so that he, through mourning, can rediscover his desire in her. This is a particularly important issue. From this starting point, death is shown as the limit for everything, and likewise, as the path for something different. Death gives mourning its quality as an event that violently shocks the psyche, and forces the subject to never be the same.

Hamlet, "the tragedy of desire," as Lacan (2014) calls it, shows this very clearly. From the moment Ophelia dies, nothing can ever be the same for Hamlet. It is necessary that he reconstructs his subjective world, his intolerable psychic reality, especially the intolerable position he discovers he holds in the world after Ophelia's definitive disappearance. Therefore, it is not only about the sudden change that subjects experience after the death of the other, but also about what these deaths reveal about and to themselves. These revelations most of the time can be so intolerable that they can halt the mourning process, as will be shown in the clinical cases presented.

What we see in Hamlet becomes relevant since the encounter that Hamlet has with the calling to Ophelia, once dead. The scene of Ophelia's burial reveals itself as a sudden, unexpected and overwhelming event that necessarily entails a shock in Hamlet. In an act of identifying himself with Laertes, manifested through his jealousy for his pain upon Ophelia's death, Hamlet finds himself, suddenly, in a very profound grief.

We stated that Ophelia had to die for Hamlet to recover his lost desire. Hamlet, without desire, subjectively dead, could only live by abruptly finding it. Once again, we encounter the paradox of mourning: a loss, a death, aids in rescuing the missing desire.

It should be borne in mind that Hamlet did not consider Ophelia a suitable object of his desire until her death. This could not have happened in any other way. It is a sacrifice that she grants him. While she was alive, Hamlet was dying in his desire. Once she is dead, Hamlet comes back to life. The multiple paradoxes that arise from mourning keep appearing in different shapes and with different nuances. And this paradox shows that only one of both desires can survive. Two incompatible desires. Nonetheless, these two desires imply life or death.

Allouch (1998) also makes evident that death is necessary to summon the other's life, the retrieval of the survivor's desire. It is about considering the real death of the object to be able to reconnect with desire: this does not necessarily imply that such an access to the impossible object cannot occur but in the real death of the object, this implies that there are certain cases in which only the real death allows such access. Undoubtedly, this involves a major sacrifice, since it demands the death of the other. If Ophelia must die to mobilize Hamlet's desire, this also implies directing said desire toward her, now absent. This is a new paradox of the incomprehensible mourning: she is only desired as dead.

In this way, we find another perspective: that of a woman who sacrifices herself to give life to another. This is the perspective of Ophelia's sacrifice. Taking it one step further, Ophelia has died because of her intolerable place in the world! Ophelia has died because of the pain that Hamlet's contempt and indifference caused. She has died because she is aware that she means nothing to him. She dies because of love, because of the absence of love by the other who was everything to her. This loving sacrifice of Ophelia in favor of the other's desire is revisited in the analytic setting, in cases of women who also carry out the same sacrifice of love as her. Cases of subjective deaths, of the revelation of the intolerable subjective position of women that is only possible after the death of the other. A loving sacrifice carried out by the woman for the salvation of the other, which may be intolerable in its revelation, ambivalent in relation to the object or may absorb their own desire. The issue of loss in a woman is linked to the annihilation of desire, to the establishment of a subjective position in the world that is related to men's desire. The death of one man will not only be a loss in terms of love but also a revelation of the intolerable position of sacrifice that women hold. This is shown in two clinical vignettes, which show the two incompatible wishes, the sacrifice of one's desire for the desire of the other, and the death of the other as the only way of reconnecting with one's own desire. Ophelia as the paradigm of women's sacrificial love.

How is it that women assume a position of sacrifice for the benefit of men? How far back can we trace this? We trace this by questioning the subjective position of women toward the fathers' desire. Also, considering the father, from the perspective of his desire, as the one who shapes the feminine psyche, which determines how women think about themselves, for they have constituted from there, not knowing another way of being or living in the world. Therefore, these intolerable revelations only occur when the absolute father, who established everything, dies. In this way, we change the statement from *Ophelia must die for Hamlet to live* to *the father must die for the daughter to live*. Or rather, the desire of women has to come to light in a subjective world that was created by the father.

From a classical psychoanalytical perspective, the topic of loss for women is studied considering the issue of the anatomical differences between the sexes and the creation of the signifier of the phallus to show the imparity and impossibility of sexual relationship. Nonetheless, and disregarding the positions that may lead to the cyclical nature of the issue of loss in women from a theoretical psychoanalytical perspective, which has already been revisited many times before, it is undeniable that something else has to be taken into account when facing different contexts and cultures. There is something more for these women who face loss, and it is related and takes part in the unconscious fabric of their lives. The social voice, interiorized, and the demand of suffering that is constantly in the foundation of the loss of the loved object for women.

Many contemporary social and cultural contexts, like those addressed in the clinical vignettes presented here, are based in traditional structures that have stuck through time: it is expected for women to suffer loss in a different way than men. Women themselves expect it to be this way, and thus experience it like this. Ophelia's sacrifice is revisited in distinct ways in the clinical context. However, and not far from Ophelia, a social and subjective structure that favors men is based, to a great extent, on the father's mandate. Fathers dominate the scene of what will become their daughters' destiny and life.

The father as the supreme authority dictate their daughter's preferences, sources of pleasure, and life conditions. Daughters, deprived of an authentically free choice, become unconsciously configured from the starting point of what another man desires in them or from them. The death of the father would involve revisiting the current stage, mobilizing memories and pieces of the relationship with that overwhelming object, and, therefore, also mobilizing one's own subjective position, and rejecting an eternal sacrifice, just like the one Ophelia had with Hamlet.

With the father's death, the relationship with him and what he took with him are called into question. Ambivalence appears constantly as one of the main features. During mourning, and not just in what Freud called "pathological mourning," or melancholia, the identification can showcase the ambivalence; not-knowing, or knowing contradictory ways about our love toward the loved object:

> According to classical psychoanalytical theory (Abraham, Freud, Klein), depression, just like mourning, hides an aggressiveness towards the lost object, and reveals the ambivalence of the depressed towards his object of mourning. I love him, but I hate him even more: because I love him, and so as not to lose him, I place him in me; but, since I hate him, this other in me is a bad ego, I am bad, I am invalidated, I kill myself. (Kristeva, 1987, p. 20)[5]

Loss, however, in the case of sacrifice, is also loss of who one was before the sacrifice, loss of desire, and the loss of a possibility of a different condition. This starts with the question of what the other desired in me, what the other person made me lack. The answer to this question can put the object of mourning at risk.

Therefore, it is necessary to point out that during mourning, there is also a sacrifice of the object. Not only because the object must leave, but because to question it means to change the state of the object. If I question he who is gone, I discover who he was in our relationship. The object stops being what it was, and this is what Freud seems to shed light upon when referring to a substitute object. The object itself is not replaced; it just stops being what it was. From the perspective of analysis, when women ask who that father was, they do so from a place where he can't answer. If what you were ideally for me is lost, then I must also lose who I was. It is a double loss, and, probably, a double sacrifice. Just like Kafka addresses a letter to his deceased father, a letter to himself and a letter to nobody. Derrida (2006) states, this letter is neither in literature nor outside literature. In the last pages of this letter, Kafka addresses himself, in a fictitious way, more fictitious than ever, the letter that he believes his father would have wanted, should have, in any case, he would have sent as an answer. "You could answer"; "You could have answered," said the son, and this also sounds like a complaint or an affront that comes as an answer to another one: you will not speak to me, in fact, you have never answered me and never will, you could answer, you could have answered, you should have answered. You have remained in secrecy. You are a secret to me (Derrida, 2006, pp. 147–148).

Just like Kafka, just like Ophelia, the fathers of two women from the clinical vignettes presented here had to die so that they could interrogate them and themselves from these violent deaths. They had to die so that these women could acknowledge their intolerable positions in the world, taking with them a passage of the all-loved object, the doubts about their fathers' love, and ending with the revelation of what has been and can no longer be. Fathers had to die so that their daughters could live. And in that hurtful but hopeful passing is where loss, grief, ambivalence toward the object, and the question about destiny overlap.

"LIBERTAD" AND THE HATRED TOWARD THE FATHER: THE INTOLERABLE REVELATION OF AN UNSPEAKABLE LOVE

Libertad's father has died.[6] After a long sickness that lasted for a year, during which she had to take care of him, he finally died. *It's good that he's finally dead!* She repeats constantly, showing signs of relief and disbelief upon the death of someone who would seemingly never leave. For her, a violent, alcoholic man has died. The man *guilty of everything* that happens to her has died. Now, she is left with her brother, who is in a vegetative state, and a violent mother who works incessantly to pay the debts that her husband left behind. Libertad remembers the constant abuses that her father heaped on her mother and on herself. She also has another brother, whom she refers to as *the drug addict*, and who, she speculates, must now be taking drugs or have been arrested for theft. It doesn't matter what happens to him.

Libertad claims she hates her father above everything, as an attempted second death that does not end with the real disappearance of the other. It is not enough that he died; it would have been better if he suffered even more. He is placed as the one responsible for all the tragedies in Libertad's life. She cannot utter one word that contradicts this manifest hatred. Mourning is not possible, since, according to her, her father's death is not a loss: it could even be considered a gain for her.

She claims that because of this man she has never been free. She was constrained to taking care of her brother forever, and constrained by her father's disease, since she also had to take care of him. Taking care of that man was what she least wanted. Freedom was denied. She could not go anywhere she wanted to, dress the way she wanted, or choose what field of study to pursue, and much more choices were imposed on her by him. But now, suddenly, her father is gone. This long-awaited unleashing also brings about the unleashing of other experiences. Now, she is no longer afraid of getting hurt by him.

She confesses something that she never told anyone before. It is a memory from when she was a child. *Sometimes, I think it was a dream, but no. It actually happened.* The blurred boundaries between dreams and reality, illusion and truth, characteristic of several forms of trauma, laid the foundations for the utterance of words describing a scene. This scene also belongs to the scope what has been rejected by conscience, but that, after her father's death, are bound to return. She suddenly decides that it is a good time to say it, since her father cannot do anything to her now that he is dead.

She remembers that she was lying in bed, crying and afraid. Facing her were her father and her brother, *the drug addict*. They were both laughing, and she was under the impression that they were making fun of her. Something had just happened. More precisely, her father had just sexually abused her, and her brother was a witness and accomplice of the abuse. She claims that it was her father, while her brother did nothing to help her, and, on the contrary, he even served as a look-out so that nobody would notice. She remembers the satisfaction on her father's face. A disgusting, tormenting face that still haunts her. She also remembers her disabled younger brother, who was yelling from a distance, as if he had seen everything. His screams lead her to think that he wanted to help her. His screams expressed rage, helplessness; they asked for help, but help never came. Libertad, while saying this, is suffering, crying and in authentic pain. She clarifies that she does not cry because of her father's death. She claims that she cries because of what he did with her and to her.

Her father had to die so that she could confess the intolerable position she had in the world. But this tormenting father transcends death. As was expressed previously, death is not enough for him to disappear. The return of images, the fear of the bedroom where he died (which was also the bedroom where the sexual abuse took place) held his presence. She countered this by avoiding being home alone, especially in that dark room, which she goes past running and without blinking. As Leader (2011) recalls, all necessary measures must be taken so that the deceased do not come back to take revenge on us.

Sadly, as in many other child sexual abuse cases, there was a clear contradiction. Keeping the other as exclusively hated could not be sustained for too long. As the one responsible for everything that had happened to her, there were also good things that happened to her. For example, she says that the happiest day of her life was her eighth birthday. Her father was there and bought a cake for her. That deeply hated man is also responsible for the happiest day of her life. The confusing ambivalence that is provoked by this object-deceased-father who is both loved and hated was the reason behind a considerable amount of time spent at clinical sessions. We could almost say that what was taking place was properly mourning. She wonders if that man, whom she hated and who hurt her so much, possibly loved her. And she loved him, too.

By acknowledging this, mourning would start, but it would soon be ended when she reconsidered her relationship with her father; asking herself who her father was meant questioning the intolerable nature of the role she had as a subject and as a woman, in a world dictated by the father's mandate: pursuing a "feminine" degree (nursing), which became truncated because she became the eternal nurse of her father and her brother. She could only eat what she was forced to cook, and she could only dress in the way she was allowed to dress. Therefore, the fundamental question of what she likes can be answered from the starting point of what she does not like, what she wants, would have wanted and can now start to articulate. The question about her desire, her singularity, invariably means unleashing herself from her father, a review of what he was for her, but above all, of what she was for him. For Libertad, the end of mourning, her unleashing from mourning, happens when she acknowledges that she has her own desire, separate and distinct from his.

Finally, the transition from the absence of mourning, to mourning, and then to the interruption of mourning takes place from her father's death, to the acknowledgment of what she was for him and, finally, being set free. *Futuromania*, as Barthes (2009) wrote in his diary of mourning. The subjective re-positioning implied in realizing that her place in the world was dictated by what her father chose for her. Her father's desire overwhelmed Libertad's desire. He had to die so that she could start living. She dropped out of nursing school and rediscovered a passion for acting (theater), for playing with characters. She started experimenting with what she wanted to be, and what she could eventually become.

"DANIELA" AND THE LOVE FOR THE FATHER: THE INTOLERABLE REVELATION OF FALLING OUT OF LOVE

Daniela,[7] twenty-two years old, cries over the loss of her father, who died of cancer recently. Sessions revolve around her deep love for him, and how much he loved her as well. Feelings of deep sadness and grief emanate from every word she speaks about him.

Daniela's words show sadness and grief over her father's loss, which is typical of mourning. Moreover, her words always speak about good memories she has of her father. She talks in depth about the day he died and about his burial, with a level of precision and detail that is surprising, showcasing how scrupulous trauma can be on the psyche. She, as a daughter and as a woman who has five older brothers, said that she was her father's "favorite." *Verneinung*, a subjective measure taken upon the loss, can operate at several levels: not only as a protection from the trauma of the death of the other, but also to justify one's position in relation to the other. The elusiveness of denial contributes to sustaining the idealized quality of the object. This man was *good in every way*. He was a good father, a good person who *fought until the end*. He wanted to live, and Daniela remembers his optimism about the future, and how he maintained his optimism until his last day.

As more sessions go by, she starts to question what her father was and what she was to him. This is a necessary and indispensable consequence of mourning: analyzing the object meticulously, thus putting the idealized quality of the object at risk. The circularity of her discourse about the day of her father's death led her to mention his last words: *The last thing he said to me was a scolding. He scolded me for wearing shorts.* This confession was not enough to tear down her idealized image of him, but it helped her realize that he was different from who she thought he was.

Thus, a series of events and memories triggered by the scolding her father did while in his deathbed started to appear, having found a space in which they could be spoken of. These were moments in which her father was not entirely good anymore, but fully flawed, and, above all, moments that showed what being the favorite, the only daughter, protected by her father, really meant. Her father used to work in the countryside, and Daniela's brothers would go there to help him. She always wanted to go with them, but her father never allowed her to. He argued that she was a woman, and that women should not work in the countryside, but should stick to doing the house chores. She dedicated herself to house chores, and would, along with her mother, look after her brothers and her father, helping them in everything they needed. Her father did not want her to pursue a university degree. He wanted her to be a decent woman who would find a good husband. Therefore, after she finished high school, she did not go to college, although she wanted to pursue a degree in psychology. She could begin to speak about her father's scolding toward her as constant: like the last one because of her shorts, many times, it had to do with her "indecent" way of dressing, her habit of going out and attending parties, and her lack of poise as "a lady." Her mother intervened so that Daniela could finally be allowed to study. She was amid admittance proceedings when her father passed away. He was never interested in knowing anything about it. Being the favorite meant that she had to do everything he wanted her to. And, for many years, she did. Now, after his death, Daniela is liberated and has two new issues. First, the question about what to do with her life now that she has nobody telling her what to do. And, second, the intolerable revelation of her position as a sacrificing woman who sacrifices her desire for the service of the other.

In one dream, in which there is a monster mask that disturbs and upsets her very much, she confesses what she had not said until then: that he is not what she thought he was and what she kept holding on to for so long. The memory of him in his coffin, before being buried, suddenly arises. They had put makeup on him, and he looked different. *That was not my father*. From absolute love, to ambivalence, to admitting that she did not love him as much as she thought. For a long time, she also hated him. He made her go through very difficult times, and now, she was someone very different from who she wanted to be. So, uttering "stop it, no more!" mourning is interrupted. He was no longer the same object she mourned. Now, it was necessary to change her position. This process is also about giving up the image of who we were for the others. Ending mourning implies renouncing to that image. As Leader (2011) said, mourning is often indicated by dreams, which, unlike others, do not require interpreting. They are more like indications of where the mourning person stands in the process, a sort of mapping of his situation.

THE END OF MOURNING AS SUBJECTIVE RE-POSITIONING

The subjective movement that Libertad and Daniela have set forth means to question the loved and hated object ("*hainamoration*," hatred and love that cannot be dissociated, according to Lacan), in such a way that the end of mourning over the father begins when there is an objectless loss. From recognizing that what has been lost is not the father but, now that they are liberated from him, they are also liberated from their intolerable feminine position in the world as dictated by the other's desire. We do not speak of mourning as interrupted, but the loss is not what they first thought it was. As was mentioned earlier, Lacan (2014) places the questioning about the object at the center of the issue of mourning.

> The continuation and horizon of the relationship with the object, if not a conservative one, it entails, if I may say so, interrogating what is at its core or to enquire about what follows in the line when trying to isolate the function of

> the *petit a*, in other words, the properly Sadean perspective in which the object is questioned at the core of its being. The issue is to what extent the object can endure that questioning. And, after all, it stops enduring it when the last lack-of-being is revealed. It stops enduring it when questioning overlaps with the destruction of the object (Lacan, 2009, p. 363).

What is addressed is the questioning of the object. To interrogate the object means to discover it as different from our original and ideal conceptions of the object. This *Sadean perspective* that Lacan mentions is, indeed, to be willing to kill the idealized object. As Cancina (2012) writes, the object has traveled certain trajectory that puts him far from the ideal. Therefore, in a certain way, it is sadistic to question the object, since the object might—or might not—survive this questioning. That is the key element of mourning. This is what sets apart the objects we mourn from those we don't. Objects that can endure the loving question about the revealed lack can follow through the path of mourning. Objects that cannot endure this question halt the mourning process and annul it. In Libertad and Daniela's cases, fathers, as objects, could not endure the test of what the object was toward them, in relationship to them. Love is questioned, and the idealization is overthrown. In a certain way, it also means killing the object. Since to question it means to reveal the impossibility of it being the keeper of one's own desire. It is an object that is not satisfactory in any way, and it is an object that cannot be a libidinal depositary at the moment. In many cases, the fact that the mourning process can begin is not enough for it to stand the test of time. For Leader (2011) this initial impulse must receive support from other resources, and, during mourning, many things that transcend our consciousness must take place (p. 93).

Once the deaths of Libertad and Daniela's fathers were subject to their questioning, becoming de-idealized and disappointing, the way was open (via these events) for things to never be the same: "That space cannot stay the same as it was before the moment of tragedy and loss" (Leader, 2011, p. 97). However, for them, what is the tragedy exactly? And what loss is being referred to? The end of mourning means that it is impossible for the object to maintain its previous state. Therefore, if there is a tragedy, this tragedy takes place after the death. The tragedy is the intolerable position of sacrifice of one's own desire in favor of the father's desire. The true loss took place, imperceptibly, long before the father's death. If the father had not died, this would not have been noticeable. At the end of mourning, mourners adopt a narcissistic stance of claiming the recuperation of the ego, an unconscious protest for the recovery of the ego. Therefore, mourning cannot continue once the subject realizes that the object actually made the subject go through a loss long before the mourning process even began. And that, maybe, their death could mean a liberation.

Leader (2011) states that Lacan thought that mourning is not founded on letting go of the object, but on restoring our bonds toward an object that is considered lost, impossible.

> The key is sorting out the object from its narcissistic cover, from the details of the human image that our love has created. If bonds toward the object are restored, and the place of the imaginary cover are separated from the object, it might be possible that another object might take its place. According to Lacan, the problem for the mourners comes when they maintain bonds with the image, through which love is structured in a narcissistic way. If we have loved someone based on the model of our own image, or we have developed their image within the field of our own narcissism, then losing that person will mean losing ourselves (pp. 122–123).

If my narcissism remains fixated on the other's image, when that person leaves, I won't recognize who I am anymore. In Daniela and Libertad's cases, the departure of the other also affects narcissism, since they hate a part of themselves in relation to the object and they still have enough self-love so as to demand the definitive loss of the object and the position in which they were placed and in which they placed themselves. Finally, as expressed by Leader (2011), "Freud pointed out that there might be a difference between those who we have lost and what we have lost in them. This beautiful and sensitive differentiation suggests that, maybe, mourning can only take place when we have been able to separate those two dimensions in ourselves" (Leader, 2011, p. 117).

This quote denotes an inverse process to that which takes place for many other women, who, just like Daniela and Libertad, find what they have lost through their lost object, who acts as an authentic thief. A thief that, unlike the thief that Allouch described, would have stolen the possibility of something else, of being something else and desiring something else. Death, then, is as tragic as it is liberating. Just like Bauab (2012) stated, mourning is not only the breeding ground for ailments, they can also be the occasion and exquisite opportunity for, in the already mentioned re-composition of the signifiers involved in the working through of loss, constitute a fertile ground to make is subjective, to elevate loss to the category of lack and, consequently, propitiate a re-distribution of enjoyment.

Like Leader (2011) mentioned: "as Joan Didion pointed out, when we mourn over losses, we mourn, for better or for worse, for ourselves. For how we were. For how we no longer are, and for how we will never be again" (p. 133). Mourning cannot go on because they now feel liberated from their position in the feminine condition from which they are escaping. Inversely to what happens in most cases of mourning, in this case, mourning must be interrupted as demanded by their own desires! It is common to hear or read phrases stating that, in a way, the death of another person can be liberating.

In this case, we are talking about a feminine position, a social position, which is conceived in a symbolic order that transcends women and, in a way, shapes them. Thus, to end mourning is a way of feminine protest. Without saying it, it is a way of putting into action an authentic form of feminism.

Faced with the void of the end of mourning, the subject is forced to ask about himself, about herself, since there is an empty space that needs to be occupied again. Mourning, as we have seen, involves a process of constituting the object. Mourners have to constitute their object separating the empty place from the fundamentally lost object made of images of people who used to fill such place (Leader, 2011). It is asking about who was my object. But at the same time, sadness, which is the new shape into which subjectivity transforms, involves a moment of deep reflection in which life acquires a new purpose. Meaning of life is made: "For the speaking being, life is life as long as it makes sense: life itself constitutes the peak of meaning. If the meaning of life is lost, life is lost: if meaning is broken, life is in danger. In moments of doubt, depressed people become philosophers" (Kristeva, 1987, p. 16).[8] In a certain way, we are also faced, like Lacan, with the problem of desire. It is the same problem as mourning, but from a different perspective. If it is not possible to place desire anywhere, mourning becomes impossible. However, and unlike what Lacan pointed out, if mourning becomes interrupted because the object is no longer what it used to be, the gap of desire is reopened, and the subject does not know where to place it. New symptoms emerge, or narcissism reemerges, in the purely unilateral and Freudian sense of mourning. A sort of "Quick, let's cover this somehow!" feeling.

FINAL THOUGHTS: FROM THE FATHER TO THE FATHERS, OR A MATTER OF PATRIARCHY

The position of women, defined from the father's mandate, has been thoroughly explored from the perspective of gender studies, and, more recently, in the psychoanalytical field, and by many Latin American feminist psychoanalysts. This is not only due to the rise of contemporary transdisciplinary studies, but also to the undeniable reality of women who are subdued to men's desires, which constitute their subjectivity. Unfortunately, this is a current matter and it is palpable in clinical consultations, in which a space has always been provided for grief generated by the loss of a man.

From the absolute desire of the father, to the absolute desire of anyone who becomes the spokesman of the father, women in multiple social contexts are brought to life determined and named by the paternal desire, not only the maternal desire, as more classical psychoanalytical perspectives indicated. Losing the protective man, which is an image that comes from the father, places man in the position of another father. The external spokesman of the superego's voice internalized in the grieving woman. After their fathers' passing, and after losing men they were in a relationship with, the question about *what do I do next?* haunts many women. This only indicates an insufficiency that was always there, and that was sustained on a double subjective responsibility, that of the man and that of the woman.

This follows along the lines of typical mourning that was described before. Herein, the question about one's own desire is based on acknowledging the desire of the father toward the daughter, as a woman and as a feminine subject. It makes us wonder about the heritage of the particular relationship that daughters have with their fathers, about the way this relationship is set up, in an utterly Freudian manner, as a repetition, not only of the object choice, but also of an impossible symmetrical relationship.

As Dio Bleichmar (2011) pointed out in her book *Women Treating Women*, there is a problem of a different subjective constitution between men and women, which brings as a consequence a different subjectivation toward loss. She questions why women tend to resort more to therapy in cases of loss, particularly cases of loss of love and of being loved. We have addressed this issue previously, and it is a notorious element in our cases. The author asks why are anxiety disorders nine times more common among women than among men? And why is it two or three times more common for women to be depressed than for men? Also, depression in women usually goes hand in hand with a certain person, a certain name. So, in the case of women, are losses experienced through a paternal reference, through the name of the father?

Chabert (2008) acknowledges the Freudian formula of women, the narcissistic woman, according to Freud's "Introduction to Narcissism" (1914): a woman who wishes to be loved, more than to love, but this is reversed with the idea of a girl as an active subject, who wishes to love the father. The girl also desires. Women also actively desire. This also summons the constant question of the phallocentric issue. Gamboa (2012) defines "phallocentric" as a male privilege through their symbol, the phallus, as signifier of lack, of difference in general, and the sexual difference in particular; as a cause of saying and then of thinking, what is to say, as the organizer of the symbolic order.

Thus one thinks of a patriarchal symbolic order, in which the desire of women, as women are subordinated, above all things, to the desire of men, where "what underlies the image of the castrated woman is the patriarchal assumption of the female sex as an inferior, less worthy and less valuable" (Gamboa, 2012, p. 56). Therefore, also from the starting point of psychoanalysis, if all of the theoretical and clinical body is based upon the image of the castrated woman, there is a destiny assigned to her in history (and not only in one's particular history). This has also constructed the world the way it is. Unlike the male body, the female body, in all of human societies and through all the means that they have at their disposal (such as science, literature, religion, philosophy, among others) has suffered the ravages of a seizure. Women are seized of the possibility and of the right to name and cipher themselves according to their own voice and to their own libidinal economy (Gamboa, 2012).

In the name of fatherly protection, and, then, of the protection that men assume that women need, a collective imaginary order has been constructed around women. This imaginary order creates subjective roles that are difficult for women themselves to challenge, thus fossilizing their knowledge, in favor of a culture that favors masculinity. Therefore, the clinical work is a possibility for escaping, as is, in some cases, the death of another who, until that moment, had named them. As Tamayo (2004) recalls, not all deaths lead to mourning. Some lead to a feeling of power, of survival. Somehow, Libertad and Daniela embody the voices of many women, such as the immortal words of Frida Kahlo when she amputated herself from Diego Rivera in 1953, by saying, "I do not want your pity, neither yours nor anyone else's; I do not want you to feel guilty about anything, either. I am writing to let you know that you are liberated from me. I amputate you from me. Be happy and do not look for me ever again."[9]

NOTES

1. "La tristesse serait le signal d'un moi primitif blessé, incomplet, vide." The translation is mine.
2. "Irréductible à ses expressions verbales ou sémiologiques, la tristesse (comme tout affect) est la représentation psychique de déplacements énergétiques provoqués par des traumatismes externes ou internes." The translation is mine.
3. Les signes sont arbitraires parce que le langage s'amorce par une dénégation (Verneinung) de la perte, en même temps que la dépression occasionnée par le deuil. J'ai perdu un objet indispensable qui se trouve être, en dernière instance, ma mère, semble dire l'être parlant. Mais non, je l'ai retrouvée dans les signes, ou plutôt parce que j'accepte de la perdre, je ne l'ai pas perdue, je peux la récupérer dans le langage. The translation is mine.
4. The "dry death" is approached by Ariès (1983) and would organize itself since around the fourteenth through nineteenth centuries; it is characterized for being the period in which the rituals of abbreviation of mourning began.
5. Selon la théorie psychanalytique classique (Abraham, Freud, Klein), la dépression, comme le deuil, cache une agressivité contre l'objet perdu, et révèle ainsi l'ambivalence du déprimé vis-à-vis de l'objet de son deuil. Je l'aime, mais plus encore je le hais; parce que je l'aime, pour ne pas le perdre, je l'installe en moi; mais parce que je le hais, cet autre en moi est un mauvais moi, je suis mauvais, je suis nul, je me tue. The translation is mine.
6. The name "Libertad" is a pseudonym used to assure privacy.
7. "Daniela" is a pseudonym.
8. Pour l'être parlant, la vie est une vie qui a du sens: la vie constitue même l'apogée du sens. Aussi perd-il le sens de la vie, la vie se perd sans mal: à sens brisé, vie en danger. Dans ses moments dubitatifs, le dépressif est philosophe. The translation is mine.
9. Excerpt from a letter from Frida Kahlo to Diego Rivera. Translation from Spanish is mine.

REFERENCES

Ariès, P. (1983). *El hombre ante la muerte.* Buenos Aires: Taurus.
Allouch, J. (1998). *Erótique du deuil au temps de la mort séche.* Paris: E.P.E.L
Bauab, A. (2012). *Los tiempos del duelo.* Buenos Aires: Letra Viva.
Barthes, R. (2009). *Diario de duelo.* México: SXXI.
Cancina, P. (2012). *El dolor de existir . . . y la melancolía.* Buenos Aires: Letra Viva.
Chabert, C. (2008). *Femenino melancólico.* Madrid: Biblioteca Nueva.
Derrida, J. (2006). *Dar la muerte.* Buenos Aires: Paidós
Dio Bleicmar. (2011). *Mujeres tratando a mujeres. Con mirada de género.* Barcelona: Octaedro
Freud, S. (1913). Tótem y tabú. In J. Strachey (Ed.), Etcheverry, J. L. (Trans.), *Obras completes de Sigmund Freud* (2nd ed., Vol. XIII), 2006. Buenos Aires: Amorrortu.
Freud, S. (1914). Introducción del narcisismo. In J. Strachey (Ed.), Etcheverry, J.L. (Trans.), *Obras completes de Sigmund Freud* (2nd ed., Vol. XIII), 2006. Pp. 65–98. Buenos Aires: Amorrortu
Freud, S. (1917). Duelo y melancolía. In J. Strachey (Ed.), Etcheverry, J.L. (Trans.), *Obras completes de Sigmund Freud* (2nd ed., Vol. XIV), 2006. Pp. 235–256. Buenos Aires: Amorrortu.
Gamboa, F. (2012). Feminidad, espanto y locura: un circuito paradigmático de lo fantasmal In Orozco, M; Gamboa, F; Pavón-Cuéllar, D; Huerta, A.E y Cantoral, A, *Configuraciones psicoanalíticas sobre espectros y fantasmas*. Pp. 55–81. México: Plaza y Valdez.
Kahlo, F. (1953). Cartas de Frida a Diego. *Revista de Artes*, 43 (2014) http://www.revistadeartes.com.ar/revistadeartes-43/lit_cartas-de-frida-a-diego.html.
Kristeva, J. (1987). *Soleil noir. Dépression et mélancolie*. París: Gallimard.
Lacan, J. (2014). *Seminario 6. El deseo y su interpretación.* Buenos Aires: Paidós (original versión 1958–1959).
Lacan, J. (2009). *Seminario 10. La Angustia.* Buenos Aires: Paidós (original version 1962–1963).
Leader, D. (2011). *La moda negra. Duelo, melancolía y depresión.* México: Sexto Piso.
Morin, E. (2011). *El hombre y la muerte*. Barcelona: Kairós
Nasio, J. D. (1996). *El libro del dolor y del amor.* Barcelona: Gedisa
Rohde, E. (2006). *La idea del alma y la inmortalidad entre los griegos*. México: FCE
Shakespeare, W. (2002). *Hamlet.* México: Editores Mexicanos Unidos. (versión original de 1600).
Tamayo, L. (2004). El fin del duelo. In *Litoral. École lacanienne de psychanalyse*, México: Epeele, 34. Pp. 163–175.

Chapter Two

Phantoms of Foreclosed Mourning

Marilyn Charles

Mourning is a lifelong process, through which loss, large and small, must be faced. Development itself entails a breaking apart, a loss of a previous mode of adaptation, to make way for the consolidation of new knowledge and skills. Disruption, rupture, and loss are present from the moment of birth. Thrust from the mother's womb into a new world of sights, sounds, and sensations we cannot make sense of, we are utterly dependent on those who forestall the too-much of daily existence and titrate our exposure down into manageable chunks. To the extent that parents are attentive to our need, then relief comes in relation to that need, and we experience a sense of efficacy and also of cause and effect. In such a universe, losses are managed and the experience of loss becomes one that is parsed as manageable. Need, desire, and curiosity—along with a history of successfully taking on life's challenges—push us past current comfort to take on the challenges that lie ahead.

Early experiences of extreme deprivation also lodge in the body, leaving traumatic trails that echo back to the lost safety of the womblike space of the mother's arms. When safety can be found, we carry that assurance, which helps us to venture outward and find other sources of refuge and repair. But there is also an inevitable alterity, a limit to be reckoned with. That limit, which initially feels externally imposed and oppressive, leaves an archaic imago of the terrible mother, who threatens to devour and engulf us if we seek refuge there. This leaves the Woman, as archetype, in a position of both fear and desire, the feelings and fantasies that myths, gods, and demons are made of (see Balter, 1969; Campbell, 1959; Cassirer, 1946).

Initially born from our mothers' bodies, we must disentangle ourselves from her in order to become ourselves. Although we can all experience a yearning for a return to an enclosed, womblike, protective state, and also a fear of being engulfed there, the path of development is different for the woman, who must both disentangle herself from and identify with the mother. Laplanche (1999a) suggests that at the core of some of these developmental dilemmas is what he terms the *enigmatic signifier* that both calls to us and subverts itself. Such a message, he suggests, both "fails and succeeds at the same time" (Laplanche, 1995, p. 665) because the unconscious of the parent speaks to the child in ways that compromise the message. Because the knowledge of the adult is beyond what is accessible to the young child, there is a transmission that "is opaque to its recipient and its transmitter alike" (p. 665) because of the unconscious message content that lies below threshold.

Death presents us with perhaps the most problematic enigma, the interrupted message that calls to us precisely because the sense of disruption, of loss, is such an integral aspect of living (Laplanche, 1997). For Levinas (1981), disruption represents a profound truth, in that meaning is exposed through it, but "the lapse of time is also something irrecuperable, refractory to the simultaneity of the present, something unrepresentable, immemorial, pre-historical" (p. 35), that reveals itself in the echo of whatever came before. Death is thus both unknowable and essential to meaning, a limit that we encounter through the echo or enigmatic message that both calls to and eludes us. In alerting toward such messages, suggests Levinas (1999), we learn something. Perhaps most profoundly, the confrontation with the inevitable alterity of death brings about "an aloneness toward which I cannot be indifferent. It awakens me to the other" (p. 161). Through the death of the other, we are called into our humanity and therefore also into our responsibility for others.

That call is something we cannot delegate without losing some of our humanity. And yet, in cultures that fear death, women are often called upon to tend the dead and thereby to gaze into the face of death. That delegation affords them the direct confrontation with enigma and also with the call for an ethics of care and responsibility. The essential enigma at the core of this call that faces us with our lack and our limit also marks our potential to move beyond the point of being captivated and held captive by the desire of the other (Lacan, 1977a).

And yet, in such cultures, women also get caught at the crossroads of very different cultural expectations; to be subservient to the needs and desires of men and become the object of the man's desires and fulfill his fantasies; versus the more difficult challenge of discovering and fulfilling her own (Stone, 2012; Thompson, 1964). The latter is complicated by the cultural messages that make that course dangerous. In spite of changing ideas about women's sexuality, cultural pressures still invite a sense of guilt that can make it difficult to find one's own desire, which also makes it more difficult to say no to the desire of the other. Those oppressive injunctions can be seen as one means for managing the power of the maternal imago.

WOMEN AND ABJECTION

Paradoxically, then, it would seem to be the very power of the woman that invites her oppression, through patriarchal structures that manage men's anxieties by keeping women in a subjugated, "protected" place. The presumption of women's inferiority has not only been a source of oppression for women but also of confusion for the individual woman who receives mixed messages regarding her potential and the extent to which she is entitled to her own feelings, particularly her feelings of aggression and desire. Structural oppression results in feelings of abjection at the social level that are experienced as a shame-inducing inferiority at the individual level. Because the source of the distress is cultural, it is difficult for the individual to successfully work through the problem, inviting, rather, a masochistic surrender to the debased, devalued identity (see LaCapra, 1999).

On the other side of this question, of course, rests the part of the woman that cooperates with her exclusion, her willingness to be placed in such a position. Kristeva (1986a) describes this dilemma in relation to Christian ideas regarding the imago of the Virgin Mother or Madonna. The price of aligning oneself with such an idealization, suggests Kristeva, is to abjure all bodily pleasure and to dedicate oneself "to the highest sublimation alien to her body. A bonus, however: the promised *jouissance*" (p. 181). Kristeva links female masochism with the self-sacrifice required in order to pass along to the child the social norms necessary for survival. For Kristeva, feminine perversion entails, not a sexual object but the protection of the unique suffering and self-abnegation required for maternity. That dilemma is further complicated by the woman's position in relation to life and to death, the two great mysteries that bound human experience. A feminine ethics, she suggests, may be required in order to deal with the problem posed to us by the fact that we die. "For an heretical ethics separated from morality, an *herethics*, is perhaps no more than that which in life makes bonds, thoughts, and therefore the thought of death, bearable" (p. 185).

For Kristeva (1986b), female subjectivity is uniquely situated in relation to repetition and eternity. The woman is subject both to internal biological cycles and also to the eternal transpersonal cycles of human life and civilizations. Kristeva contrasts a *logic of identification* that locates itself within the dominant discourse of the society, with a *dynamic of signs* that refuses linear temporality in favor of an aesthetic, spiritual discourse. The latter can be seen, for example, in the choice of Antigone to obey a law that called to her from her human relatedness beyond the law of the land. The call to an allegiance to an internal truth marks a crucial ethical injunction that we also see in psychoanalysts such as Bion and Lacan, who place a personal ethics, Bion's *truth instinct* (Grotstein, 2004; originally described in terms of *pas-*

sion in Bion, 1977) or Lacan's (1992) *desire of the subject* at the heart of the developmental project that is psychoanalysis.

The story of Antigone is complicated because she does not merely obey an injunction that is conditioned by the criminality of her brother, but also one that is conditioned in relation to the crimes of the mother (Walsh, 1999). Walsh invites a reading of the story of Antigone in which, "in recognizing our mothers as selves, ethicity no longer depends upon the strength of our adherence to a lie that refuses maternal desire as criminal, but rather upon our acceptance of maternal love as beautiful, flawed, ambiguous, and human" (p. 121). Such a stance, she suggests, would be "a powerful antidote to the violent, suffering, isolated self forced upon us in the psychoanalytic, philosophical mirror" (p. 121). Although psychoanalysis can offer us insights, we can see in the story of Antigone, written by a man, how she is offered to us as a sacrifice in the name of love, and in the name of beauty (Shepherdson, 2008).

In contrast to the truths offered through the man's gaze, there is a truth at the core of the woman's experience, marked by the regularities of life, death, and the intervening cycles of human lives, that potentially affords insights beyond the cultural forces that impose meaning structures that both illuminate and limit awareness. The mystery of the woman that makes her "unclean" or "untouchable" at certain times in certain cultures also alienates her from herself. The attempt to link with the positive aspects of what is offered can also put her at risk, such that her power becomes her prison (see, for example, Charles, 2008, 2011, 2019).

One challenge for contemporary women is to recognize how we have been positioned and then, to the extent we desire to do so, to challenge those limits and attempt to transform them. That transformation process depends on our ability to differentiate between culturally imposed limits and those that are essential, in terms of our biology and physiology, and also to consider the ramifications of making one choice versus another. Such a transformation process is inevitably complicated by our language structures that define and proscribe meanings. Kristeva (1986a) notes that although language is a fundamental bond between people, it is also at odds with other ways of making meaning that are more driven by affect or "the infinitesimal significations with the relationships with the nature of their own bodies" (p. 199).

Lacan (1977a) positions lack and limit at the forefront of the human developmental challenge. From his perspective, it is only in grappling with limit that we discover our own desire that might give direction and purpose to our life. For Kristeva (1986b), as well, desire can only be understood in relation to lack, to the "privation of fulfillment and totality; exclusion of a pleasing, natural and sound state: in short, the break indispensable to the advent of the symbolic" (p. 198). To imagine what we might become, it is important to be able to find our place in the agreement; in Kristeva's terms, the symbolic or social contract that "is based on an essentially sacrificial relationship of separation and meaning" (p. 199). This contract has been seen as imposed on the woman by the man, which may in some sense be true, but the larger problem is that the woman agrees to it. How, then, might she oppose whatever is illegitimately imposed, given that it is only through the possibility of opposition that a choice might be made?

Much like Fanon (1952; see also Hook, 2012), who suggests that abjection cannot be repaired without attention to the logic of embodied meanings, Kristeva (1982, 1986b) suggests that such opposition must come in an embodied form, not through the pillars of received knowledge but rather through the personal feelings that arise from facing the limit. This leads, she suggests, "to the active research, still rare, undoubtedly hesitant but always dissident, being carried out by women in the human sciences; particularly those attempts, in the wake of contemporary art, to break the code, to shatter language, to find a discourse closer to the body and emotions, to the unnameable repressed by the social contract" (1986b, p. 200). Kristeva further suggests that a force has been unleashed in women in which the "major social concern has become the sociosymbolic contract as a sacrificial contract" (p. 200). Kristeva's position here is similar to that of Lacan (1977b), who writes that "the function of language is not to inform but to evoke" (p. 86). Language, he notes, poses a particular problem in that it speaks and hides in relation to our ambivalent desire to know and to be known. And yet, inevitably, we reveal ourselves: "the symptom is metaphor whether one likes it or not, as desire is metonymy" (Lacan, 1977c, p. 175).

THE WOMAN AS MOURNER

This sacrificial contract, through which women become relegated to the position of mourners, is the topic of my chapter here. In many societies, women have been the repositories for grief, tending the dead and providing vehicles for a mourning process. Being relegated to this position leaves women at the juncture between life and death, that frightening potential space that both entices and frightens us. Relegating her to that position, however, leaves the man further displaced from the body in its creative and deadly aspects, and increases his aversion to death—and to bodily reminders of death. Joseph Campbell (1988) suggests that myths evolve, in part, in order to link mind with body, which necessarily includes a recognition of death, the ultimate marker of loss and limit. Myths mark our essential helplessness and vulnerability (Arlow, 1961), including the complexities of developmental transitions from dependency to autonomy and maturity, and then to the later dependency of increasing age. They provide models for maturation, to help the man and the woman to move from childhood to adulthood within the frame of that particular society's cultural practice.

Notably, suggests Campbell (1988), the boy needs some ceremony of initiation in order to become a man, whereas the girl is inducted into womanhood more directly, through menarche. Along with the original dependency on the female that the man must separate himself from, there may also be something about the woman's more direct relationship with nature, creation, and death that invites in the man a sense of both mystery and fear. In relation to that enigma, Freud (1925) positioned the woman outside the direct line of social constraint in his depictions of the Oedipal dilemma. For Freud (1926), she remained the "dark continent," as indeed she must; one can be given anchors and guideposts but the road to self-discovery inevitably lies within.

And yet, in the search for meaning—and for safety—we also must seek answers from without in order to anchor and organize our experience. Campbell (1988) notes that the position of the shaman, whose wisdom comes from direct experience, marks the allure and aversion to direct knowledge. For Campbell, the shaman is the character who uses their externally sanctioned authority to invite recognition of internal truths, in that way serving a similar function to that of the psychoanalyst today.

> But instead of relieving the boy of the deities, the shaman is adapting him to the deities and the deities to himself. It's a different problem from that of psychoanalysis. I think it was Nietzsche who said, "Be careful lest in casting out the devils you cast out the best thing that's in you." Here, the deities who have been encountered—powers, let's call them—are retained. The connection is maintained, not broken. And these men then become the spiritual advisers and gift-givers to their people. (1988, p. 89)

Those who speak from beyond consensual knowledge are both desired and feared, but also potentially form a bridge between internal and external truths in relation to one's own authenticity. Human development depends upon the external vantage point that helps to contain and to organize our experience, but always in relation to our emergent capacity to make our own meanings in line with an internal sense of truth.

Historically, however, the interdependence of man and woman has resulted in formulaic and somewhat rigid separations of role, which may have worked in previous times but have become more complicated in contemporary culture, where the dividing lines between roles are less clear. And yet, there is an essential truth to those earlier, circumscribed relationships that we still grapple with. We need both power and protection in order to thrive, and the cycles of life and death require that children be protected, nurtured and challenged. Although in today's world a parent of either sex can play the role of "mother" or "father," once the child is born, traditionally the woman has needed the man's protection in order to be the primary source of shelter for the child.

As an example of these interrelated functions, Campbell (1988) offers the bushman who stands as servant to the woman who represents life. "The woman is life and the man is the servant of life," (p. 86) he says. In order to pass into manhood, the man circles around the woman, the deep recesses of human mind and being, fearing to be lost there but needing to find something that is essential to his manhood. According to Campbell, the man has to become small in order to pass into God's place, and it is the community of men that holds the place for the reentry of the man from his trance state into the world of the living. We see in this ritual the attempt to recognize one's dependence; paradoxically, the need to be interdependent so that one can stand on one's own, grounded in the types of deep truths Kristeva (1986c) terms the *chora*.

Kristeva describes the chora as a rhythmic articulation rather than a disposition, "a nonexpressive totality formed by the drives and their stases in a motility that is as full of movement as it is regulated" (1986c, p. 93). Following Plato, Kristeva describes the chora as "nourishing and maternal" (Kristeva, 1986c, p. 94), organized through an ordering rather than according to a law. In her words: "the kinetic functional stage of the *semiotic* precedes the establishment of the sign" (p. 95). In this way, in line with Bion's truth instinct, Kristeva posits an organizational framework that structures human meaning-making.

Campbell (1988) positions the duality between man and woman in terms of necessary and complementary functions. "Society is always patriarchal. Nature is always matrilinear" (p. 101), he says, suggesting that whereas hunting societies are individualistic, directed outward, planting mythologies are turned inward, toward the seed and its cycles of death and rebirth. "In the forest and planting cultures, there is a sense of death as not death somehow, that death is required for new life. And the individual isn't quite an individual, he is a branch of a plant" (Campbell, 1988, p. 102). This leaves us with the paradox, in planting and harvesting societies, that the power resides in the woman and yet, "motherhood is a sacrifice" (p. 114) for the good of the whole. "Since her magic is that of giving birth and nourishment, as the earth does, her magic supports the magic of the earth" (p. 101). The woman is also identified with danger—with sin and corruption—but also, from this framework, with the possibility of transcendence and transformation; a denial of the death that she also stands for.

CONFRONTING LACK AND LIMIT

We see in this example the attempt to face lack and limit, to move directly toward, and thereby to pass through and overcome, the fear located in the dark continent symbolized by the woman who represents both life and death, the void that can also be pregnant with possibilities, if we can only face it (Charles, 2000a,b). From a psychoanalytic perspective, Lacan (1977a) highlights for us the particular ways in which lack forms and formulates the terms—and the price—of existence. Beyond the relationship between the primary drives that are linked to embodied survival needs, there is the relationship with lack that drives our interchanges with one another and with meaning itself. Notably, the human being is born uniquely incapable of self-protection or preservation, dependent upon others for survival.

From the perspective of patriarchal societies, woman has been positioned as the lack, the other; that which is both elusive and necessary to the survival of the species. In some ways, we all stand as prospective sacrifices in that survival, moving inevitably toward our ultimate disappearance, enforcing at some developmental moment a switch from self-focus to attention on the survival of the other who will carry forward something of us after we die. In this way, there is a lack that is at the core of all living beings, in that we are finite and limited, and move inexorably toward death.

From the perspective of his-story, the lack is located in the other, as in tales of creation in which the man is at the center, the woman merely an appendage to or derivation from his being. In that story, the lack is located in the woman, who is defined as that which is other. Necessary to survival but inevitably alien, she stands as the I that accuses the man as he is of being insufficient. The impossibility of surviving entirely on one's own points back to the lack, the point of instability that reconfirms our inevitable dependence on the other. That reading of the creation myth, however, problematizes the woman's acquisition of knowledge—and her sexuality—as though any lack must necessarily be located in her. Phillips (1986) suggests that although psychoanalytic treatments of this myth disclose "a struggle to overthrow the tyranny of patriarchy," they fail "to acknowledge Eve's decisive role in the rebellion or agree that as half of the human fraternity, she must necessarily share the power at its conclusion" (p. 13).

For the woman, there is a somewhat different relationship with lack. She needs a man for survival of the species but, unless she needs protection from one man, she could accomplish this goal with any man. How, then, would the man ensure his own survival, that someone would carry on *his* name, *his* genes? Patriarchy stabilizes the instability inherent in the inevitable alterity of the woman by offering her protection in return for affirmation of the dependence that marks her lack. If the man and the woman can agree in a partnership where each recognizes the important and essential role played in not filling—but rather compensating for or balancing—the lack in the other, then we have some stability.

From that place, we know the ground on which we stand, and we can be grateful for what is given and generous with what is taken. If, however, we cannot face and come to grips with our inevitable interdependence on precisely those others who have something we lack and lack something we have, then we are in a mess. Like a malformed wheel, we circle erratically ever further from the goal we cannot clearly have in mind because one eye opens to see the object of our desire while the other eye closes to not see how the object is constituted in relation to whatever is lacking.

This is the form of the dilemma into which we are born, that we are dependent on others who only partly fill our needs while busy filling their own, which, at its best, builds our capacity to tolerate the inevitable frustrations that accrue so that we might build a life on ground that affords some place to stand and from which we can also move. Complicating this difficulty is history, through which course through us the developmental failures and adaptations of previous generations, which form the rules that have enabled survival but also foreclosed development, and thereby become the constraints on our own becoming.

THE USE OF AN OBJECT

Winnicott (1971) helps us out here, in offering us, through metaphor, another basic pattern in development that he captures in his depiction of *the use of an object*. Through this lens, he marks the important passage from oneness to twoness. Winnicott invites us to consider this point where we move from a relationship with objects that either frustrate or fulfill our needs to a recognition of persons, separate and apart from ourselves, with their own experiences and existence.

In Winnicott's formulation, the child flails in relation to his own needs and desire. The parent (or analyst) must be able to remain empathically present in relation to precisely the desire he cannot fill. It is in our ability to remain empathically related to the desire we cannot fill that the possibility emerges of a meaning that can sustain us in spite of our frustration. That thread of meaning puts a limit on the frustration. It both attenuates the distress and tells us that it will end. Time becomes, not endless, empty, and unendurable but limited and marked by the meanings that make it survivable. Time can feel eternal without being eternal. But there is this problem: that exactly what is most adaptive in us and pushes past the obstacle, the point of difficulty, also loses focus and blurs and skates past precisely the locus of our stumbling. Like the proverbial frog in the frying pan, we are in danger of adapting to the very thing that kills us.

So, in this volume, we are talking about women and about grief and the possibility of mourning, which invites us to think about the woman in relation to the lack she hopes to both fill and overcome, through which process she might find and lose herself; lose the self that has limits by finding an illusory self with none. Because herself, her life, and her meaning are at stake, it matters where she finds herself in relation to the basic human struggles that face us all, and also the particular historical, cultural, and familial contexts into which she has been born. Without some second sight, some perspective through which to capture herself in motion, she is in danger of losing herself in the very process of finding herself. Identity develops in relation to the life story as it evolves over time. This means that our growth is enhanced—or limited—by our ability to integrate new ideas as we encounter them.

THE TALE

Such is the dilemma depicted by Jennifer Fox (2018) in the film *The Tale*, through which she looks backward at the story she has told herself regarding her life. She uses this backward glance as a way of gaining perspective on the narrative she has created from the events that occurred during the time of her own emerging pubescence. We see how she initially resists any retelling of her story, preferring her adaptation even though it forecloses the possibilities of alternative readings so essential to development. Notably, Fox is invited into this revisioning by her mother's encounter with the tale as it had been written by the young Jenny, forcing an encounter with a Real that the adult Jenny resists. Once, however, the possibility of another reading of her own history is raised, she cannot entirely close the door that has been opened.

There is an immediacy to the story as it unfolds. The audience is invited in as participant-observers, as fragments and bits of meaning intrude, disrupting the narrative as it has been told and forcing tension into what had previously remained a seamless rendering of her life events. Through the film, the director quite brilliantly shows us ways in which meanings intrude and invite, first resistance and then curiosity. As meanings shift, so do the memories. Vividly and graphically, we are confronted with the impossibility of continuing to construct meanings in the ways they had been shaped. Relationships and intentions shift in relation to the more fully evolved and developed meanings that the adult Jenny wrestles back from her recalcitrant child self. The cinematic form affords a means for representing the at-times complicated relationships we have with previous versions of ourselves, ways in which a childhood or adolescent adaptation can foreclose development in a particular area somewhat invisibly. Particularly with shameful or traumatic experiences, there can be an unconscious resistance to even recognizing the gap.

As the story evolves, we see the desperation that shaped the child's distortion and distention of self and experience, in relation to lack and to the illicit and impossible promise of its fulfillment. In this way, the film invites us to consider ways in which we subvert our own well-being to avoid facing uncomfortable self-knowledge, and invite our own destruction through the false promise of fulfillment of lack. This film highlights the particular relation of the woman to lack and to desire, which is the track we are here treading.

In the film, as we often see in the consulting room (and in our own lives), the child is "loved" but ignored by the parent who is too preoccupied to alert sufficiently to the child's needs or distress. The mother is lost in relation to the demands that she tries to adapt to without being able to sufficiently think about, to reflectively consider the meanings and therefore also the ethics of the choices she is making.

Without reflection, there can be no ethics and we are caught in a lawless and dangerous universe, the universe bequeathed to young Jenny. In successive revisionings of pivotal moments in time, we see the parents preoccupied with other things that keep their attention turned from the daughter's unaspirated questions. Without sufficient parental engagement, Jenny is free to foreclose on her own development and to jump past important developmental milestones, to try to bridge/deny the lack rather than coming to grips with it. Denial must always fail, because we trip over whatever we fail to see, which brings us to the importance of mourning.

THE TRANSGENERATIONAL TRANSMISSION OF FORECLOSED MOURNING

Abraham and Torok's (1994) exposition of Freud's (1917) work on mourning and melancholia highlights the difference between a mourning process that includes a reckoning with trauma versus one that tries to jump past and so inevitably stays at the surface. For Lacan (1977a), the crucial issue is to face loss, recognizing that pivotal in the experience of loss is the confrontation with lack and with limit. Laplanche (1997) suggests that there is more at stake in the early negotiations between parent and child than Winnicott can help us to recognize, that along with a call for development there is also something seductive in these early exchanges.

For Laplanche (1997), what is most crucial for us to recognize in seduction is the call from the other, the enigmatic sign from the adult's unconscious that signals to the child something that is below threshold for each. We can see this type of message in the look of love from mother to baby that orients the child toward the mother and her message. Along with whatever may be consciously known, this look also satisfies needs not consciously known by either participant, thereby even more firmly binding each to the other. We see this type of call in *The Tale*, when the coach's look calls to Jenny in a way that she cannot refuse, moving her beyond her own inhibitions and limits to accede to the desire of the other. That call is the paradox that Lacan points to, in which the search for the Other who will fill the gap is an impossible search, for when a person "presents himself to fill the gap, he does so as an imposter" (1977a, p. 311). How, then, does the woman come to terms with her own lack and limit when she is invited to become the enigmatic signifier for the man who represents the possibility of a jouissance with no lack or limit?

The film invites us to focus on what seems, to young Jenny, to be the look of love, an appearance that, as we later see, may hide the function that is being served. Lacan (1977a) stresses the importance of the distinction "between the principle of sacrifice, which is symbolic, and the imaginary function that is devoted to that principle of sacrifice, but which, at the same time, masks the fact that it gives it its instrument. The imaginary function is that which Freud formulated to govern the investment of the object as narcissistic object" (p. 319). The symbolic phallus marks a limit, whereas the imaginary phallus can be used to fulfill a lack in a way that signifies jouissance, which then "explains both the particularities of the woman's approach to sexuality, and that which makes the male sex the weak sex in the case of perversion" (p. 320).

For Lacan (1977a), perversion "accentuates to some extent the function of desire in the man, in so far as he sets up dominance in the privileged place of *jouissance*, the object *o* of the phantasy (*objet petit a*), which he substitutes for the Ø. Perversion adds a reabsorption of the ø that would scarcely appear original if it did not interest the Other as such in a very particular way. Only my formulation of phantasy enables us to reveal that the subject here makes himself the instrument of the Other's *jouissance*" (p. 320). Perversion, for Lacan, marks the illegitimate satisfaction of desire, a jouissance that is accomplished at the expense of another; in the film, the fulfillment accomplished by the coach through his domination/seduction of the child, Jenny.

Perversion denies the inevitability of the confrontation with lack, with loss. And yet, it is through that very confrontation that we can fine-tune our perspective on the possibilities that might be available to us. There is pleasure in the mastery of a challenge, and there is anxiety created in the face of the failure to confront the challenge. This, I think, is the locus of Bion's (1977) *seventh servant*, the *truth instinct* that can guide us in our ambivalent efforts toward and against the point of difficulty. This truth is also pointed to by Jane Van Buren (2007), who suggests that there are unconscious meanings that cannot be parsed by the individual because of previous generations' failures to bring them into consciousness. What is passed along, then, is a truth that haunts us because we fear to encounter it. These truths become the phantoms described by Maurice Apprey (1993, 2003) and Abraham and Torok (1994) that carry transgenerational meanings that cannot yet be known.

The unknowability of such meanings undermines development and can even, at the extreme, drive us mad. In their book *History Beyond Trauma*, Davoine and Gaudillière (2004) illuminate ways in which history courses through us, such that no symptom can be understood without referring back to the meanings that have shaped the individual life. This is also a point that Lacan (1974–1975) comes to in his metaphor of the *Borromean knot*, the ways in which the individual life and mind are shaped by the particular confluence of the interlocking rings of the Real, Symbolic, and the Imaginary, the ways in which experience, culture, and the human mind come together to uniquely configure meanings for that individual.

If we can see the pattern of human development as a transpersonal process, and also the layers of culture, family, and history as they impact the individual, then we have some way of recognizing both similarities and difference, and perhaps grasping this unique individual's relationships to meaning and to development. That confluence inevitably brings us back to the confrontation with limit and with lack, through which identity develops.

For those whose histories include a foreclosure of mourning, there is the added complication of trying to face some obstacle that cannot be recognized by the parent. Perhaps this dilemma is endemic in all development. Every parent would like to protect the child from pain = limit. The parent who has faced loss and limit recognizes the points where this is impossible, and so helps the child to recover from such encounters. When some knowledge is barred, however, the parent's vulnerability becomes an added encumbrance for the child, one that is hard to surmount because breaking through that imposed limit involves a rupture with the parent that cannot be repaired because it cannot be recognized for what it is. Rather, the limit shifts to another realm where it remains hidden behind the pain of the other that has been invoked through the violation of the parent's illicitly established taboo. For example, Jenny's mother cannot face something in relation to her husband, and also in relation to her own mother. In subverting her legitimate authority as a person to have her own perspective, she blinds herself to precisely the suffering her daughter needs her to see.

The mother has more children than she can manage and brings in her own mother to assist her. She pays the price exacted because she has not established herself as a legitimate authority in her own mind, body, and home. That price is not only exacted from her but, more importantly, also from her daughter, who cannot find in her mother an identification that insists that she face difficult truths. In consequence, Jenny's foundation is insufficient, leaving her looking for the thing she needs outside of herself. She is seduced by the promise of "having it all" because her relationship with her mother has not forced a reckoning with limit and with lack and therefore with the possibility of asserting herself, her needs, and her desire in relation to that of the other. Instead, her desire is subverted into a desire to fill the desire of the other. In this move, her own desire disappears and, with it, most terribly, herself.

In the film, adult Jenny looks backward and discovers that foreclosing on her own desire in order to fulfill that of the other, rather than positioning a victory in relation to the problem posed by the other, represents merely another facet of failure. She has refused the particulars of the life of the mother but has conformed to its pattern in the failure to come to the type of reckoning with lack and limit that would enable a real relationship with another separate yet connected human being. Rather, she is invited into a relationship that becomes perverse because of the confrontation that has been foreclosed.

Such foreclosure becomes addictive because we close our eyes at precisely the moment when we are presented with the opportunity to see the something-more that would confront us with our lack. That confrontation, albeit painful, also offers the possibility of growth because there is ground under our feet rather than the fantasy we have turned to in order to soothe an honest distress that demands resolution.

That type of pattern is a function of perverse power dynamics in which dominance is used to ease one's own distress at the expense of another. In his novel *Another Country*, James Baldwin (1962) points to this dilemma, brilliantly showing us how each character is caught in the Imaginary in relation to his or her own lack or limit. The rupture cannot be repaired because the encounter with another separate being cannot be achieved. Each character yearns to be redeemed by a love that is foreclosed by her inability to encounter it. In this way, he points us back to the problem of abjection as a human struggle in which we are all both caught and implicated, that must be faced in order to set ourselves free from the blindness that becomes self-authorized.

From this perspective, mourning is foreclosed because of the inversion through which we seek out in the other something that can only come from within. Laplanche (1999b) points to the paradox in Freud (1917) regarding the reluctance to renounce the lost object, which he terms an "enigmatic block of mourning" that remain untouchable (p. 250). He links this paradox to the reluctance to recognize that mourning inevitably has infantile reverberations and narcissistic consequences. In his attempt to explore the enigmatic aspects of mourning, Laplanche turns to Penelope, who wove and unwove her fabric, suggesting that she is not only buying time but also, perhaps, that "she only weaves and unweaves *in order* to weave, to be able to weave a new tapestry" (p. 251). This reading of the story links mourning to the type of remembering we hope to accomplish in psychoanalytic self-discovery. In this story, for Laplanche, there is a recognition of the need to move from a perverse relationship with taboo to a legitimate recognition of limit, noting that Penelope, through her ritual of mourning, "sets aside the reserve of the *taboo of Ulysses*, the reserve of the *name of Ulysses*" (p. 252).

In consequence, shifting away from Freud's focus on the problem of detaching the libido from the representation of the object, Laplanche (1999b) likens psychoanalysis to the process of "unweaving so that a new fabric can be woven, disentangling to allow the formation of new knots" (p. 254). Looking through that lens, we can see Jennifer Fox's film as this very type of exploration, an act of mourning through which a new tapestry can be built. In line with Levinas (1948), Laplanche suggests that if we change our focus from the enigma *of* to the enigma *in*, "the enigma leads back, then, to the otherness of the other; and the otherness of the other is his response to his unconscious, that is to say, to his otherness to himself" (p. 255).

Laplanche (1999b) reminds us that there is a shell game being played, in which what we experience as though it were an external threat is actually inherent in our own subjectivity, our relationship with ourselves. "Psychoanalysis can only run after mechanisms in which the subject would still be active, all the while *pretending* to be passive" (pp. 256–57). He proposes a "fundamental inversion" (p. 257), in which the person positions herself as though her origins are formulated through otherness, through whatever is implanted into us. Psychoanalysis, then, entails "a going back over which dissolves, which resolves, and not a going back to the so-called ultimate formula of my being. Beyond translations and past constructions, beyond the weaving it undoes, analysis goes back along the threads of the 'other': the other thing of our unconscious, the other person who has implanted his messages, with, as horizon, the other thing in the other person, that is, the unconscious of the other, which makes those messages enigmatic" (p. 258).

THE ENIGMATIC MESSAGE OF MATERNAL ABJECTION

In *The Tale* of Jenny and the tales of women who report having been ensnared by men in positions of power, we can see a trap that is part of the sociocultural context of Western culture. Patriarchy positions the man in a place of power in relation to the woman who he can protect but also possess. The sexual relationship between men and women is one of intrusion by the man, which positions the woman as either intruded upon or embracing and enclosing, perhaps even trapping and engulfing the man. Each, then, poses a potential satisfaction but also a potential hazard for the other. How, then, does one fulfill one's needs, one's desires, without becoming trapped by the desire of the other?

One resolution to the problem is for each to recognize the other's power and the other's weakness. In that way, we might perhaps fill the lack in the other without doing violence to whatever is there. In the sexual act, for each there is a loss. Staying with the topic at hand, for the woman there is the loss of her virginity, her self-sufficiency and also, with pregnancy, the loss of herself as a singular being whose focus can be most primarily on herself. There is now a further twoness to be reckoned with, beyond the twoness of the sexual act, beyond the twoness of an adult partnership. In this twoness, the other's needs prevail to the extent that this other cannot fend for him or herself. Thus, the maternal position is, to some extent, one of an enforced deferral of self and needs to the other, to both the other whose seed is planted within her, and to the being who will evolve from that seed.

How, then, does the mother pass along to the daughter a message that counters the enigmatic message of abjection, a message that, according to Laplanche, she cannot help passing along because it is carried in her unconscious? Perhaps one clue to this dilemma can be found in Laplanche's (1999c) consideration of *Nachträglichkeit*, which he translates as *afterwardness*, suggesting that what is missing from Freud's elaborations of this concept is a recognition that there was a message missing from the other, that "the past already has something in it that demands to be deciphered, which is the message of the other person" (p. 265). For Laplanche, "Freud's concept of afterwardness contains both great richness and a certain ambiguity, combining a retrogressive and a progressive direction" (p. 265). In this way, he accounts for the ambiguities of these dual directions inherent in the concept of Nachträglichkeit, in the call from the adult that speaks forward but can only be understood in retrospect from what he terms "the implantation of the enigmatic message" (p. 265).

Thinking now to the position of the mother whose story is one of a dangerous world, there is the added difficulty of not just nurturing one's child but also of protecting that child from danger. When danger has exacted its price across the generations, the legacy of the mother is to exact that price from the daughter as well, in the service of her survival. Toni Morrison's (2008) novel, *A Mercy*, well illuminates the ongoing price of that survival, whatever the intention of the mother. In that novel, the mother has such restricted choices that there seems to be no good choice, and yet, as we can see only in retrospect, she *might* have given her daughter the word, the words that might have contained meanings through which the daughter might have maintained contact with the love of the mother and, through that thread, sustained the core of her own humanity.

Briefly, here is the story. The main character, Florens, is a slave in the United States in the seventeenth century, owned by a man who is also struggling to survive in a new country. Florens's mother is absent, having, in Florens's mind, chosen her brother over her, abandoning the devalued daughter. As the story progresses, we learn that the mother's intention was not to abandon her daughter but rather to save her from the assaultiveness that might be her future. She therefore leaves her with a master who seems kind and decent. That gift, however, that mercy, cannot be received by the daughter, who feels only the lack in herself that caused the mother to abandon her. That lack is present in Florens throughout the novel, and ultimately destroys her and those she loves, in relation to a fundamental alienation from self, an otherness that cannot be understood or repaired (see Levinas, 2000)

In a review of Morrison's later novels, Jean Wyatt (2017) suggests that at the core of Florens's dilemma is a failed communication, an enigmatic message that Florens is unable to successfully elucidate over time because of the absence of any words through which to make sense of and repair the rupture caused by the apparent rejection by her mother. In Florens, we see a character utterly broken by a traumatic moment in which she loses, not only her mother, but also the sense of being loved or valued by that mother. The memory of rejection replaces any access to her mother's love, which, in cruel paradox, was the reason that the mother gave up her child. In this way, Morrison illuminates the horror in slavery of parents' structurally imposed inability to protect, much less adequately care for, their children.

For Wyatt (2017), Florens's dilemma is illustrated by her stunted language, such that "in the act of reading, a reader has to experience a formal version of the impeded communication that is central to the novel's plot. To a degree unusual even in Morrison's carefully crafted words, form expresses content" (p. 125). Florens is utterly caught in a present tense that is also the traumatic moment, frozen in time, showing us viscerally and directly the impact of trauma that is not softened—or interpreted—through the mind, heart, or language of another. Ultimately, love, for Florens, is neither redemptive, reparative, nor even possible because, when challenged, she becomes frozen in the traumatic moment that ever threatens to repeat itself in the present as an utter annihilation of self, meaning, and possibility. Utterly destroyed, her rage erupts into the destruction of those around her.

MOTHERHOOD, MOURNING, AND THE POSSIBILITY OF REPAIR

From Bion's (1977) perspective, we can see the enigmatic signifier in relation to a meaning that is present but barred because the parent is not able to fully metabolize/contain certain meanings. If we think of the early function of the mother, to translate meanings from experience into the words that not only recognize the experience but also help to manage it, then whatever cannot be translated remains outside of language, in the realm of mystery, the realm of both trauma and of the enigmatic meanings that call to us because they affect us but we cannot understand them.

From Van Buren's (2007) perspective, women's speech that is not authorized, but rather is denied expression in the public realm, is expressed through less conscious processes such as rituals, customs, and myths. These containers enable us to hold and communicate complex truths of human experience that must be grappled with without necessarily being spoken about. The crucial issue, in terms of development, would seem to lie in whether these meanings are merely displaced into metonymy, or whether they can emerge in the realm of metaphor, where meanings can multiply and build upon one another, and be used in the service of meaning-making. The latter would seem to be the realm of Winnicott's (1971) distinction between the type of fantasy that flattens and goes nowhere versus a dream that can be used in creative ways because it is layered, with meanings that relate "to past, present, and future, and to inner and outer," self and other (p. 35).

From a Kleinian perspective, the mother is the locus, not only of care and comfort but also of primal anxieties (Klein, 1946). Bion (1977) adds to our notions regarding the hidden—and in some ways forbidden—realm of the mythic or archetypal dimension of human mind and imagination through his term *thoughts without a thinker*, in this way recognizing the existence of precisely those thoughts we ward off and cannot encounter. From a Kleinian perspective, it is precisely whatever we ward off that then returns to haunt us from the outside, experienced as an external oppression from which we cannot escape.

Van Buren (2007) proposes the term *illness of the signifier* to mark "the manifest or symptomatic outcome of the failure of realizations to fulfill their emotional destiny" (p. 5). She suggests that these failures are most profound to the extent that the refusal is in relation to a deep emotional truth. We find ourselves again at the crossroads of the possibility inherent in the mother/child relationship, in which, in coming to a moment of potential recognition of a truth that may be profound and difficult, the mother might overcome her resistance in the service of her care for the other. Whether she sustains her link to the daughter in such moments or refuses it has profound ramifications not only for the relationship but also for the daughter's becoming.

Van Buren (2007) invites us to reclaim the significance of the maternal mind and meaning that is too often split off and devalued, to refuse the internal estrangement that occurs in relation to our vulnerability to the exigencies of life and to one another. Although death may represent the ultimate unknowability, life, too, is at some level strange, and terrifying in that essential strangeness. To ward off the terror of whatever seems too terrible to know, we may refuse certain thoughts or "become captivated by lies, distortions and misconceptions" (p. 6). The woman's body, from whence we come, is one point of essential estrangement, particularly to the extent that we cannot recognize both the regressive and the developmental pulls in which we become tangled. And yet, evoking the rhythmicity of Kristeva's (1986c) chora, "the signifiers of the mother's body appearing in dreams, phantasies and myths are the Rosetta Stones guiding us through the evolution of mindedness in our own human brains and bodies" (Van Buren, 2007, p. 7).

In contrast, the woman's path toward a constructive mourning is problematized in patriarchal cultures, in which the messages of the mother become subversive. Such messages are often spoken through metaphor, which allows us to both speak and deny the message or signification of the speech. Laplanche (1987) suggests that these messages become enigmatic not only because the child does not have the code through which to translate the message but also because the adult has lost contact with and has no conscious access to those underlying meaning that then remain hidden. This creates a situation in which we recognize that we are being addressed but there is no way of recognizing the meaning because of "the possibility that the signifier may be *designified*, or lose what it signifies without therefore losing the power to signify" (p. 45).

Lacan (1977d) links the *significance of the phallus* to the need to protect ourselves from engulfment by the mother. If we think, then, of the male need to be able to enter into the woman without being engulfed by her, then there is this moment of both desire and terror that must be managed. At precisely the point of possible merger, the woman must be conquered, "put in her place." We develop myths and metaphors in order to help to contain our anxiety, to put our fears "in place" (Charles, 2010). We see one such metaphor in Campbell's (1988) exposition of the bushman, who must find a way to enter the territory of the mother's body in order to find a differentiation from it that will hold. The labyrinth is another such metaphor that closely parallels the psychoanalytic journey into the void. Psychoanalysis, however, is an *accompanied* journey into the unexplored universe of intense dependency and engulfment represented by the woman's body as the source of life and the repository of unconscious thoughts, feelings, and desires (Charles, 2000a,b).

Van Buren (2007) notes the complex relationship between the distress of the child who feels that she is being sacrificed to a cruel destiny and the mother's desire to be the savior rather than the persecutor. The appeal to the mother, then, is conditioned by the enigmatic signifier of the child's suffering as accusation in relation to the mother's needs for containment such that "the parents use projective identification to unburden themselves; their offspring become the warehouse for their sacrificed infant aspects" (p. 35). The offspring then either take on the projected designation or reject the parents along with the projection. This is what we see with Jenny, who, in throwing off the yoke of the mother without awareness of what she was indeed rejecting, was blind to the complexity of her own needs and desires. Without the protection of the mother to set limits and boundaries, the child was subject to traumatic use by the man for whom she fulfilled a narcissistic illusion. Because the mother still feels dangerous, as though she threatens to take away something from the daughter rather than protect her, the daughter's needs are increasingly hidden, not only from her mother but also from herself. The victory she snatches away from the mother proves to be empty, indeed, and we see, along with Jenny, that she has only succeeded in sacrificing herself.

Part of the developmental legacy transmitted from mother to daughter is the difficult progression from child into woman in a culture that both idealizes and denigrates the female body. That denigration can be seen as the inevitable consequence of an idealization that shuns recognition of embodied meanings. Opposing the perspective that assumes that nature can be dominated and overcome, the woman's body reminds her perpetually of her embodiment. That cut to the illusion of omnipotence makes development possible, if we can accept the cut as an inevitable limit rather than a sign of shame, failure, abjection, and degradation. Evoking Bion's (1977) ideas of *passion* as a marker of a fundamental truth instinct, Van Buren (2007) suggests that the major force to be reckoned with on our developmental journey is our fear of the emotional truths that press on us from the "deep and formless infinite" (p. 144).

Ambivalence toward women has often left them anxious, precisely in relation to what cannot be passed along when the mother is ambivalent about her own place as a woman and the father cannot fully endorse the daughter's womanhood. The parents' failures to come to terms with their own limits and lacks, and come to a more reflective and appreciative acknowledgment of ways in which they both suffer and benefit from what is and is not present in one another, leaves a lack of modeling toward healthy relationships. The daughter then also suffers from the absence of an internal model for a vibrant and resilient, growth-enhancing relationship.

Women are also plagued by destructive imagoes of femininity that face—or attempt to elude—lack by embracing it. Anorexia and the endorsement of the prepubescent, emaciated female body in media, coupled with the excessive emphasis on sexuality, create for the young woman an impossible dilemma between an eternal childhood and a raging sexuality that is also potentially ravaging because there is no pathway through which to find one's way and make one's own choices. Rather, without the limits and possibilities afforded when there is attentive parenting that also leaves room for growth and difference, the young woman is at the mercy of split-off, unintegrated representations of self, with no way to make her own mindful choices.

CONCLUSION

These failures in mourning can be traced to enigmatic, unelucidated meanings passed along the generations, and also to an ambivalence over giving up on the possibility of a jouissance that does not recognize lack or limit. To the extent that women have been the repositors of a mourning that cannot be fulfilled, in accepting this position we collude with our own oppression.

The call to beauty can captivate us—and destroy us—if we cannot recognize that it also effaces us. In this call, the woman is positioned as an absent presence—or present absence, the essential aspect being our erasure as a subject who could advocate for her own desire and therefore recognize the other's limits, in spite of the fear of the Medusa stare that might turn the man to stone. Butler (2000) suggests that this alterity shifts the woman's grief into a register where it cannot be legitimately fulfilled. That impossibility occasions an ethics that is determined by fate but speaks from outside of it, a commentary on our exclusion. It is, perhaps, in the act of speaking that we refuse to be complicit in our effacement. If, as Butler contends, Antigone stands as a marker of the grief that is refused a social avenue for mourning, then positioning the woman as the devalued vehicle for a mourning that is imposed on her—and courses through her but cannot be reckoned with by her—makes both grief and development impossible.

Psychoanalysis affords a means for encountering and moving beyond the fears that substitute a self-presentation, a symptom, for the self who is constrained but also liberated by facing her limits and her lack. And yet, the meaning structures of psychoanalysis have been largely writ from the male lens, to which I remain to some extent a mystery. This paradox leaves me working at finding myself through the various meaning structures that are offered to me, most of which draw from male threads. Many of those threads, such as Bion's (1977) press toward an internal truth signified through our affective engagement with it, and also his language regarding the pursuit of knowledge rather than the drivenness of desire, speak to embodied truths that men have reached toward but could only capture through their half of a conversation that has been foreclosed. There can be no dialogue to the extent that the woman remains the object of, rather than another subject in, the conversation.

As a profoundly embodied truth, Laplanche's (1999a) enigmatic signifier, which calls to us from the unconscious of the other, seems highly significant as a meaning structure, beyond the place he positions it in his discourse. This ultimate embodiment and particularity of meaning is also present in Lacan's (1974–1975) later work, in which he invites us to look at ways in which we lose ourselves in a presentation to the other that focuses on seeming rather than being. Through his exploration of the Borromean knot, Lacan highlights the inevitable, ineluctable, idiosyncrasy of being, marking ways in which the symptom is both a distress call and a clarion call, if we can be sufficiently respectful of our own distress to inquire into it, to know *further* rather than to seek an understanding that preempts the very possibility of that internal exploration.

Some attempts to illuminate what has been left unexplored, such as Klein's work, are hampered by her attempt to fit her observations too neatly into a package that needed to be extended. Others, such as the work of Kristeva, offer ideas, such as the chora, that profoundly speak to the woman's experience, but remain outside the canon. Perhaps this dialogue is one that will be inevitably unwieldy, limping along on two legs that fit imperfectly together. That gap may be an important reminder of the difference between the sexes, and between one person and another, that must be encountered and reckoned with in order for a unique subject to more fully come into being.

Following Klein's expansion of Freudian theory, Kristeva posits the mother's body as that which "mediates the symbolic law organizing social relations and becomes the ordering principle of the semiotic *chora*, which is on the path of destruction, aggressivity and death" (1986c, p. 95). Perhaps, in trying to understand our origins, we are necessarily drawn to the problem of the mother in whom we are formulated and yet who remains mysterious to us except insofar as we can discover keys to those mysteries within ourselves. In the confrontation with separation from the mother, there is, for Kristeva, a break between the semiotic and the symbolic, between signifier and signified, that makes possible not just relationships but personhood. From this perspective, one can see the failure to mourn as a failure to come to grips with the essential lack and limit at the core of human being.

And so, in contemplating the complex issues underlying the question of women and mourning, we find ourselves up against the woman as mystery, perhaps most notably configured in the character of Antigone. As I was finishing this chapter, I found myself compelled by Antigone, coming up against the issue of the beauty of Antigone and her powerful self-sacrifice that was already preordained—a beauty held by the male gaze, the male who also sacrifices himself for this beauty. I am presuming that Antigone ends the story there because although she cannot elude fate and destiny, she can keep the fate from extending further into future generations. She can take a stand for something that calls to her, even if her acts are misread and used for their own purposes by those who come after. In contrast to the Law that is called into being in the Name of the Father, one reading of Antigone's name is "in the place of the mother" (Butler, 2000, p. 22). In *this* story, it is the daughter who must take a stand for her own ethics, one that has its roots in the semiotics of enigmatic meanings passed along through family and culture. So, then, there is this demand from the next generations that calls to us whether we like it or not; we will be used, one way and another. And so, as we age, ever more apparently in the hands of fate and destiny, we are called upon to accept the inevitability of being carried along *and also* to face whatever ethics call to us.

The lessons from cultural vehicles of embodied meanings, such as those afforded by myth, film, and literature, help us to experience vicariously, from the safe distance of displacement, some of the challenges that may be too difficult to take on directly in our daily lives (Charles, 2015). The call, however, from the suffering of our children, insists that we take on the challenges demanded by the enigmatic meanings that otherwise speak to us silently, demanding obeisance to a martyrdom of suffering, through which we participate in the illusion of an impossible jouissance that can only be enjoyed at our own expense and, more importantly, at the expense of our daughters, to whom we bequeath precisely what we have failed to face. During my graduate studies, I looked at the experiences around leaving home for three generations of mothers and daughters. I found that those mothers who had not had receptive, engaged mothering from their own mothers were not able to offer to their daughters what they had lacked. The best they could do, in such circumstances, was to set them free (Charles, Frank, Jacobson, & Grossman, 2001).

The chain of unresolved mourning can be labyrinthine, ensnaring our children in enigmatic knots they can neither disentangle nor entirely break through. It is worth considering both what we might offer to our children that might help them to engage in this difficult process of becoming oneself, in spite of the hazards entailed in facing lack and limit, and also, when all else fails, how we might set them free. Ultimately, Jenny's mother offered her that invitation, and she took it up, directly asserting her claim to the legitimacy of her own telling of the tale. Notably, she did not seek consensus or confirmation but rather challenged those present to rethink the telling of their own tales that had been subverted in relation to a corrupt authority who was being illegitimately lauded. She allowed herself to not be effaced or abased by the other but rather to stare back.

REFERENCES

Abraham, N., & Torok, M. (1994). *The Shell and the Kernel.* N. T. Rand (Ed. & Trans.). Chicago & London: University of Chicago Press.

Apprey, M. (1993). The African-American experience: Forced migration and the transgenerational trauma. *Mind and Human Interaction*, 4:70–75.

Apprey, M. (2003). Repairing history: Reworking trauma. In: D. Moss (Ed.). *Hating in the First Person Plural: Psychoanalytic Essays on Racism, Homophobia, Misogyny, and Terror,* pp. 3–27. New York: Other Press.

Arlow, J. (1961). Ego psychology and the study of mythology. *Journal of the American Psychoanalytic Association*, 9:371–393.

Baldwin, J. (1962). *Another Country.* New York: Dial Press.

Balter, L. (1969). The mother as source of power: A psychoanalytic study of three Greek myths. *Psychoanalytic Quarterly*, 38:217–274.

Bion, W. R. (1977). *Seven Servants.* New York: Jason Aronson.

Butler, J. (2000). *Antigone's Claim: Kinship between Life and Death.* New York: Columbia University Press.

Campbell, J. (1959). *Masks of God.* New York: Doubleday.
Campbell, J. (1988). *The Power of Myth.* New York: Viking Press.
Cassirer, E. (1946). *Language and Myth*, S. K. Langer (Trans.). New York: Dover.
Charles, M. (2000a). Convex and concave, Part I: Images of emptiness in women. *American Journal of Psychoanalysis*, 60(1):5–28.
Charles, M. (2000b). Convex and concave, Part II: Images of emptiness in men. *American Journal of Psychoanalysis*, 60(2):119–138.
Charles, M. (2008). The masquerade, the veil, and the phallic mask: Commentary. *Psychoanalysis, Culture, and Society*, 13:24–24.
Charles, M. (2010). When cultures collide: Myth, meaning, and configural space. *Modern Psychoanalysis*, 34:26–47.
Charles, M. (2011). What Does a Woman Want? *Psychoanalysis, Culture, and Society*, 16(4):337–353.
Charles, M. (2015). *Psychoanalysis and Literature: The Stories We Live.* Lanham, MD: Rowman & Littlefield.
Charles. M. (2019). Women and Madness in Context. In: M. H. Brown & M. Charles (Eds.). *Women & Psychosis: Multidisciplinary Perspectives*, pp. 11–35. Lanham, MD: Rowman & Littlefield.
Charles, M., Frank, S. J., Jacobson, S., & Grossman, G. (2001). Repetition of the remembered past: Patterns of separation-individuation in two generations of mothers and daughters. *Psychoanalytic Psychology*, 18:705–728.
Davoine, F., & Gaudillière J.-M. (2004). *History Beyond Trauma: Whereof One Cannot Speak, Thereof One Cannot Stay Silent*, S. Fairfield (Trans.). New York: Other Press.
Fanon, F. (1952/2008). *Black Skin, White Masks*, R. Philcox (Trans.). New York: Grove Press.
Fox, J. (Director). (2018). *The Tale* [Motion Picture]. United States: HBO Films.
Freud, S. (1917). Mourning and Melancholia. *The Standard Edition of the Complete Psychological Works of Sigmund Freud, Volume XIV (1914–1916)*, pp. 237–258. London: Hogarth Press.
Freud, S. (1925). Some Psychical Consequences of the Anatomical Distinction between the Sexes. *The Standard Edition of the Complete Psychological Works of Sigmund Freud, Volume XIX (1923–1925)*, pp. 248–258. London: Hogarth Press.
Freud, S. (1926). The Question of Lay Analysis. *The Standard Edition of the Complete Psychological Works of Sigmund Freud, Volume XX (1925–1926)*, pp. 183–258. London: Hogarth Press.
Grotstein, J. S. (2004). The seventh servant: The implications of a truth drive in Bion's theory of 'O'. *International Journal of Psycho-Analysis*, 85:1081–1101.
Hook, D. (2012). *A Critical Psychology of the Postcolonial: The Mind of Apartheid.* New York: Routledge.
Klein, M. (1946). Notes on some schizoid mechanisms. In: *Envy and Gratitude and Other Works, 1946 – 1963*, pp. 1–24. London: Hogarth Press 1975.
Kristeva, J. (1982). *Powers of Horror: An Essay on Abjection.* L. S. Roudiez (Trans.). New York: Columbia University Press.
Kristeva, J. (1986a). Stabat Mater. In: *The Kristeva Reader.* T. Moi (Ed.), L. S. Roudiez & S. Hand (Trans.), pp. 160–186. New York: Columbia University Press.
Kristeva, J. (1986b). Women's Time. In: *The Kristeva Reader.* T. Moi (Ed.), L. S. Roudiez & S. Hand (Trans.), pp. 187–213. New York: Columbia University Press.
Kristeva, J. (1986c). Revolution in Poetic Language. In: *The Kristeva Reader.* T. Moi (Ed.), L. S. Roudiez & S. Hand (Trans.), pp. 89–136. New York: Columbia University Press.
Lacan, J. (1974–1975). *Seminar XII: RSI.* C. Gallagher (Trans.). http://www.lacaninireland.com/web/published-works/seminars.
Lacan, J. (1977a). The subversion of the subject and the dialectic of desire in the Freudian unconscious. In: *Écrits*, A. Sheridan (Trans.), pp. 292–325. New York: W. W. Norton.
Lacan, J. (1977b). The function and field of speech and language in psychoanalysis. In: *Écrits*, A. Sheridan (Trans.), pp. 30–113. New York: W. W. Norton, 1977.
Lacan, J. (1977c). The agency of the letter in the unconscious or reason since Freud. In: *Écrits*, A. Sheridan (Trans.), pp. 146–178. New York: W. W. Norton, 1977.

Lacan, J. (1977d). The signification of the phallus. In: *Écrits*, A. Sheridan (Trans.), pp. 281–291. New York: W. W. Norton.
Lacan, J. (1992). *The Ethics of Psychoanalysis*, J.-A. Miller (Ed.), D. Porter (Trans.). New York: W. W. Norton.
LaCapra, D. (1999). Trauma, Absence, Loss. *Critical Inquiry*, 25:696–727.
Laplanche, J. (1987). *New Foundations for Psychoanalysis*, J. House (Trans.). New York: Routledge.
Laplanche, J. (1995). Seduction, persecution, revelation. *International Journal of Psycho-Analysis*, 76:663–682.
Laplanche, J. (1997). The theory of seduction and the problem of the other. *International Journal of Psycho-Analysis*, 78:653–666.
Laplanche, J. (1999a). A short treatise on the unconscious. In: *Essays on Otherness*, L. Thurston (Trans.), pp. 84–116. London & New York: Routledge.
Laplanche, J. (1999b). Time and the other. In: *Essays on Otherness*, L. Thurston (Trans.), pp. 234–259. London & New York: Routledge.
Laplanche, J. (1999c). Notes on afterwardness. In: *Essays on Otherness*, pp. 260–265. London & New York: Routledge.
Levinas, E. (1948). *Time and the Other*, R. A. Cohen (Trans.). Pittsburgh: Duquesne University Press.
Levinas, E. (1981). *Otherwise than Being or Beyond Essence*, A. Lingus (Trans.). The Hague: Martinus Nijhoff.
Levinas, E. (1999). *Alterity and Transcendence*, M. B. Smith (Trans.). New York: Columbia University Press.
Levinas, E. (2000). *God, Death, and Time*, B. Bergo (Trans.). Stanford: Stanford University Press.
Morrison, T. (2008). *A Mercy*. New York & Toronto: Alfred Knopf.
Phillips, J. A. (1986). "Mother incest so familiar to us": Psychoanalysis and the Eve myth. *American Journal of Psychoanalysis*, 46:6–14.
Shepherdson, C. (2008). The atrocity of desire: Of Love and Beauty in Lacan's Antigone. In: *Lacan and the Limits of Language*, pp. 50–80. New York: Fordham University Press.
Stone, A. (2012). *Feminism, Psychoanalysis, and Maternal Subjectivity*. London & New York: Routledge.
Thompson, C. (1964). *On Women*. M. R. Green (Ed.). New York: Basic Books.
Van Buren, J. (2007). *Mothers and Daughters and the Origins of Female Subjectivity*. London & New York: Routledge.
Walsh, L. (1999). Her mother her self: The ethics of the Antigone family romance. *Hypatia*, 14:96–125.
Winnicott, D. W. (1971). *Playing and Reality*. New York: Basic Books.
Wyatt, J. (2017). *Love and Narrative Form in Toni Morrison's Later Novels*. Athens, Georgia: University of Georgia Press.

Chapter Three

Devil! Sing Me the Blues . . .

Story of a Life Struggling to Be Born

Shalini Masih

More than three decades ago, eminent Indian psychoanalyst Sudhir Kakar (1982) explored the insecurities and vulnerabilities that plague the Indian psyche in his groundbreaking work, *Shamans, Mystics and Doctors*. Perhaps intuiting a need for some kind of resolve, culture makes available a language populated by the "supernatural." Ghosts, like a child's imaginary friends, float amidst us, for us to "use" them, to be inhabited by them, sometimes, utter prophesies, heal the sick, state solutions to distress, demand obedience; and at other times, personify "destruction" in its most crude form. The large number of women possessed by spirits testifies to their struggles for being recognised as "subjects in their own right." As a girl grows, her blossoming body soon comes under the captivity of societal chains that thwart a fuller unfolding of desires to look beautiful, be admired, to exercise sexual choice, and to strike in rage. Confronted with the fragility of maleness in our society, its fear of the emergence of a phallic part in woman, most women choose invisibilization. Dutiful, she is revered as *Devi* or Goddess. Rebellious, she is condemned as *Dayan* or Demoness. When possessed by spirit, she can relish the sweet taste of freedom, helped by traditional belief in a "supernatural" order, creating moments of birth for the unborn parts of the Self.

What are the forms in which ghosts hover among us? Will there be a door creaking open or a pair of eyes glaring from a distance one moment, right in your face the very next?

THE TIES THAT BIND

Avni recalls her first day in marital home sitting uncomfortably in a quaint room, trying to find comfort in company of her own thoughts. Her ostentatious attire and body clad in it—itchy skin striving to breathe under all the cloths and jewelry, defiant hair locks willfully escaping from her bun, shoulders stooped—hyper aware of unfamiliar subservience she was being put through. Memories of her parental home embraced her in a warm cloak of nostalgia, gifting smile to her lips and tears to her eyes, this offering she dropped the very instant she snapped out of reverie into sharp giggles and beneath the gazes of young and elderly women in the room who sat around her, blocking space for ventilation for body and for feelings. The matriarch mother-in-law, noticing the unadorned ears, demanded the reason. Unaccustomed to carrying the weight of customs and heavy jewelry, her earlobes were swollen and bled. *"A new bride's ears should never be unadorned,"* said the matriarch, *"everyone will notice . . . You will have to wear them for a couple of days . . . It doesn't matter . . . Bear the pain."* She almost threw up; her body remaining true to a wish to reject what was being pinned on it. For the next two hours she submitted her body to older women as they dressed up the new bride as though she were a lifeless doll. She stood in a blouse and skirt, her hands going up, her stomach sucked in on their commands, skin recoiling from their cold touch on her body. *"It will be over soon,"* she kept telling herself as two women struggled to pierce an earring through the narrow reluctant hole in her swollen sulky earlobe.

Her ordeal was interrupted by her husband, *Mohan*, asserting that she should be left to carry herself the way she liked, making room for his wife to the displeasure of his own mother. Although helpful, such an assertion rarely helps a couple in Indian society to come together more closely; and subsequently *Avni* and *Mohan*[1] had to live a fragmented narrative of coupledom.

Avni, an attractive and talented woman in her early thirties, felt humiliated in the conservative space of her marital home. They laid down nonnegotiable rules about how a daughter-in-law and a couple should live their life. Her every attribute was judged, every move closely watched. Here was the clichéd relationship of the cruel matriarch mother-in-law and the silent suffering daughter-in-law. Her husband usually emerged as her voice.

Her childhood in an upper middle class family was marked by emotional poverty, neglect and preference for male child over her. Her marriage was a love marriage against the will of both the families. The reason for disapproval was *Avni*'s hailing from a "modern" family and *Mohan* from a conservative one. Neglected in parental home, she fought intrusion in marital home. *Mohan* was a good-natured man and loved *Avni* for who she was, fiercely protecting her choices. Trapped like a damsel in society's high tower she was expected to be an ideal daughter-in-law. Adorned by attires of her desire she was labeled a whore; choosing career over motherhood she was selfish and taking break from household chores she was lazy. In familial thinking sexuality could only culminate in "motherhood." If she and *Mohan* lovingly exchanged sweet nothings, they were stamped shameless. "A couple's intimacy," note Kakar and Kakar (2007), "is implicitly rebellious and defiant, it not only attracts sanctions from those who see themselves as representatives of the family order but also arouses guilt in the couple's constituents—the husband and/or the wife."

In some rare moments she felt the need to write poetry or short essays. But nothing she wrote felt good enough. Her internal landscape lay plagued by self-loathing worsened by persistent lack of acceptance and humiliation from her in-laws. Persistent vigilance pierced through her sanity, making her increasingly vulnerable to anxieties of persecution. Soon, even her trace became unbearable to that "inside" which was getting corroded by toxicity "outside." Unbeknown to her, she adapted to being squashed like a bug. Her rescuer, *Mohan*, his strength was also dwindling. Unseen and beaten down to the point of invisibility, both often suffered pangs of loneliness. Although the couple moved away to a different city, the parent-in-laws would dump even more toxicity with each visit. Forlorn, hurt, and powerless, the couple spat venomous grudges, maligning each other. Lacking capacity to fight on her own, she expected him to be more assertive. He expected her to be more adjusting. Months would pass before the flames of rage cooled down and flames of passion returned. Until then superficial coldness percolated the space between them, masking the seething embers of unspoken hostility. Their marriage was becoming a radioactive wasteland.

In all of this *Avni* and *Mohan* were unwilling to erase the "boundary with the family, re-embracing its ideological underpinnings." (Kakar & Kakar, 2007). Stuck in the quagmire between adherences to traditional roles and desire to take flight toward modern aspirations, *Avni* did not even have the presence of ghosts and ghouls to accompany her with companionship, to facilitate the assertion of her needs. Lear (1998), reflecting on the tradition of the Enlightenment and rationality, grasps the use of knowingness as a defense to deny the sense of being existentially alone; he notes that we have been abandoned by the gods and their secular avatars, by *pitr* as ancestral spirits are addressed in Indian culture. Bereft of ghosts and ghouls of the supernatural order, *Avni*'s feeble attempts at connecting with her Self in a bid to process her pain opened the gates to many grotesque images from the past.

OPEN THE GATES OF HELL

Chronic humiliation from mother-in-law had thinned down the strength she drew from her inner ideals. More tangible presence was needed. She wondered whether it was time to let her parents know about the dread with which she went on from one day to next. A traumatic incident made her decision easier. There was enough Eros binding the couple for them to steal moments away from familial mandates and sneak out for a date. On returning from one such evening, the couple was bombarded with admonition which led to physical violence on Avni:

> *I am in pieces . . . Trying to gather my fragments. There was a huge drama at my home between Mohan, myself and his parents. They were saying many mean and hurtful things to us . . . I was told that I am the root of every problem and so I began to walk out of the house. She* (mother-in-law) *held me, pushed me around but when I told her not to do so she completely denied what her body was doing to mine. I couldn't understand the two contrasting communications that were coming my way. Mohan might have felt enraged at his mother. The very next moment he entered a state of frenzy. It was pure fury! Smashing everything around into smithereens. He was trembling and screaming and then collapsed on the floor. A lull followed. I tried to physically contain him. He wouldn't let me or anyone else near him. His mother then started to apologise to us, hysterically touching our feet. Both of us kept sitting for nearly 2 hours on the floor in the middle of all the shattered glass. I couldn't feel if it cut into our skins or not. The internal hurt was more. He then asked me to walk out of his life and house . . . that we had achieved together whatever we could . . . that I should save myself. I couldn't believe what he was saying and checked with him a couple of times.*

She retaliated the first time and walked out of her house in the middle of the night. I cringe in fear picturing a young woman walking in a deserted colony of Delhi. This fear has been pushed in me by those nocturnal beings that flock the dark allies of this city, ready to prey upon unaccompanied women, making this city gain its notorious reputation as a rape capital of India. As she left the house, *Mohan* also followed, leaving his family behind. He also suffered painful disillusionment at hands of his parents. All his efforts to bridge gaps in relations fell flat. The shards of insidious humiliation cut through the desire that bound them as couple.

Months passed. In a bid to seek support she poured her heart out to her parents. They listened, expressed concern but the very next moment began to discuss excitedly about her brother's achievements. In one stroke, her hurt was erased with their glistening preference for the son. The parental was the "good" she craved and the in-laws the "bad." This indifference from the parents shattered this spectacular split. Relaying her sense of utter shock she said, "*I felt negated . . . Like I was not there . . . Like I was nothing . . . Invisible . . .*"

She sought recognition of her pain in parents' eyes. Their gaze reflected preference for son. She felt devalued to a nobody, a negation of "I." Here was an encounter with the "negative." In as far as one adheres to the psychoanalytic adage "Anatomy is Destiny," it helps us make sense of the sense of invisibility that a girl child carries in Indian culture. Alizade (1999) notes, the anatomy begins to make fate. The phallus adheres anatomically to the penis, visible protrusion narcissistically overvalued. The vulva of the woman imagines a psychic space of "not having." In Freudian frame womanhood is seen woven around the spindle of "lack" of the penis which the little girl hopes to find through the oedipal father. Cultural preference for male child consolidates the inscription of invisibility in a girl by her "not having" a penis and "not being" a boy. According to Gerson (2011), to experience oneself as devalued and not being seen by the other throws one into a pre-symbolic world which "carries the terrors of loss of communicative ability and self-delineation."

Both *Avni and Mohan*, faced with indifference from *Avni*'s family and overwhelming intrusion from *Mohan*'s, fell into abjection. The humiliation struck squarely at the desire that bound them as couple. It was to destroy, as Gerson (2011) notes, the continuity and commonality between the subject of "objectionable" desires and the objects of his or her desire. The insidious nature of this destruction is regularly accomplished by making the desiring subject experience the desire itself as the source of humiliation and subsequent isolation. Painful memories of desires having suffered the fate of humiliation returned to haunt, allying with hurt and toxicity of the present, deepening fissures. "Reminiscences of humiliations," notes Gerson (2011), are ones "in which one's desire and/or capacity to desire was not received and thus was rendered mute." Glimpses of *Avni*'s mute self began to emerge from her history.

In infancy she suffered prolonged absence of the mother. In one such story about her infancy she was told that not knowing how to soothe the wailing infant, her father would put mother's nightgown next to her. Comforted by mother's odor she would fall asleep. Or perhaps it was exhaustion from wailing? She grew into a clingy child. Freud (1917) brought to light the fate of loving emotional energy which retreats into the ego after having suffered neglect and causes the ego to split with one part establishing identification with the abandoned object. This object is held endlessly captive or clung to. Hostility and erotic love come together in sadism toward the disappointing object. The result is an internal horror story of a critical, diabolic split off part of the ego haunting the corresponding part identified with abandoned object. Horror and abuse in internal world is preferred over facing the void. "There is no loss; an external object (the abandoned object) is omnipotently replaced by an internal one (the ego-identified-with-the-object)" (Ogden, 2002). No loss, no mourning, a dynamic sets in wherein, the pain of loss and by extension every other emotional pain is persistently evaded. Without any grieving monument to loss, any process to mark the disappearance, there is just arid emotional terrain. The work of binding, facilitated by Eros, could not happen successfully, when faced with the fear of being alone, *Avni*'s clinging to the mother indicates a groping after—"What to bind to?" It is as if, when left alone, even this mother, with a slim capacity to give, can be taken away if she is not clasped.

A prolonged separation from the mother occurred at the age of four. Left in the care of her grandparents and other relatives, *Avni* refused to receive them. Instead, she went into a mute sulk. She chewed a bite from her breakfast on her way to school and back. It substituted for the breast that went missing. The evenings were pleasant. Father would return from work. She had him all to herself. The lump of food in mouth was replaced by words as father was held captive by charm of his daughter's innocent narration of endless stories about her day. A muse was born as that character in internal world, who one could endlessly erotically enthrall and suck the juices of admiration. In his animated gaze, she came alive, creating word-babies with the father. This was how her day and evening were divided. However, one wonders if in a twilight zone in her internal world the desire for the father was followed by fear of the absent mother who was not only gnawed at with fangs of rage but was also the rival replaced in the evening as father-daughter sat blanketed by the excitement of stories she created. Failing to reach what lay behind her sulk, the grandfather condemned her as diabolic, banning family members from holding her in their maternal laps. Eigen (2001) writes, "An object responding to murderous/parasitic/creative urges with overabundance of anxiety, persecution, hate, apathy throws the self back on unmodified aggravated urges." The muted self gets crystallized. When object-seeking tendencies are failed, capacity to be nourished by psychic work also gets wounded. Seeking becomes diabolic.

It is common occurrence in our culture, one inherent to the permeability of self that we invade a child's inner space, in order to appropriate certain aspects, aligning them increasingly, with the norms "outside." The child learns to hide instinctual impulses lest she risk annihilation. S/he becomes a "tricky little devil." Narayanan (2015) sees in a sulk captured both the "component of punishment to the perpetrator" as well as a plea to be rescued from an Other. Perhaps *sulk* is the endless *sucking of the milk*, the illegitimate offspring of pathological mourning, carrying the wish to suck the breast dry and not stop there. A step further to clinginess which is driven by fear, sulk gets its fuel from rage and greed—parts of her that grandfather failed to contain and instead saw as diabolic. When the mother returned after few months she looked oddly fat and refrained from lifting *Avni* in her arms. Her joy dampened. Months later with the arrival of her younger brother, she watched father's love shift to the male child celebrated by all. One wonders if being dethroned by a male child was experienced as revenge from the damaged and retaliatory mother for closeness with the father. Recurrent nightmares carried grotesque images of two male faces—one starved to the point of becoming a skeleton and the other face was swollen; both covered in pus-filled boils, like demonic versions of Laurel and Hardy, perhaps reflecting starvation, greed and rage. Slowly pushed toward the edges of invisibility, *Avni* returned as mother's extension by caring for little brother. In subsequent years, she witnessed the parents fighting and sided with the mother who was the victim to father's violence. This move toward mother and away from the father was highly conflictual—in masculine identification she was mother's partner, in maternal identification, caregiver; perhaps she saved the mother from guilt in this way. In adolescence, as she grew into a woman's body she recalled disgust in her father's gaze and words. His admiration was reinstated as she turned into a tomboy, leaving me to wonder if it was to save the father from horror of her and his own sexuality. In some rare moments she turned toward writing poetry or art only to one day come to face the elder sister's envy who threw all of these creative works away, apparently by accident. Mother's complacency in this matter was experienced as her becoming an ally of the envious sister. *Avni* stopped writing and painting. Tessman (1982) reflects on the desire for father's acknowledgment of the feminine in daughter helps in formation of an ego ideal as motivational force and his acceptance of her excitement around her creative efforts later gets transformed into internalized experiences of vitality in one's work. To savor beauty of body and mind, recreating art with the internal muse-father was yet again followed by attacks.

There was enough neglect to support some distance and rebellion. In adulthood when she began to rebel against her family and pursue her desire for *Mohan*, her father was next to brand her as diabolic. Pursuit of desire became progressively linked with guilt. Although she did marry *Mohan*, she compensated by shrinking to make room for others. Visible, she became exposed to be squashed again. Hidden, but also deriving narcissistic juices as a caretaker, she continued to grow distant from a need to be taken care of as a child. A dream became an ally here, *"I am handing over a little baby girl to a woman. Just when this woman is about to hold the baby she actually drops the baby girl. The baby girl magically grows legs mid-air. The very next moment she is standing on her two legs. She gestures to the woman to say that she is okay, that there is no need to worry."* When the need to depend is repeatedly crushed a hologram of premature birth gets created. Tustin's (1981) idea of "precocious two-ness" brings forth consequence of premature psychological birth in a stunned, shunted, hardened self. Tustin links with Bion's (1962) concept of "nameless dread" of premature two-ness as the infant's "preconceptions" are not greeted by the lap of "realization" and end up suspended in a meaningless limbo exuding terror that cannot be pinned to any source, because it cannot be thought. Vulnerable one moment, independent and stoic the very next, ever evading scatter. Why risk being dropped when you can conjure up limbs to stand on and also evade the terror of separation and loneliness? Perhaps it was this magical capacity that made those around her take her for granted, seek nurturance, sucking her dry but also be suspicious toward her and doubt her emotional pain. Having profound dependency needs and yet helpless in the face of this reflex like capacity for pseudo-independence she would survive and emerge unscathed, ready for more. But after the recent gash of neglect from parents opened up past hurts, being stoic no longer worked. She was more aware of the costs involved. Flashes from emotional and physical violence barged in the psyche like unwelcomed guests, their shadows fell on all current relationships.

BETWEEN CLIFF AND THE DARK CLOUDS

Eigen (2018a) writes, "It is not true that the devil never appears in a mirror; sometimes bits of self-knowledge do come through." Grudge blew on the embers of wounds, keeping them from healing. The foulness of rotting wounds was no longer confined to the chambers of her internal world, but, like Mist of Death personified in Greek mythology as Achlys,[2] it crept into relationships with people and creative work. Writing once brought joy and a sense of worth. "*It is eerie . . . Knowing that it is you who wrote something, yet feeling intellectually distant from it . . . Like the work is a blob in memory . . . Slowly fading away . . .*"

What was once familiar and pleasurable now felt far, a sign of the unbinding at work. With urgency she would approach writing but find the blank whiteness of her laptop screen staring back at her. Perhaps this whiteness (Green, 1970) was of a space deeper than all the depression and rage, where all efforts to mourn collapsed due to lack of a psychic structure to support it. Internal space was held captive by a dark force, appearing as a Muse at first only to transform into demon—the admiring-father-turned-rejecting "unconsciously merged in with the early withholding and hostile mother" (Kavaler-Adler, 1993). Muse-demon kept fresh the rage that enveloped unmet cravings.

The trauma of unfulfilled cravings and engulfment by one's own primitive rage was re-lived in marriage. The Devil that kept her from procreating a life *out of desire* for *Mohan*, also took on the face of the matriarch mother-in-law.

An image of rotting, maggot infested leftover food became external manifestation of rotten insides corroded with acidic concoction of hostility and pain. Sleeping and eating increased. Was she becoming a baby again? *Mohan*'s love held her together. Weeks passed, like clouds floating endlessly casting shadows over the inner landscape, evoking host of feelings which she responded to with numbness only to be rattled by a nightmare. "*I dreamed that my skull is cut out from the top. I can see my own brain . . . Exposed . . . I look closer . . . There are maggots crawling inside my brain . . . I woke up in frenzy . . . Shaking them off from my head and face . . . My mind is infested with maggots."* Rage, like maggots, gnawed away all potential. At one level she felt psychically crippled to use her experience creatively, at another, she yearned to become a mother but feared for her child's future in her familial milieu. She felt possessive for a child who she had not even conceived yet. Eigen (2018b) notes a "loose equation tends to hold in dreams: bugs = babies = madness as destruction . . . Babies are born into a world that does not know what to do with them." Perhaps it was her dread of aliveness, her own as well as her baby's, and also the harm to it that she anticipated that kept fresh the sense of toxicity infused by her environment. Both the internal and external world were not safe abodes for a child. In reverie my mind floats to Winnicott's (1971) use of Tagore's words: "On the seashore of endless worlds, children play." This image lay in striking contrast with the image of a three-year-old Syrian boy washed ashore from the Mediterranean Sea highlighting an overarching concern—the world unsafe for playful children. The best way to save the baby's life was to prevent its birth, keep it pinned in its inorganic or unborn state. Instead, she nursed maggot-babies in the cradle of her rage.

Sharing Bion's astute sensitivity to life in death, Eigen responds to an interviewer,

> For him (Bion), marriage and raising children meant life. Yet death struck in childbirth. He, too, said he died in the First World War, in grotesque mutilations on the field of battle. A death that lingered as his baby girl grew. In one incident he recounts, his little daughter was trying to reach him while he was sitting staring into space in their garden. She tried to crawl to him, crying, but could not reach him. He was in a frozen state, paralyzed. Finally, unable to bear the scene, the housekeeper picked the little girl up and comforted her. Years later this girl, a grown woman and mother, died in a car accident in the Italian mountains, a daughter with her. (Eigen in conversation with Kaniel, Kara-Ivanov, R., 2013)

Like her baby, *Avni*'s self clothed in words was not allowed birth or expression. In identification with her baby, *Avni* was unwilling to relinquish the symbiotic ties with the mother of early infancy. The fantasy baby was akin to the lump of food she chewed on her way to school. I recall young women patients brought up in similar familial matrix where the mother suffered brutal humiliation by her mother-in-law. One young woman began to cut when she was seven years old while the other lacked control over her bowel movements well into adulthood. These symptoms were closely linked with dread one went through in trying to appease the wounded mother.

Incapable of navigating destructive aspects of aliveness, a "bugged" or rotting mind gained power over the potential mind-womb pulsating with aliveness and its fluctuating intensities. A general futility of life persisted with eerie calm, wiping life clear of meaning, spirally into full-blown thoughts of suicide, with not even a hint of helplessness to grant any hope of recovery. She began to plan to take off to a cliff and enjoy the view for some time before taking "*a leap into the dark clouds.*" Wish for transcending life and self lay cocooned in this fantasy, "*I want to die in a way that I won't know the difference between flying or* [*sic*] *dying. It will be the utmost freedom.*"

While writing about her, carrying a sense from the time before words, with its failed ecstasies and flourishing agonies as well as her need for freedom, an image sprouts like a stammer between word and its meaning. It is as if, like the seashore, the cliff is the surface of the mother's body, bearing signs of birth and sought to bear the thrust as the daughter's body launches itself into the dark clouds where lies the yearned-for embrace of the father's admiration.

HELLO DARKNESS

Enabled by *Mohan*'s love she oscillated between death and meaning, fighting thoughts of suicide.

> *Spirit sinks . . . I am trying to not think of suicide . . . I often have these urges to scream . . . I would dig my face in a pillow and just scream . . . Until my throat turns bad and my voice begins to split . . . It then reaches wailing . . . Then fades into a whimper . . . In that state I have noticed that my body squirms . . . Like something is going to explode . . . Earlier I used to do it when I would be alone . . . Only now have I begun to let myself go in presence of B . . . I feel it won't stop if I go on . . . That I will crumble and evaporate . . . His embrace brings me back . . . I keep telling him to make it stop! And he repeats—"I am here. I am here." And after its over my body feels drained . . . So much that I can't even lift my hands . . . He says that he sees my rage when I am in that state . . . I feel light . . .*

Her screaming, squirming body reminded me of those of women possessed by demonic spirits from my research field. Scream was the catalyst for the muted self. A wailing infant yet again, this time *Avni*'s squirming body had the comfort of the blanket of *Mohan*'s warmth. Bolognini (2011), through the myth of Peleus hugging Thetis to gain her love, reflects on "antecedent formative phase of the container" and notes, "To contain someone, one must be or have been contained." What escaped *Avni* due to her hostility was that in the background of *Mohan*'s maternal capacity was her mother-in-law having given him an experience of containment and love.

However, the destructive force within fought back. Images of decomposing face emerged demanding that *Avni* dreamt them. The noose tightened. She was becoming a nobody, the very image of the negation she had suffered at the hands of her families. In suicide, Benjamin (1988) saw an attempt to find recognition. The terror of non-recognition became evident through another nightmare, "*I am looking at my face in the mirror. It is covered with many red boils and blisters. They begin to burst one by one . . . Pus oozing out of them . . . It is painful and an unpleasant sight. I look for my mother or Mohan . . . Gradually boils appear on my tongue as well.*"

The grotesque images from recurrent nightmares of childhood returned. Only this time, rage and greed, hitherto cast away to anonymity, had her face and threatened to gag her, making her incapable of giving it any form in words. She was the diabolic that the other's gaze reflected and that she needed to dream.

With medication, crying spells were controlled. She began to weep in sleep. Her husband's embrace was the lap that allowed for scatter. For the first time in life she did not have to grow limbs magically to save (m)other the trouble. One night in sleep she wept. *Mohan* held her again. However, when he turned her toward him her eyes were open, face emotionless, only her tone was weepy. The bizarreness terrified him, making him believe his wife was indeed possessed by a ghost which now threatened to possess him. Having seen a glimpse of the dark force that resided in her internal world as her most intimate companion, *Mohan* was terrified. Meeting terror with fury, he began to attack the possessing ghost in her. Hit by his fury, she woke up and saw him. Utterly confused and wretched, she looked at the contagious too-muchness of her needs that *Mohan* succumbed to. She dug her face in a pillow and screamed her last scream. Winnicott (1969) writes of the final unuttered scream when the baby gives up and swallows the potential thing that could reach the mother or the non-event of a session, the scream the patient does not scream.

In his meeting with Eigen, Bion spoke about marriage as having "someone to speak truth to and mitigate the severity to yourself." The spouse receives one's dark side in the same fashion as a therapist receives the patient's. This event was a rendezvous *Mohan* had with the demon who resided in *Avni*'s internal world as her most intimate companion. In her work on women artists and their relationship with their creative works, Kavaler-Adler (1993) writes about a demon lover as internal diabolic father. According to her,

> only when the idealized father figure is taken inside the woman's psyche at the level of primitive omnipotence, where he becomes a god or mammoth muse upon whom early symbiotic longings are focused, does the father of necessity turn into a demon . . . Incorporating him at this level, in an attempt to compensate for the lack of an adequate good maternal object, causes a symbiotic illusion including wishes that must inevitably meet with traumatic failure. If wed to this frustrating and omnipotently idealized figure a woman is addicted

to an internal object, which she holds on to in an attempt to seek rescue or repair.

As a clingy child, *Avni* entered the phase of prolonged absence of the mother with a sulk. The lump of food in mouth was replaced by words as father returned home in evenings and was held captive by charm of his daughter's innocent narration of endless stories. The father held out the promise of "rescue through erotic enthrallment." A muse was born in the internal world as that character who one could endlessly suck the juices of admiration from. This romance was short-lived, ruptured by arrival of the mother dethroning *Avni* by bringing a male child who was preferred more, envious attacks from sister, father's disgust at the growing woman's body and having to take on the role of a tomboy to save father from horror of his own sexuality and of a caretaker to save the mother from pain and guilt. In compromises, terror of separation and loneliness could be avoided. However, primitive rage held sway. There was an urgency with which creative writing was pursued as a shot for redemption but she lacked the agency to see it through and would reach a point of blankness. Perhaps this blankness was of the painful realization that the extended limb was merely a hologram, that one was actually dropped. When she did manage to write something her works ended up as many aborted beginnings, like her Self. In creating something she intensely pursued the internal Muse, as if begged for a flow of creative juices, only to appear as a Demon or the admiring father who turned rejecting. Like *Ravana*, this demon had many faces—rage, greed, absent mother, damaging mother, damaged by aggressive attacks and retaliating, who was sucked dry from, father who was revered and desired, who instead celebrated a male child, who was experienced as turning hostile when *Avni* allied with the victim mother and the father who was disgusted by his own and his daughter's sexuality. "The sadomasochistic after image of the rejecting father unconsciously merged in with the early withholding and hostile mother" (Kavaler-Adler, 1993). With rage and cravings as its allies, the demon-lover possessing her made it difficult to receive *Mohan*'s love or to relish the nourishment that came from writing poetry. About her own work, Flannery O'Connor reflected, "I have found, in short, from the reading of my own writing, that my subject in fiction is the action of grace in territory held largely by the devil."

The internal enemy drills a hole in memory where all good memories get sucked in and forgotten. Seized by cravings she pursued love but rage, supported by splitting and idealization, prevented the loved other to come together as whole, albeit imperfect, object. The trauma of unfulfilled cravings, abandonment and engulfment by one's own primitive rage was relived in marriage. The demon that kept her from procreating a life out of desire with *Mohan* had the face of the matriarch mother-in-law. Later he told her that the experience of terror and fury for him was one in which he felt he abandoned his body and watched it go in frenzy. Like the grandfather and father, had *Mohan* also failed in offering maternal care? One wonders if via the mysterious process of projective identification, her stubborn sulk casted an image of father-with-breasts onto these men who were apparently secure in their familiar grooves of masculinity only to be dislodged into coming face to face with the femininity that obscured them. Perhaps the oedipal father was approached with unmet cravings from the pre-oedipal time.

BUG'S LIFE

Limbs had to be formed to take charge of the situation. However, there was a textural shift. I felt that *Mohan*'s love had created enough ease for her disappointment to not spiral into recriminations and reactions of rage. He was both—nurturing and limited—and needed her love. She began to take care of him. However, growth was still weak to fight internal darkness that showed suicide as an easier route. It was becoming unimaginable to *live through*. She was sinking again and in this fall a moment served as an anchor. She sat brooding on her loneliness when her eyes fell on a bug. She squashed it dead. Staring at the lifeless carcass of the bug held between her fingers, she felt an intense impulse to eat it. Was she turning into a whimpering, crawling bug, like the ones her Self was infested with or perhaps, like Gregor of "The Metamorphosis" (Kafka, 1915), she *was* the bug? Maggots and bugs—what was the psyche speaking? Eigen (2018c) helps us listen. The worm is associated with humiliation, baseness, sneaky aggression, a sense of unworthiness. Like a bug she was repeatedly squashed by others. She struggled to fight the impulse to eat it and could resuscitate through the fear of going crazy, to be reduced to a bug. Eigen (2018c) writes in praise of the worm, "We need to let the worm into our self-image more openly. It is not so bad being a worm . . . Too much pride in who one is can be as stifling as too little. We need the worm for balance. We need to taste the earth, let it go through us. We need to be close to the ground, not just high above it. To play down strength is malicious or silly; to play down weakness is delusional." In feeling fear for her sanity, *Avni* had touched ground.

Getting a grip she announced, "*I am on my own.*" Was it also a statement to the demon lover that loneliness as a threat would not work? Disappointment did not blow up to disillusionment, rage, and sulk. One wonders if grips of the internal Devil had begun to loosen as a bad-yet-present object, gripping and clung to ward off the void underneath. Loneliness as a threat had stopped working. A solemn fearlessness took over. Knowing that she was now "on her own" felt freeing, especially in situations which made her nervous earlier. Slowly she resumed writing poetry, this time not to impress but to convey that which seized her insides begging for life *in* expression. The internal demon-lover fought back her attempts to dream it.

One such interrupted dream,

> *I am in my home. Mohan is not around. I am alone. I feel like there is someone in the house. Scared, I call a friend. She asks me to check all the doors and the windows. All the doors are locked except one which is slightly ajar. I panic and go to my room to peep from a window if my dog is alert. He is unconscious, frothing from the mouth. It seems he has been poisoned. I got panicky and then there is this loud sarcastic voice saying—Go ahead. Be Erotic and lead them Stalkers. Suffer!*

The voice declared that *Avni* got her comeuppance for pursuing her desires uncannily echoing those familiar voices which blame the attire of a rape victim for her "deserved" fate. In empowerment one is alone. The woman in her sought the other's admiring gaze as she took strides toward exhibition in a bid to reformulate her Self. The persecutory voice was of an undreamt "murderous superego" (Bion, 1992) constituted by the object's failure to support "object seeking tendencies, magnification of the horror of not being able to reach another's insides with one's own, reaching only traumatizing outsides" (Eigen, 2018d). It was terrifying to come together as a person. Her internal resources that could bite into experience of terrors of visibility were rendered poisoned, depleted. It was a battle between what one possessed (sexualities as we cherish pleasure in various parts of our body and creative works) and what wishes to become akin to a dervish,[3] leaving body and flying off the ajar openings without anyone noticing it.

THE HOWL

When Freud (1920) was painting the canvas of his concept of "death instinct" it had an eastern hue—"The 'Nirvana' principle expresses the trend of the death instinct." Unlike the Hindu understanding of Nirvana to mean release and transcendence of the *Aatman* from the cycles of pleasure-displeasure, into fusion with *Paramataman*, Freud's use of the term remained confined to an understanding of death instinct as a demonic force woven in the very fabric of psychic life and geared toward reducing all excitation to zero. Soma comes in to deflect this force outward in aggression. The demonic force was further chiseled under Kleinian fire where it emerged as modulated by internal object relations. Annihilation anxiety expressed work of the death instinct and deadness was a defense against annihilation. Bion (1965) wrote of a force that is anti-life and never stops destroying. Bion, Winnicott, and later Eigen shifted focus to psyche's capacities to support its own aliveness which depended on its having known that support from a responsive Other in the past.

Like many domesticated women in Indian culture, *Avni* was far from her instinctual wild core. The Devil inside employed “fear of loneliness” as adhesive to internal toxic attachments. However, having realized that she was on her own, she could receive the limits of the other. Reality demanded that the tension between relishing one’s needs and renouncing them be held.

Blake wrote about “a Moment in each Day that Satan cannot find.” In this crack in time emerged dreams of a white and grey She-wolf: *“calm face and fiery orange eyes like contained fire.”* Everything about her was alive. *Avni* was drawn toward its beauty and ferocity with which it protects its pack. In urban consciousness she-Wolf is reminiscent of Raksha,[4] fiercely protective mother of a man-cub, Mowgli, of *The Jungle Book* (Kipling, Drake, & Frenzeny, 1898). *Avni*’s Wolf appeared like she was about to say something, but never did. Was psyche feeding images as proto-states to be sung to by the howls of maternal lullaby? Jungian analyst Estes (1992) writes, “Wolves and Women have much in common. Both share a wild spirit. Women and Wolves are instinctual creatures, able to sense the unseen. They are loyal, protective of their packs and of their pups. They are wild and beautiful. Both have been hunted and captured. Even in captivity, one can see in the eyes of a Woman, or a Wolf, the longing to run free, and the determination that should the opportunity arise . . . they will be gone.” Were *Avni*’s howls or screams from the wild nocturnal instinctual part in her waiting to be embraced?

By howling a Wolf also calls out to its pack. This is very reminiscent of how Bion (1970) saw scream, substituting breast, as a link between personalities. One wonders if *Avni*’s screams served to link mind and body. Perhaps, through images of swollen ear lobe, maggot-infested brain, face covered in pus oozing boils, screams in the pillow-breast, body squirming or insides squirming on thought of digesting a bug, mind and body were coming together? Was it a shape-shifting process for a woman turning into a wild wolf? To touch raw vitality in rage is something mind cannot achieve without an extension into the body. Freud (1893–1895, 1915, & 1940) thought of body as being object of our instincts which choose the body for discharge. Instinct was a link between the body and mind. The mere frame of *Avni*’s body could not contain the infinity of feelings, making suicide seem as the only way to escape the fading sense of self. She needed to build capacities to be seized by the wild aliveness while remaining in her body.

To be alive meant to embody ferocity and maternal warmth. In psychoanalysis, biologically determined instincts form the psyche-soma in conjunction with inter-subjective experiences beginning from the psyches of the parents and their facilitation of a potential space between child and the mother. Under the weight of these external constellations psyche organizes its patterns and ways of experiencing and relating inside with outside. Maternal abandonment, insistent control, and impingement from environment serve only to enhance the split between mind and body.

Avni yearned to be a mother or rather to create her own extension that could be kept safe from the ongoing corrosion of the Self. Fearing loneliness ensuing from separation from the internally held object she kept the child and her thoughts captive in eternal pregnancy in her mind-womb. In Freudian thinking, phallocentric theoretical axis of womanhood proceeds toward substitution of the father's wanted and envied penis by the wish for a child with him, especially complicated in our culture with preference for a male-child. Compared to her brother, *Avni* felt negated, nothing. The "negative" is inscribed on the woman's body at birth for "not having" a penis and "not being" a boy. To the extent that she feels humiliated under this inscription, the woman begins to share the contempt of the phallic order for a gender which lacks. From an organ that was *not* there Erikson (1964) through his writing on "inner space and outer space" and later Alizade (1999) through her addition of a "nothingic order" to the phallic order, weave a story of womanhood around the potential to give birth. Alizade (1999) saw "nothingness" as seething with possibilities and fertility. "It is nothingness that insists and finds the subject, evoking the archaic, the uncanny and the demonic, leaving an invisible and mute trail . . . it symbolizes enigmatic ignorance and the inevitability of human limitations, and is established through the 'not-being' exemplified by fluidity," which marks the internal feminine somatopsychic universe. In Bionian thinking also "no-thing" calls for "accretions of meaning. Meaning is a 'no-thing,' not a thing. Tolerance of no-thing is linked with modulated openness and learning from experience" (Eigen, 2018c). Realizing that she was on her own opened a new vertex which gave relevance to a familiarity with finitude. Annihilation was inevitable. So was revival. Shifting gaze to the potential in her "inner space" the woman is released from need to depend on an Other to ward off annihilation anxiety. Her need to depend on the other shifted. She found her own territory which was not build on envy toward the male-child. She began to see *Mohan*'s breakdown as enabled by a faith in her love for him. A *womb of and for her own* became visible to her where she did not feel the need to appropriate her Self. The "negation" inscribed on her mind-body self became progressively more positive. "Loneliness becomes an indispensable requirement in the decline of the female Oedipus," notes Alizade (1999) A new Oedipal path was being carved with the learning of an auspicious "No." Her recognition of what she *does have* was slowly becoming evident as she began to feel freer in voicing her thoughts or writing them. She began to write, not to appease the (m)other, but to give birth to what gripped her. Earlier *Avni* feared others would attack her baby and her thoughts as they did her. While in the lukewarm darkness of her mind-womb, thoughts kicked and tossed around before she penned them down. Thoughts, as babies, were nurtured with love and sent out in the world enabled by a tenacious preparedness with which she would defend them if they were humiliated. With same tenacity she defended her desire for a child, out of love for *Mohan*, rather that out of compliance to superego social mandate. She slowly acquired inner autonomy to assert with her in-laws that she would not welcome them in her house unless they acknowledged the damages they have done to the couple. To *Mohan* she was able to say, "*I do not want you to be my shield. If your parents wish to complain about me they should do it with me. I will handle it.*" Her taking responsibility of protecting her honor also freed *Mohan* from the burden of his conflicts.

Avni and *Mohan*'s story brings to mind the Hindu myth of *Savitri.* A dedicated wife, *Savitri* was married to *Satyavan* who was destined to die. When *Yama*, the God of Death, arrives, *Savitri*, unwilling to lose the love of her life, asks for her husband's life and reminds *Yama* of "a perspective of saintliness resident in Death." In its saintly avatar, Death supports the three heads of Time—Past, Present, and Future. Death being that which unbinds is bound by a desire to be communicated by *Savitiri.* Nagpal (2011) reflects, "Hearing those moving words in which *Savitri*'s own sense of deadness upon having lost her husband in the prime of her youth begins to come alive touches him deeply, and the boon is granted. Death truly renews life even as its own deadness is recognized in undesignated places where the two walk together in no hurry to leave and await the dawn of saintliness."

In this case study, darkness has emerged as a necessary unbinding, space of nothingness opening the doors of psyche to newer emotions in order to clinch a sense that "love can outlast the arrival of composure" (Nagpal, 2014).

To conclude, I put together these reflections on *Avni*'s struggles to come alive, to finally see her inner space as packed with potential to nurture life, her mind as a space to nurture thoughts and the image of Bion frozen at the sight of her daughter's aliveness approaching him. I am reminded of a question Eigen (2016) asks, "Is psychoanalysis in process of being born? Is it in gestation? Gestation and birth together? Bion speaks of psychoanalysis as embryonic, sometimes a baby, and wonders what it may become. He speaks of the embryonic aspects of personality. But at times goes further, emphasising the relationship with what is not conceived, our relationship to the unknown."

I end with a sequence from the unfinished movie on Bion's Memoirs which depicts this tussle in conceiving a relationship between the mothering and the embryonic and unknown parts of the personality.

> MOTHER: Though the body dies the virus shall live forever. Did God make a mistake when He allowed the human animal to reproduce?

SOMITES: Any foetus could tell you that. I wish you'd stop tossing about.

MOTHER: How can I help it with you thrashing around?

SOMITES: I've got a stomach ache.

MOTHER: You are my stomach ache.

SOMITES: I can kick my way out of here easily.

MOTHER: That pressure on my spine—

SOMITES: That pressure on my optic pits—

MOTHER: Calm down: I've got an idea you may abort if you kick around like this.

SOMITES: I am an idea of yours.

MOTHER: Only an idea?

SOMITES: I see a great light.

MOTHER: It is the darkness of the womb.

SOMITES: I'm getting absorbed.

MOTHER: My feelings are getting idea-lized.

NOTES

1. Avni and Mohan are pseudonyms used for the research participants.
2. "Reading your mention of Achlys, the female death-spirit of the original, eternal night, I wondered, what then is Thanatos? I was very surprised to realize Thanatos is the personification of the peaceful death, and not just any death, which makes me wonder if it has to do with Freud's choice to draw together Thanatos and the eastern Nirvana, as some unmaking that advances in silence. As you point out, the destructive fire of strife in Klein's perspective seems to take Freud's death drive even further way from the unbinding freedom of cutting repetition in Hindu understanding of Nirvana as an exit path" (Hafner, 2018).
3. In Sufi tradition, a dervish, in a bid to reach humility, takes a vow of poverty and austerity. He engages in dancing, whirling, or howling as a way to touch the Divine in a state of trance.
4. When translated from Hindi, the word *Raksha* means "Protection."

REFERENCES:

Alizade, A. M. (1999). *Feminine Sensuality.* London: Karnac Books.

Benjamin, J. (1988). *The bonds of love: Psychoanalysis, Feminism, and the problem of domination*, New York: Pantheon.

Bion, W. R. (1962). A Theory of Thinking. In *International Journal of Psychoanalysis* 43, 306–310.

Bion, W. R (1965). *Transformation.* London: Karnac Books.

Bion, W. R. (1970). *Attention and Interpretation.* London: Tavistock.

Bion, W. R. (1992). *Cogitations.* London: Karnac Books.

Bolognini, S. (2011). *Secret Passages: The Theory and Technique of Interpsychic Relations.* London/New York: Routledge.

Eigen, M. (1999). *Toxic Nourishment.* London: Karnac Books.

Eigen, M. (2016). *Image, Sense, Infinities and Everyday Life*. London: Karnac Books.

Eigen, M. (2018a). *The Electrified Tightrope*. New York: Routledge.

Eigen, M. (2018b). *Toxic Nourishment*. New York: Routledge.

Eigen, M. (2018c). *Psychic Deadness*. New York: Routledge.

Eigen, M. (2018d). *Damaged Bonds*. London: Routledge.

Erikson, E. (1964). Inner Space and Outer Space: Reflections on Womanhood. In *Daedalus, The Woman in America*, 93(2), 582–606.

Estes, C. P. (1992). *Women who run with the wolves: Myths and stories of the wild woman archetype* . New York: Ballantine Books.

Freud, S. & Breuer, J. (1893). On the psychical mechanism of hysterical phenomena: preliminary communication. *S.E. II*, 1–17.

Freud, S. (1915). Instincts and their Vicissitudes. *S.E. XIV*, 111–140.

Freud, S. (1917). Mourning and melancholia. *S.E. XIV*. 239–258.

Freud, S. (1920). Beyond the Pleasure Principle. *S.E. XVIII.*

Freud, S. (1940). *An Outline of Psychoanalysis.* Wiltshire: Redwood Press Ltd.

Gerson, S. (2011). Hysteria and Humiliation. In *Psychoanalytic Dialogues*, 21(5), 517–530.

Green, A. (1970). The Dead Mother. In *On Primitive Madness*. London: Hogarth Press, 142–173.

Hafner, D. (21–01-2018). *Personal Communication.*

Kafka, F. (1915). *The Metamorphosis,* German by Johnston, I. (trad) [1999].

Kakar, S. (1982). *Shamans, Mystics and Doctors*. New York: Knoph.

Kakar, S. & Kakar, K. (2007). *The Indians: Portrait of a People*. Penguin Books India.

Kaniel, Kara-Ivanov. R (2013) *Therapist from the Depths: A Conversation with Michael Eigen*. Tikkun Magazine.

Kavaler-Adler, S. (1993). *The Compulsion to Create: A Psychoanalytic Study of Women Artists.* London and New York: Routledge (2nd and 3rd eds published as *The Compulsion to Create: Women Writers and Their Demon Lovers.* New York: Other Press, 2000; New York: O.R.I. Academic Press).

Kipling, R., Kipling, J. L., Drake, W. H., & Frenzeny, P. (1898). *The Jungle Book.* London: Macmillan.

Lear, J. (1998). *Open minded: Working out the logic of the soul.* Cambridge, MA: Harvard University Press.

Nagpal, A. (2011). A Hindu reading of Freud's Beyond the Pleasure Principle. In Akhtar, S. & O'Neil, M. K. *On Freud's Beyond the Pleasure Principle.* London: Karnac Books.

Nagpal, A. (2014). *Sigmund Freud—A Relational Guru*. (Video) Retrieved from https://youtu.be/1aa03DDpNYM.

Narayanan, A. (2015). The non-fiction of my Feminism. In *The Stolkhome Review of Literature special issue "Feminist Non-fiction.'*

Ogden, T. (2002). A new reading of the origins of object-relations theory. In *International Journal of Psychoanalysis.* 83, 767–782.

Tessman, L. (1982). A note on the father's contribution to the daughter's ways of loving and working. In *Father and Child*, ed. S. Cath, A. Gurwitt & J. M. Ross. Boston: Little, Brown.

Tustin, F. (1981). Psychological birth and psychological catastrophe. In *Dare I Disturb the Universe*, ed. J. Grotstein. London: Maresfield Library, 181–196.
Winnicott, D. W. (1971). *Playing and Reality.* New York: Basic Books.
Winnicott, D. W. (1969). Additional note on psycho-somatic disorder. In *Psycho-Analytic Explorations*, eds. C. Winnicott , R. Shepherd , & M. Davis. London: Karnac, 1989.

Chapter Four

Killing Death with Silence

Women in the Colombian Post-Agreement Era

Angélica Toro Cardona

Freud (1915) stated that we have tried to kill death with silence in *Reflections on War and Death: Current Topics* to depict the incapacity of the human beings to represent their own death. According to Freud, there is an unequivocal tendency to put death aside and eliminate it from life.

Faced upon the impossibility to inscribe in the unconscious the register of our own death, we resort to fiction and art as means to reconcile with it through characters whose death is not definitive, or which would be marked by a dignity that will justify it. According to Freud (1915), this would be the only way in which death becomes acceptable: after all the vicissitudes we encounter in life, whatever remains is an untouchable life. In war, we do not find this to be the case. War radically changes men's attitude toward death; here men truly die. In war, death cannot be denied, and it is necessary to believe in it. War imposes the imminence of death, which stops being a contingency to become a certainty. According to Freud, we should draw a line between two groups to study this phenomenon: those who put their lives at risk in the battlefield and those who stayed behind at home and do not have any other choice but to wait for death to snatch one of their loved ones away. At war, both group are confronted by the evidence of death: those combatants who, willing to risk their lives, choose to go to war, as well as those in which case war came to them not as a choice but as a reality that irrupts, bringing the onslaught of death.

We can also consider another kind of separation: that between men (who historically have been protagonists of war) and women (whose participation has also been important but was given less attention). We will then approach the particularities of the feminine aspect on that encounter with death within the framework of war. Sventlana Alexievitch, who received the Nobel Prize in Literature, points out in her book, "La guerre n'a pas un visage de femme" (2016), the war does not have the face of a woman, that the female war has its own colors, smells, lights, and spaces. It has its own words. For the purposes of the present chapter, we will study these phenomena in the specific case of women involved in the domestic armed conflicts in Colombia, which is considered to be one of the longest and most serious conflicts in the world.

Women have played an essential role in this conflict, such as combatants—40 percent of women in the case of the *Fuerzas Armadas Revolucionarias de Colombia* (FARC) (Revolutionary Armed Forces of Colombia)—and as victims. According to the *Unidad para la Atención y Reparación Integral a las Víctimas* (2015) (Unit for the Victims Assistance and Integral Reparation), the victims of the armed conflict in Colombia have amounted to 7.9 million, almost half of them being women.

Following Freudian indications, we study the matter of mourning and loss in the case of two specific groups or categories particular to women within the framework of this armed conflict. On one hand we have the combatant women, active members of the armed front, especially from FARC, and on the other hand, the victims, whose bodies have constituted a scenery of war, or to whom death has already taken one or more loved ones away. Based on these two basic postulates—that the war experience is lived in a singular way by women and that the role of women has been essential in the armed conflict—we try to understand how the matter of mourning and loss is presented to each of them on opposite sides of the Colombian armed conflict.

WOMEN WHO RISK THEIR LIVES ON THE BATTLEFIELD: THE WAR CONTEXT IN COLOMBIA

To analyze the matter of mourning in the case of ex-combatant women, it is necessary to present some contextual elements about what has been the armed conflict in Colombia. The FARC was a guerrilla and insurgent extreme leftist organization inspired by Marx's and Lenin's ideologies. Considered to be the oldest guerilla group in Latin America, this organization had a leading role in an armed conflict with the national government that lasted more than 50 years, thus becoming one of the key actors of domestic conflicts in Colombia. After the September 11 attacks, the FARC was included in the list of terrorist organizations of the United States and the European Union.

Counting with approximately 7,000 members in their lines, of which 40 percent are women, the FARC and the Colombian government conducted negotiations lasting for four years, taking place in Oslo and La Habana: from its official opening in October 16, 2012, until September 26, 2016, when the *Acuerdo para la Terminación Definitiva del Conflicto* (Agreement to Definitely End the Conflict) was signed. This first version of the agreement, which should have been countersigned through a plebiscite, was not approved by popular vote, forcing the parties to a renegotiation that resulted in the final version of the agreement, countersigned at the *Congreso Nacional* (National Congress) on November 24, 2016.

The definitive signing of this agreement, which puts an end to the armed conflict between the FARC guerrilla and the Colombian government, marks the beginning of the post-agreement era. It is worth mentioning that we do not stress on the post-conflict situation since there is another multitude of armed groups—both left and right wing—which are still at war.

After signing the peace agreement, the FARC started a transition process toward civil life, ending in August 2017 with the establishment of its own political party. Thus, the *Fuerzas Armadas Revolucionarias de Colombia* (Revolutionary Armed Forces of Colombia) became the *Fuerza Alternativa Revolucionaria del Común* (Common Alternative Revolutionary Alternative Force).

This transition process implies for each and every one of the demobilized troops the need to find a singular response to face the new statute. They are no longer combatants, insurgent, or members of an armed organization, but civilian militants of a political party in the process of being created. Such transition process, in which social and psychological consequences are just starting to become visible, attracts special attention in the case of women. We talk, then, about women who have spent many years set on the Colombian jungle to the detriment of their lives as women, lovers, mothers, daughters, and sisters.

THE THIN LINE BETWEEN THE VICTIM AND THE EXECUTIONER

To start considering these femininities in a suspended state, in the case of ex-combatants, it is necessary first to pose a paradox: many of these women have been victims of many types of violence. They have lost their loved ones at the hands of other armed groups, have been victims of forced recruiting and sexual assault, or have been forced to abort inside guerrilla lines.

In the particular case of the armed conflict in Colombia, there seems to be no radical separation between the victim and the executioner, but the same individual can eventually move from one position to another. The condition of victim in themselves is considered as a risk factor that increases the possibility of becoming part of the armed group. We can depict this element with the testimony of a female guerrilla fighter, who voluntarily joined the

FARC at the age of thirteen: "*When we are like this, at home, we witness how they abuse children, how we are denied the chance to study, for example, when children get sick, we are not taken to a hospital because we are poor. We see poverty, inequality, misery and that makes you sad, then that is why I joined the FARC*" (La cara femenina de la guerrilla, 2016).[1]

We can see how sadness due to violence and poverty, as well as the feeling of not counting on the care and protection needed, are definitive factors that favor joining the armed ranks. The feeling of belonging and safety that an organization or an armed group can provide can counteract the feeling of abandonment or hopelessness that one can feel toward parents.

Similarly, taking up arms can also be a subjective answer toward an important loss: the desire of vengeance, when you have been a victim of any of the armed groups, is a risk factor for an individual to join the enemy's ranks. In this sense, the act of taking up arms can be thought as a way to elaborate the process of mourning. Before the evidence of the loss of a loved object, the libido that used to be linked to this object is displaced to invest the armed fight. In this war, there are neither heroes nor grandiose feats, these are just human beings involved in an inhumane task (Alexievitch, 2016).

THE WOMEN'S BODY AS A WAR TERRITORY

We have already stated that women have played a primordial role in the armed conflict. We will find it necessary, then, to stop to look into detail what has been their participation from both sides of the conflict. First, it is important to pose that this violence, which women have been victims of within the context of the conflict, has been primarily sexual, and it has taken place both inside and outside the line of war. A kind of violence that targets directly to the self of the woman, in every aspect that concerns her femininity, attacking the body in her sexual and reproductive dimensions; and with the objective, in most cases, to make it bearer of a political and bellic message.

The report *La Guerra Inscrita en el Cuerpo* (2017), The War Inscribed in the Body of the *Centro Nacional de Memoria Histórica* (National Center of Historical Memory) (CNMH) presents an inventory of the different connotations sexual violence can have within the framework of the conflict, and that researchers have defined as a battle between men that is fought in the body of women, meaning that a woman's body is attacked in its feminine essence, but at the same time, it is reduced to a statute of the object. An object whose only function is the transmission of a message which is addressed to the enemy.

Thus, in many cases recorded by the CNMH, the act of sexually assaulting the enemy's women aims to humiliate and to display a superior and dominant position in which women become a territory to be conquered. It is about proving that the body of the women, similar to the territory, has an owner.

The assaulted body of the victim can also be the battlefield; it is the means through which armed members send a message of terror to the communities as a warning of what might happen if they collaborate with the enemy. Sexual violence can also be used as an exemplary punishment, wherein victims are women who are suspected of collaborating with the enemy or that oppose by resisting certain violence and domination practices.

In accordance with the above-mentioned report, these practices imply a castration and mutilation message sent to the enemy, showing them that they were not able to protect their women and that their honor is stained. The reviewed studies coincide in stating that in the internal logic of war, what is at stake at first instance it is not the women's honor, but rather, the true target that is aimed for is the honor of the enemy. Furthermore, the expropriation, exploitation, colonization, and dispossession dimensions highlight the statute of the object that acquires the woman's body in the context of war to the detriment of the subjective dimension.

It is exactly here that psychoanalysis has to enter the picture and asks, from a particular perspective, the psychical consequences of this event to each of these women, with the intention to rescue precisely that statute of subject which they have been stripped of. How can we consider the matter of mourning and loss in these women? Based on the victims' testimonies, we can affirm that this experience constitutes a traumatic event in general, an encounter with reality where they cannot find any resort to symbolization, and, in order to get out of there, it is necessary to work on the elaboration of mourning.

Although, in the specific case of sexual violence, the loss of a loved one has not occurred as such, we agree with what Freud (1917) describes in *Mourning and Melancholia* that what is at stake here is the loss or impoverishment at the "ego" level. What we have called an expropriation of the body implies for the individual a profound pain that is lived as an irreparable loss.

Such is the case mentioned in the report *Expropiar el cuerpo: seis historias sobre violencia sexual en el conflicto armado* (To Expropriate the Body: Six Stories About Sexual Violence in Armed Conflicts) of a countrywoman who was kidnapped by one of the FARC fronts: "*There was no way of escaping, she was being watched all the time: while she was forced to cook, they would touch her; when she was allowed to take a bath, she had to be naked in front of everyone. She was raped any time they wanted. —It was the worst of tortures, she mourns, still crying. I would have rather being murdered right there instead of having them doing those things to me*" (CNMH, 2018, p. 104). In front of the instrumentalized, exposed and outraged body, a pain appears in front of which life loses all meaning.

In *Mourning and Melancholia*, Freud (1917) defined mourning as the reaction toward the loss of a loved one or an abstraction that acts on its behalf, like homeland, freedom, an ideal, and so on. For women who have been victims of sexual violence, it is not about the loss of a loved one but the loss that has to do with the being and that destroys an ideal of the female body as the object of desire of the other. The body of the woman is reduced to a statute of object for the satisfaction of the executioner, without there being a possible mediation of the order of the desire.

As a partial conclusion, we can state that there is a dimension of the loss that has to do with being a woman, as if the rapist had murdered a part of her. The process of mourning in this case, then, is about psychically elaborating the loss of the body that used to be owned before the vexation and to be able to invest libidinally that what we might call a new body. After being raped, most women find it quite difficult to establish a new relationship with another man. The guiltiness dimension, which is highly present in women who have been victims of sexual violence, shows up as a common denominator in all mourning processes. We will resume later on the matter of guilt inherent to loss.

After considering the matter of violence over the victim's body, we can assess the forms that this kind of violence takes in the body of combatants, through practices that directly address women in the maternity dimension.

MATERNITIES IN SUSPENSE . . .

The first image of mourning and loss is related to the maternal desire in women who are ex-combatants. A desire most of them had to give up or, at least, put aside until the end of the armed conflict. According to the reports from International Amnesty (2004), contraception and forced abortion have been recurrent practices inside these armed groups. Such methods, imposed to combatants as an imperative measure, whose subjugation conditions their stay in the organization, were a generalized policy inside the FARC. Guerrilla life was then considered to be incompatible with family life, and particularly with maternity, as testimonies from ex-combatants prove: "*We did not even consider the possibility of having children . . . How will someone have children in a place where gunshots are being triggered from everywhere?*" (Tobella, 2015).

Women who got pregnant were forced to abort or else to trust their families or farmer families to raise their children, something similar to give their children for adoption against their will. Even if the organization has categorically denied carrying out these kinds of practices, the testimonies of several dissident guerrilla fighters give account of it. "*Since you arrive, they put devices in your body and inject you. Pregnant women have to abort. It is the commander who decides whether you have the baby or you must abort. Some women escaped because of this. If they get caught, they are killed, regardless of their age*" (Amnesty International, 2004).

In this situation, guerrilla women had to elaborate the mourning for their maternal desire: the mourning for a child they never had or for the interrupted maternity due to a forced abortion as well as for the definitive separation from their newborn who had to be given to other people. This is the case of a commander from the 34th front of the FARC. After trusting her child to her family when the baby was three months old, she admits that a guerrilla fighter cannot provide her child with the love of a mother babies deserve when they are born and adds that sometimes it is better not to have them, because they are left there and the love becomes the battle we are fighting here. We could think of an affective displacement since it is not uncommon to listen to these combatant women talk about war as if it was a love story (Sutyrin, 2016).

"YOU ARE NOT HERE TO GIVE BIRTH TO CHILDREN . . ."

However, for women to whom that sort of substitution or displacement is not enough, the interdiction of maternity is lived as an extremely violent experience, as we can see from the following testimony of a dissident guerrilla fighter: "*You know that you haven't come to the FARC to give birth to children, you know the rules. 'If you don't know them, learn them' they told me. I started to cry, I begged, I told them I wanted to have my child, asked him to please understand that I wanted to be a mother*" (Infobae, 2017).

This situation causes, on the one hand, the deep pain of the loss and, on the other hand, a feeling of guilt for not being able to avoid abortion. A mother's pain for whom avoiding their children's death was not possible, since in some cases, abortion procedures were carried out even late in pregnancy. It is necessary for them to mourn their children, whose death was not chosen or whose lives were not meant to be.

CHILDREN OF PEACE

As proof of that repressed maternal desire, let us briefly consider another phenomenon: the baby boom that occurred in the guerrilla forces in the last few years. With the negotiations and the subsequent signing of the Peace Agreement, and bringing with it the end of the control over maternity by the organizations, hundreds of guerrilla fighters have given birth to the so-called *hijos de paz* (children of peace). This phenomenon can be compared with the baby boom that occurred in some Anglo-Saxon countries by the end of the Second World War, with the particularity that, in this case, the protagonists were not men coming back from war but the women who were in the battlefield until then.

"*One being in the guerrilla wants to have a baby . . . you start asking yourself, when will the conflict be over so that I can form my home, to have children?*" (Tobella, 2015). A suspended desire that can finally come true and that represents a dynamic that would surely have interested Freud. The life impulse as a civilizing function that opposes to the imminence of death.

TO EXCLUDE FROM DEATH IS TO EXCLUDE FROM LIFE: FORCED DISAPPEARANCE

We have seen how women combatants must elaborate their losses linked to the sexual abuse they have been objects of, to the interrupted maternity or the impossibility of it, as well as how the life impulse is manifested as an effect of the end of war. Let us focus again on the victims to analyze another important phenomenon in the context of war: the forced disappearance.

Forced disappearance has been a war practice whose main precedent is the Nazi decree, Natch und Nebel (Night and Mist), of December 7, 1941, that established the guidelines of the Third Reich for repression and the physical elimination of politicians opposing the regime, which is defined as the disappearance of the enemy and the denial of knowledge about their whereabouts (CNMH, 2016).

In Colombia, during the last forty-five years, forced disappearance has taken more than 60,000 victims. In the report *Hasta encontrarlos: el drama de la desaparición forzada en Colombia* (Until We Find Them: The Drama Behind Forced Disappearance in Colombia) of the CNMH (2016), this practice is defined as a modality of violence intentionally shown in a context of extreme rationalization of violence, which consists of the combination of the victim's deprivation of liberty, their removal of legal protection, and the concealment of information regarding their whereabouts, where the national states may be responsible, as well as the illegal armed groups that incorporate this modality to their practices within the framework of their criminal activity.

Disappearance, as well as torture and sexual violence, sends a message of terror: the total annulment, the symbolic and real suppression of a human being. An obliteration of the person that also erases any traces of their bodies. The reason we are interested in this phenomenon of forced disappearance is because we can see an important clinical element regarding mourning and the feminine. In the absence of a response from the State to establish the whereabouts of the disappeared people, many of those who are suffering try to find the truth of the facts by their own means, undergoing highly unsafe conditions and visiting guerrilla or paramilitary camps, prisons, among other places, to directly question the armed actors.

But in most cases, it is women—wives, mothers, daughters, or sisters—who start by themselves these searching quests that many times involve risking their own lives. According to the report *¡Basta ya!*, by the *Grupo de Memoria Histórica* (Group of Historical Memory) (GMH, 2013), a woman in Montería said that she even took the risk of going to a paramilitary camp to look for her brother. This risky decision faced her with new humiliation and threats.

The drama these women have suffered takes us by analogy to the Antigone tragedy, which Lacan used in his teaching. Let us briefly remember that in Sophocles' tragedy, Antigone defies King Creon's ruling that prohibits funeral rites on her brother Polynice's body. Such prohibition, which carried a political message, consists of leaving the corpse without burial in the place where the person died, as an exemplary punishment over the body of the person considered to be a homeland traitor. Knowing her life is at risk, and in spite of the many warnings, Antigone decides to carry out the burial, and as a consequence, she is sentenced to death.

This sacrificial position, that of the heroine who does not yield her wish, denounces the totalitarian power that attributes a right over the bodies, even after death. Antigone claims the prevalence of the divine laws over the human laws (Naveau, 2011). It is interesting to set a parallelism between Antigone's tragedy and the women that risk their lives in Colombia to recover the remains of their loved ones to give them a burial. Three main aspects guide our reflection:

First, we recognize in there a feminine position: as defined by Jacques-Alain Miller (1999) in his seminar, he presents a psychological repertoire, which he called "A Sexual Repertoire," where he characterizes the feminine and masculine positions based on their relationship with castration and loss.

Indeed, the female position appears as that in which loss has already taken place since castration is a consummated fact for women. This is how fearlessness, boldness, rebelliousness, and even indolence are characteristics of the feminine position, she who has already lost everything and has nothing left to lose (Miller, 1999). Although fearlessness can also be a masculine characteristic, it is not about the same relationship with risk for men. Paraphrasing Miller, we can affirm that the risk, in its relationship with femininity, is a risk that goes further than fear and shudder; where men face the castration anxiety, women, devoid of that ballast, are able to take a blind risk.

This loose relationship with risk can be found both in Antigone—whom we will describe together with Miller (1999) as she who does not understand reasons and follows her own path, since she has as a compass the body of the dead man—and in the women who decidedly go in search of the executioner: "*After about 15 days my mum went up to their camp (. . .) then, my mum arrived there. There, they asked her, 'Why are you here? What can we do for you?' and my mum said: I came here to ask you why you have killed my boy*" (GMH, 2013, p. 324).

This wholehearted search for the truth, where victims are capable of anything, even to face death, responds to a strain that touches the deepest part of their feminine essence. There are no adjectives in Spanish to name the parents whose children have died or to name that person whose loved one has been a victim of forced disappearance. Upon this hole at the level of the signifier, it is essential to find other signifiers to skirt that gap—like the story of what happened to that loved one—and other representations—like the fact of knowing what was such body's fate.

In his article *Des deuils si coupables*, Michel Hanus (2015a) stated that these risky behaviors are linked to a feeling of guilt inherent to mourning. Thus, the suffering people might feel that they have not loved the other person enough, that they have failed them in some occasions, or that they have experienced hostile feelings toward them; they might even feel they failed at keeping them alive.

The deep pain of the suffering person, according to Hanus (2015a), has an expiration value of the feeling of guilt and often goes hand in hand with taking risks, most of the times in a passive or involuntary manner: negligence, risky behavior, illnesses, accidents, recklessness. We can think that both Antigone and these women who look for their loved ones experience an underlying feeling of guilt linked to the impossibility of rendering justice, which generates in the suffering person a feeling of debt that obliges them to continue an incessant search. Nevertheless, it is necessary to indicate that we find a decisive element when analyzing the testimonies: the fact of taking risks not in an accidental or passive manner but in a totally deliberate and fully aware manner.

Both in Antigone and with these victims, this determined desire of reestablishing the truth implies a tragic dimension.

The second element in common is *the suffering imposed by the holders of power in the absence of the impossibility of carrying out the funeral rite*. This indicates Creon's prohibition in the case of Antigone, whose plan was to degrade the corpse down to the statute of garbage, and in the case of the Colombian victims, with the absence of a corpse to bury in view of their total ignorance about its whereabouts.

This event makes victims suffer in deep sorrow, leaving them in a sort of limbo that will not allow them to complete the mourning process and work through what Freud called *normal mourning*, that in which the loss of the object is overcome, after reality states its verdict: the object no longer exists and the ego is carried away by the sum of the narcissistic satisfactions that being alive provides and unties the bond to the lost object (Freud, 1917).

There is no normal mourning for those who are looking for their disappeared loved ones because even if they suspect their death, there is no corpse that allows embodying that reality to go through it symbolically. In the absence of the corpse, the disappeared person acquires a particular statute since there are neither concrete elements in the reality that account for their death nor for their life. There is only absence and emptiness, which are a source of anxiety and, most of all, of guilt for the survivors.

In her article *El dolor por un muerto-vivo* (The Pain for the Dead-Alive), Sandra Zorio (2011) explains how the disappeared person acquires an ambivalent character as it could be the dead one to whom it is impossible to bury or the alive one going through great difficulties and pain (kidnapping, torture, sexual exploitation, forced confinement by an armed group). The testimonies in the aforementioned article depict to what extent the suffering person is condemned to a feeling of guilt. In the case where the disappeared one is still alive, the fact of advancing on search tasks could put them in danger; however, stopping the search feels like negligence since the possibility of helping is lost. Furthermore, with uncertainty and lack of information, the suffering people are longing for the confirmation of death, which also makes them feel guilty: "*Every time I went to the hospitals, I used to beg God to find them dead and, when I didn't find them, then I felt as bad as if I had killed them. Then I begged God for forgiveness and asked him not to find them in the next hospital. That was torturous*" (Zorio, 2011, p. 88).

That is to say, wishing for the confirmation of the death of a loved one is lived unconsciously as if you were wishing for their death, in addition to the feeling of not having been able to protect them and avoid their disappearance. This is how, even being almost certain of their death, given the absence of their corpse, the dead is neither the dead whose loss is confirmed nor the living person whose coming back home is longed for. Present and past are mixed in the speech of those who suffer: "*I start thinking . . . if my son died, what have they done to him? How did they kill him or torture him? What his suffering is like? If I had found him, at least I would have known that I saw him dead for real. But, this way, it is impossible to be at peace, my heart bleeds every time I think of him, every day*" (CNMH, 2016, p. 261).

These testimonies show the importance of the corpse in the process of mourning. At this point, we go back to the first part of this article wherein we agreed with Freud about the impossibility to inscribe death in the unconscious. The body of the deceased fills the impossibility of representing the un-representable character of death (Zorio, 2011).

In his article "Les traces des morts" (The Traces of the Dead), Hanus (2015b) poses the three main functions of the remains of our loved ones: to be certain of the reality of their death to be able to progressively leave them, to be able to pay homage to them, and lastly, to be able to keep them in our memory.

We will depict this element with the story *Sin nombres, sin rostros ni rastros* (Without Names, Faces, Traces) by Jorge Eliecer Pardo (2011): "*Since my brothers have disappeared, I wait by the river tonight for a corpse to arrive and make it my dead. They have taken someone away from all of us in the harbor; they made someone disappear; they murdered someone close to each of us; we are orphans, widows. That is why we are always waiting for the dead who come from the turbulent waters, among the palisade, to make them our brothers, fathers, husbands or sons*" (p. 317).

Finding the corpse is necessary to inscribe the deceased in a historical dimension, to be able to tell the others, the new generations, that our loved one existed, and to frame the end of their existence based on signifiers, with precise elements from the topologic and chronologic point of view: when they died (their birth and death dates), how they died, and where they were buried.

That is to say, the corpse is necessary when the death of the loved one is uncertain but also when it is known to be certain. In any case, we can see the courage of these suffering people, just like Antigone, in a quest to rescue their loved ones from limbo, getting them out of the statute of waste and to restore them to the order of the deceased, being as courageous and determinant as a woman can be. We conclude with the story of one of the victims:

> *I knew where my husband's corpse was discarded and I decided to go by myself to get it . . . many years later, when the authorities told me that there was neither a formal complaint nor records of him being killed . . . I went with my older sons to the place that used to be our land and that today is inhabited by new owners. We entered, and they would not let us dig . . . I told them. "It is for your own sake. We take our dead and we do not bother you again. I am looking for my dead and I swear that, before leaving, I will take out my shoes and show you that I am not even taking dirt . . . I will leave it there . . . I just want my dead.*" (GMH, 2013, p. 324)

The abovementioned story takes us directly to the third point of this parallelism between Antigone and the victims of forced disappearance, showing the importance of the corpse to signify the death of the loved one as well as the *need for a funeral rite* to elaborate the mourning process and to reconcile with the death, paraphrasing Freud (1915) in *Reflections on War and Death*.

This implies that once the whereabouts becomes known, finding the corpse is not enough, and Antigone's tragedy is proof of that, since it is necessary for a funeral to be held as a sort of transition rite marking the crossover between the living and the world of the dead. Performing the rituals for the disappeared people is a way of restoring their human dignity.

According to Hanus (2015b), the main function of the funeral rite is to pay homage to the dead and to accompany them in their journey to the other side, ensuring that both their body and soul are properly cared for. Moreover, this rite also has the function of accompanying the survivors, the suffering ones, in their mourning and giving them the chance to publicly express it, to share it with others, and feel the support of the community they belong to. And in this last instance, the rites' purpose is to join and consolidate the social group that was destroyed by the death of one of its members.

Overall, we have stated that for the griever to accept their process of mourning, it is necessary for them to be certain that the other one is dead. The corpse of the dead allows to embody this loss and to represent it symbolically; it allows for the clearance of this field full of ambiguities, that in the case of the disappeared people we have compared to a limbo. To symbolically go through loss, individually and collectively, the corpse needs to go through a funeral rite. The griever knows that the object no longer exists and needs to share this painful experience with their congeners to seek for comfort. Only then, as Freud (1917) stated, the ego can renounce to the object, declaring it death.

TO RECONCILE WITH DEATH THROUGH RITE

To speak about the funeral rite as a transition rite implies considering death as a transit movement toward the other side, that is to say, toward a place or state where the dead still exists, not as a body but as a soul. At the beginning of our reflection, we mentioned that to Freud, the only condition that would lead us to reconcile with death is the idea of an "untouchable life" left for us after life, that is, a life after death.

To give an example of the importance of the funeral rite as a transition rite, we have selected the tough testimony of a woman, who was a victim of sexual violence and whose son died in the field due to lack of food and medical care. After confirming the death of her son and without being able to find comfort in others to share her suffering, she improvised her own funeral rite:

> *"The child! The child is dead!" No one. Nothing. Then she went inside and with the taciturn peace of who has nothing to wait for, she boiled some orange sections, took the corpse of the child in her arms and gave him a bath. She put the child on the table and wrapped him in swaddling clothes as if dressed; she thought he looked like an angel. She went out and picked up some pieces of cardboard from the floor and drew a pair of wings. She cut them and also wrapped them in swaddling clothes. She put her angel on them, lighted two candles and stood there, staring at him, until the sun came out.* (CNMH, 2018, p. 35)

She transforms her dead son into an angel and puts wings on him so that he can fly to the land of the dead. This angel, that states another part of the testimony, has protected her and allowed her to survive the war.

FROM VICTIMS TO SURVIVORS: LIVING TO TALK ABOUT WAR

Throughout this chapter, we have elucidated the matter of mourning and loss both in the victim and in the executioner. We have mentioned that many times, one individual can easily jump from one position to the other. We have also noted that some victims even risk their lives to find the whereabouts of their loved ones. And, above all, we have identified the important participation of women in the Colombian armed conflict. In all the sources reviewed for the purpose of this investigation, the authors highlight the courage and fearlessness women show when the threat directly attacks the being of them: "*But if there is something relevant in the experience of women, is that their strength is often times linked to maternity, the love for their children, or the affective link to other loved ones*" (Ruta Pacífica de las Mujeres, 2013, p. 88).

To conclude, we should consider the case of those women who have gone beyond the state of victim and decided to take an active role as a solution to process loss: the survivors. We owe Primo Levi and his narrative works on his experience in war, the consideration of the survivor statute as the person who is called to take an active role, making a reconstruction and memory exercise. Primo Levi (2015) does not exalt the statute of the victim, although, he recognizes the importance of giving them their dignity back and taking into consideration their suffering. He says every victim must be sympathized with, every survivor must be helped and sympathized, but their behaviors must not always be set as examples.

There is a stance which we find fully compatible with the ethics of psychoanalysis, since it considers the dimension of subjective responsibility and encourages the victim to find a unique solution to their tragic experience. The survivor has an individual and collective responsibility: an individual need to reconstruct themselves to keep on living, but also, a collective duty to provide their own version or piece of the truth so that it can be transmitted along the collective memory of the community they belong to.

In this regard, it is particularly relevant the experience of the *Ruta Pacífica de las Mujeres* (Women's Peaceful Route), a feminist movement that has been working for more than twenty years for the negotiated process of the armed conflict in Colombia, denouncing the particular impact of violence on women.

In its report *La verdad de las mujeres víctimas del conflicto armado en Colombia* (The Truth of Women Who are Victims of the Colombian Armed

Conflict), this organization collects testimonies of women who have moved from the victim to the survivor position in a transition that oscillates between death and life: they feel that they are dying but they keep on living stating that, out of extreme fragility, they extract the strength that allows them to continue living. Such strength, from the order of the desire, allowed them to elaborate a new response to their pain. To get out from the painful position, women have moved their learning from their violence experiences. They have learned to become strong through bonds and support. They set a limit on the swirl of succumbing into pain. They have accepted the irreversibility of the facts without forgetting them. They have learned not to let themselves be stripped of their dignity (Ruta Pacífica de las Mujeres, 2013).

Just as it is necessary to restore their dignity to the dead through burial and funeral rites, survivors also require to restore their dignity through new anchor points that give another sense to their existence. To that end, they also need to reconstruct the truth of the facts: "*I have spent years looking for her, without knowing anything new. I used to think that my daughter had left because she was angry with me. But this was not true. He clearly told us that they took her and then killed her. I hugely thank that man; I bless him because he took that horrible suffering away from me. Now at least I know she is dead and that I will be handed over the remains to give her Christian burial, and that is a relief*" (GMH, 2013, p. 293).

TO LOSE EVERYTHING IN ORDER TO GAIN LIFE: THE ENCOUNTER WITH THE EXECUTIONER

During the first hearing of the *Jurisdicción Especial para la Paz* (Special Jurisdiction for the Peace), Rodrigo Londoño, Timochenko, former commander in chief of the FARC, declared that "We are compelled to Dantesque realities from which we are sure irreparable damages, pain, anguish and loss stem from many Colombian and foreign families. We apologize to all of them, we will do even the impossible so they can know the truth of what happened" (Ortega, 2018).

We learned from the teachings of Lacan (1973) that this quest for the truth is marked by impossibility. In his XX seminar, which focused on the matter of female enjoyment, he stated that there is something of the truth that is of the order of the unnamable, the whole truth is that which cannot be said. It is what can only be said on the condition of not pushing it to the extreme, of telling half-truths.

In the Colombian case, the main scenario for this reconstruction of the truth is the restorative justice system created in the context of the Peace Agreement, called *Sistema Integral de Verdad, Justicia, Reparación y No Repetición* (Integral System of the Truth, Justice, Reparation and Non-Repetition). Conformed by three agencies: a *Comisión para el Esclarecimiento de la Verdad, the Convivencia, and No Repetición* (Commission for the Clarification of the Truth, Coexistence, and Non-Repetition); a *Unidad para la Búsqueda de Personas dadas por Desaparecidas* (Searching Unit for Disappeared People); and a *Jurisdicción Especial para la Paz* (Special Jurisdiction for Peace) (JEP). From these, they must derive the measures of integral reparation for the construction of peace and the guarantees of non-repetition.

However, the truth of war can never be fully clarified, and this longed reconstruction must be understood as a product of the joined fragments of truth both from the victims and from the executioners. According to JEP reports, more than 3,500 ex guerrilla fighters and about 1,750 officers will be called by the *Sala de Reconocimiento de la Verdad* to appear before the victims. Unlike the cases considered above, in which women take their own initiative toward the encounter with the executioner by risking their lives, within the frame of transitional justice, this encounter is regulated by a legal framework. Indeed, along the negotiations, the victims were actively involved in the process, which is considered to be an unprecedented event.

Just as we mentioned before, in these encounters with the victims throughout negotiations, the two roles can coexist within the same individual: the victim and the executioner. The leader of the victims of sexual violence, who in 2014 told her story before her victimizer, stated that by the end of the event, a guerrilla woman approached her and "*she told me that she felt a lump in her throat as she was listening to my story*" (Arenas & Arrieta, 2014). This led her to believe that she had felt identified with her. Another victim, to whom a guerrilla leader asked for forgiveness, said that, "*this is the most important and transcendental encounter of my life*" (Reyes, 2014).

The JEP is an encounter setting for victims and victimizers, where both aim at clarifying the facts. The victim needs to clear up the truth to process her suffering, whereas the victimizer also needs this space to process his guilt. Both the victim and victimizer find a place that contributes to their mourning process.

During one of the first JEP hearings, one of the accused stated that "We hope the victims can rebuild their lives, and also us as appearing parties" (Ortega, 2018). Victims are still mostly represented by women: mothers, daughters, and sisters searching for a truth that can only be partially spoken. There is something unfathomable in the victim's pain and in their experience of war, as well as something unspeakable in the moving act of the executioner.

The survivors are these women who, such as an analysis subject would do, accept the challenge of *naming the unspeakable and forgive the unforgivable*, taking the expression from Pastora Mira, representative of the victims at the negotiations table (Ramírez, 2017). Humanizing the executioner seems to facilitate their mourning process, which according to Freud takes the ego to give the object up, declaring it dead and offering it the gift of staying alive (Freud, 1917)

Coming back to Primo Levi (2015), we want to highlight the importance of listening to the executioner, as we tried to put it in this text. The oppressor is still such. The same happens with the victim. They are not interchangeable. The first must be punished and condemned (but, if possible, he must also be understood). The latter must be sympathized with, and also assisted. However, in the light of the impudence of the fact that has been irrevocably committed, both need a shelter, a defense, and they instinctively search for that. Not all, but most of them. Almost always and for the rest of their lives.

In conclusion, we could say that even though "we have tried to kill death with silence," the testimonies provided by the victims and executioners show that it is also a human need to make the dead speak and to tell us something about that unbearable but inescapable reality so that it becomes less foreign and troubling. We need to speak to the dead as a way of believing that they have not left us completely. We try to kill death with silence, but is necessary to talk about it in order to give it life. To dialectize the horror of war, it is imperative to speak of death, to speak to death, and to make death speak.

NOTES

1. All translations from documents in Spanish from the editor.

REFERENCES

Acuerdo Final para la Terminación del Conflicto y la Construcción de una Paz Estable y Duradera (2017). Available at: http://www.altocomisionadoparalapaz.gov.co/procesos-y-conversaciones/Documentos%20compartidos/24-11-2016NuevoAcuerdoFinal.pdf.

Alexievitch, S. (2016). *La guerre n'a pas un visage de femme*. Paris: J'ai lu.

Amnistía International. (2004). *Colombia, cuerpos marcados, crímenes silenciados. Violencia contra las mujeres en el marco del conflicto armado.* Madrid: EDAL.

Arenas, N. & Arrieta, L. (2014). *El encuentro con las FARC a los ojos de las víctimas.* In *La silla vacía*. Available at: http://lasillavacia.com/historia/el-encuentro-con-las-farc-los-ojos-de-las-victimas-48430.

Centro Nacional de Memoria Histórica (2016). *Hasta encontrarlos. El drama de la desaparición forzada en Colombia*, CNMH, Bogotá.

Centro Nacional de Memoria Histórica. (2017). *La guerra inscrita en el cuerpo. Informe nacional de violencia sexual en el conflicto armado*. CNMH, Bogotá.

Centro Nacional de Memoria Histórica. (2018). *Expropiar el cuerpo. Seis historias sobre violencia sexual en el conflicto armado*. CNMH, Bogotá.

Freud, S. (1917). Duelo y Melancolía. In J. Strachey (Ed.), Etcheverry, J.L. (Trans.), *Obras completas de Sigmund Freud* (2nd ed., Vol. XIV), 2006, pp. 273–304. Buenos Aires: Amorrortu.

Freud, S. (1915). De guerra y muerte. In J. Strachey (Ed.), Etcheverry, J. L. (Trans.), *Obras completas de Sigmund Freud* (2nd ed., Vol. XIV), 2006. Buenos Aires: Amorrortu.

GMH (2013). *¡BASTA YA! Colombia: Memorias de guerra y dignidad.* Bogotá: Imprenta Nacional.

Hanus, M. (2015a). Des deuils si coupables... !. In *Jusqu'à la mort accompagner la vie* (121), pp. 65–72.
Hanus, M. (2015b). Les traces des morts. Nécessité pour les proches et pour la société de savoir où se trouvent le corps ou les cendres des défunts. In *Jusqu'à la mort accompagner la vie* (121), pp. 31–36.
Infobae (2017). *De niña fue reclutada por las FARC y ahora cuenta su calvario.* Buenos Aires, Argentina.
Levi, P. (2015). *Trilogía de Auschwitz*. Barcelona: Ediciones Península.
Lacan, J. (1973). *Encore. Le séminaire livre XX.* Paris: Le Seuil.
Miller, J. A. (1999). Un répartitoire sexuel. *La cause freudienne* (40), 5–26.
Naveau, L. (2011). Lacan avec Antigone. *La Cause freudienne* (79), 231–234.
Ortega, C. (2018). Arranca la verdad de la Farc en la justicia especial para la paz. *El tiempo.* Available at:
http://www.eltiempo.com/justicia/jep-colombia/las-declaraciones-de-timochenko-en-la-primera-audiencia-de-la-jep-243256.
Pardo, J. E. (2011). Sin nombres, sin rostros ni rastros. *Desde el Jardín de Freud* (11), 317–320.
Ramírez, J. (2017). Perdonar lo imperdonable. *El Colombiano.* Available at: http://www.elcolombiano.com/opinion/columnistas/perdonar-lo-imperdonable-NG7282078.
Reyes, E. (2014). Víctimas de Colombia hablan de su drama ante sus verdugos en Cuba. *El País.* Available at:
https://elpais.com/internacional/2014/08/17/actualidad/1408268734_992932.html.
Ruta Pacífica de las Mujeres. (2013). *La verdad de las mujeres víctimas del conflicto armado en Colombia (versión resumida)*, Available at: https://www.rutapacifica.org.co/descargue-los-libros/208-la-verdad-de-las-mujeresvictimas-del-conflicto-armado-en-colombia.
Sutyrin, N. (Producer) (2016). *FARC, La cara femenina de la guerrilla. RT "TV-NOVOSTI".* Available at: https://actualidad.rt.com/programas/especial/222071-selva-colombia-femenina-farc.
Tobella, A (2015). *Tras décadas de control de la maternidad, las FARC viven su propio baby boom.* Red Mundial de Radio. Available at: http://redmundialderadio.com/tras-decadas-de-control-de-maternidad-las-farc-viven-su-propio-baby-boom/.
Unidad para las Víctimas. (2015). Informe: *Mujeres y conflicto armado.* Available at: http://www.unidadvictimas.gov.co/sites/default/files/documentosbiblioteca/mujeres.PDF.
Zorio S. (2011). El dolor por un muerto–vivo. Una lectura freudiana del duelo en los casos de desaparición forzada. *Desde el Jardín de Freud* (11), 251–266.

Chapter Five

On the Construction of Maternity

Paola J. González Castro

In our contemporary societies, maternity and the feminine condition are constantly articulated with mourning and loss. Something of the feminine is lost with the birth of a child so a mother may be born as well. The sociocultural conditions under which the puerperium is inscribed are the support throughout this process of subjective mutation. Even though these symbolic supports cannot completely protect maternity against its vicissitudes, these at least are the pillars which cover, or unprotect, women in this redefinition.

Within the Nahua worldview, the pregnant woman symbolically dies during delivery, just before returning from the underworld as a warrior or mother, having crossed a threshold from which there is no turning back.

Culture has usually equated femininity with maternity, as if the reproductive capacity that inhabits the biologically feminine subject implied a univocal and natural condition from which to define women as mothers, as if the natural condition of the feminine being was located in maternity. Thus, one can speak of a maternal instinct, an archetype of the mother whose main role would be to veil the fatal possibilities of the reappropriation of the object, in its infanticidal or perverse aspects. Psychoanalysis has moved away from this idea and shown that, where language rules, instinct is not enough to support the various configurations that would derive from a symbolic condition.

For the mothers who have been unable to be inscribed inside the symbolic and imaginary registers of their time, as well as for those who happen to inherit the feminine as a mere hollow emblem, with symbols and ideals of maternity without roots, the death and symbolic rebirth entailed in maternity may involve a greater burden for their narcissism than the one that can be endure, leading to the appearance of severe maternity-related destabilizations.

Facing the enigma opened by the child's birth, one can be lead back to an archaic problem, a pre-Oedipal moment of havoc in the mother–daughter relationship. A return to a period of suspension and dependence on a genealogy of mothers where silence without resonance predominates. It remains to be known if a woman, in maternity, manages to create a new answer to that silence, which sometimes reveals itself as mortiferous.

UNPROTECTED MATERNITIES

Modernity has transformed maternity, introducing new frontiers to human biology, allowing or avoiding procreation, separating the sexual act from conception, and providing configurations so complex that they advance faster than international legislations: gamete and embryo donations, surrogate motherhood, artificial insemination, in vitro fertilization. The list is long, and the problems related to filiation for those conceived under their techniques are not minor.

The technical and biological aspects of the maternal event are highlighted, thus undermining desire as foundation and driving force of this experience. One by one, the rights of pregnant women, of the parturient, of puerperal women, are violated. Nowadays, in Mexico, cesarean births are privileged even without any medical need for the procedure (43% of cases at national level, reaching as high as 80% in private health institutions) (Juárez, 2017). Exclusive breastfeeding during the first six months of life occurs in barely 14 percent of the cases (UNICEF México, n.d.). The financial participation of women with at least one child is of 43 percent, increasing to 70 percent in the case of single mothers. Most births take place in hospital facilities, and only 7 percent of women have home births or give birth at birthing centers.

These figures are paradoxical if we consider that Mexico is a country with a significant ancestral tradition in medicine and midwifery. Among the original indigenous people, we can find extensive knowledge, techniques, and traditions in regard to birth which have been passed on from generation to generation. The secrets of life, health, and plants were combined around midwifes, legendary and leading figures who today are nowadays treated with disdain.

In regard the current puerperium treatment, the medical system is the one which holds power over the woman's body and birth. There are no favorable conditions to put the midwife's ancient millenary traditions into practice, except from some places in which these are rescued through midwifery vocational training and some others in which traditional births are respected. There is clearly an abyss between cities and towns in regard to births and their medicalization.

The signifiers mobilized during this period are very particular and point toward a disease that will be "alleviated" after giving birth, as if pregnancy would have been a disease sutured by birth. And in this new state of relief, completeness, discharge, an idealization of the maternal figure is gestated.

The sinister hospital practices during birth oppose this maternal ideal: the immediate separation policies, forced sterilization and unauthorized cesarean births, as well as little breastfeeding support, offenses and harassment during delivery; these are, in many cases, the conditions in which women have been subjected to modern asepsis. In five years, 2.9 million cases of obstetric violence have been registered in Mexico (Voces Feministas, 2017).

In this way, reality and ideals remain distant, in opposite conditions. The psychical component of maternity is set aside. Women's word and desires remain suspended in favor of a health system eager to turn birth into a disease for which the cure is a cesarean birth. Fortunately, not only is the body present in maternity, but also the unconscious which, through a singular and strictly coded language, presents itself in varied forms in response to the motions of maternity.

The maternal symptomatology, which ranges from depression to severe destabilization that may take place during this period, are problems that must be understood, prevented, and treated, given their immediate and long-term consequences they have on the further development of boys and girls; due to the psychical consequences on the mother and also the impact that this libidinal retreat has in relation to what is being constituted in both mother and child.

In Mexico, the psychic phenomena associated with maternity have been barely studied, giving priority to a hormonal, environmental, and genetic approach in its development. Depression (both moderate and severe), as the most widely studied maternal phenomena, has a prevalence of 20 percent in women with a child aged under five; of these more than two million women, only 17 percent speak of their sadness and maternal depressive symptoms with doctors or other health care professionals. Indeed, only 15 percent receive appropriate medical or psychological treatment (de Castro, Place, Villalobos, & Allen-Leigh, 2015). In Mexico, the factors related to maternal depression include being the mother of a girl, having more than four children, suffering from food insecurity at home, the baby's low weight at birth, and being a victim of violence (de Castro et al., 2015). This daunting situation clearly leaves maternities unprotected. We can't set aside the weight that society and generation transmission have in the construction of this symbolic function.

A MOMENT OF DEATH

Within the Nahua worldview, the rituals surrounding pregnancy and childbirth, as well as care of postpartum women (or of those who died in childbirth), reflected a system of understanding of the world order in which the opposing principles such as life and death, the feminine and the masculine, the high and the low, and the light and the darkness are intertwined, confront each other and follow one another to prepare the way for life itself (Alcántar-Rojas, 2000).

The conception this society had on childhood was far from the one of European societies, for which, at that time, children were perfectible, impure beings who were scarcely involved in society. Nahua children, as soon as they were given a name, became full subjects of rights with an appointed specific role in society; they were respected and surrounded by love; paternity and maternity were exercised in a conscious and participatory manner (Quezada, 1977). Conception was regarded as a divine gift, a splendid, rich feather, which is creature that needs to be perfected and will end up in that girl's womb (Sahagún, 2013). The Nahua society did not consider procreation as a mere biological fact but a process covered by the veil of mysticism through which transcendence was achieved. It is also important to underline that not only did the parturient woman receive physiological care, but the midwives' role also involved the psychosomatic care of the puerperal woman (Quezada, 1996).

The rituals surrounding this event facilitated the woman's passage "to a new state" (Alcántar-Rojas, 2000) in which both the family and the society cared for her health, as well as the baby's health, in its condition of extremely valuable divine gift; such divine veil is doubled as a result of the pregnant condition that veils such a *precious gem* from the viewer.

The woman's transition to such new state is announced during a public ritual. Her family and friends shared their words and advice with her, anticipating the fragility and uncertainty that will accompany the pregnant woman during the next moons. Toward the end of pregnancy, a midwife was allocated to the mother-to-be through a careful ritual. Such midwife would be in charge of giving advice and comfort and guiding her during childbirth, during the definitive transitional moment after which the woman is reborn in a new state of things (Alcántar-Rojas, 2000); its significance lay in the event itself rather than in the result.

Giving birth is equivalent to a battle, and ever since its start, the woman was considered a warrior who had to fight the battle in solitude, only in the company of the midwife that had been at her side for some time. Regardless its winner (life or death), the warrior would be crowned with the honor of parenting or the honor of accompanying the sun in its road to the West in its daily struggle to be reborn from the place of the dead (Quezada, 1996).

In the Nahua worldview, giving birth (and especially for the first time) provided women with the insignia of change to be deemed as a woman-warrior, who has been reborn after a brief death.

What we want to highlight through this path to the Nahua tradition surrounding becoming a mother is the moment of birth, also referred as "a moment of death" or *imiquizpan*. From this moment of death, the woman was reborn as a mother and warrior, as we have previously stated, honored with the upbringing of her children or as a company for the sun in its path to the feminine part of the sky that gives rise to sunset.

The concept of *imiquizpan*, a moment of death needed to give life, is presented as a useful concept to illustrate the psychic grief the female subject is faced with during maternity. These first postpartum moments are conceptualized as a road to a new construction that will redefine what had so far been understood as normal and through which women's lives have to be reorganized upon, now as mothers; such transition becomes more evident when giving birth for the first time and during the first postpartum moments (Martell, 2001).

FROM THE FREUDIAN TRIEB TO THE ARCHETYPE OF THE MOTHER

When Freud (1915a) sketched out the metapsychology of the human mind's genesis, he based his ideas on Darwinian hedonism and Bradford Cannon's famous "fight or flight" binary. Flight involves the reduction of the unpleasant external stimulus through the distance that is placed between the source of the stimulus and the subject. Alternatively, we can find the fight response and its variations in function of the control over the environment. The modification of the causative agent through eating, drinking, sleeping/dreaming, or getting into conflict would involve supplementary possibilities for "flight."

According to Freud (1915b) the unavoidable nature of the internal stimuli would promote mental development, thus resulting in two unique diverging options: development or oblivion. This way, children start distinguishing bit by bit those discreet stimuli that could be avoided from those continuous stimuli that cannot be avoided unless a caregiver intervenes. Experience will soon teach the difference between the internal and the external to this mind under development, and the functionality of the flight response. Later on, the child will try to replicate their caregiver's actions, succeeding in mitigating his needs, leading him directly toward an instinct of mastery and the evolution of his psyche. Freud stated that instincts and not external stimuli are the true motive forces behind the advances that have led the nervous system, with its unlimited capacities, to its present high level of development. There is naturally nothing to prevent our supposing that the instincts themselves are, at least in part, precipitates of the effects of external stimulation, which in the course of phylogenesis have brought about modifications in the living substance (Freud, 1915b).

Based on this model of the mind organized in function of the pleasure and displeasure principles and the evolution axioms, Freud strives to determine the precise psychological nature of instincts. In 1911, he refers to a psychic border representing organic forces in "Formulations on the Two Principles of Mental Functioning" whereas, in 1915, he declares that instincts cannot turn into objects of thinking; only their representation may have access to thought (Freud, 1915b). In 1926, "Inhibitions, Symptoms, and Anxiety," the theory on instincts remains a "dark region" for psychoanalysis and for Freud himself.

We must consider the difficulty of the German *trieb* in its translation into English, which has in many occasions been equated with instinct. When Freud uses the German term *instinkt* in his article "The unconscious" (1915c), he specifically refers to instinct in animals: "If inherited mental formations exist in the human being—something analogous to instinct in animals—these constitute the nucleus of the Ucs" (p. 195). This differentiation between the animal instinct (*instinkt*) and human drive (*trieb*) may be due to the postnatal plasticity of the so-called human instincts and the deviation that language introduces in the human being and, as a result, the Freudian theory finds support in Lamarck, which allows it to explain the human instinct from an epigenetic point of view. Nevertheless, the Freudian elaboration of the relationship between instinct and psyche locates certain aspects of the instinct as being represented or transformed into an acceptable herald of a certain somatic insistence.

The idea of an archetype as a mythological concept of collective images inherited not just through history and culture can be understood as Jung's (1936) response to the Freudian theory that locates drive as the engine of the psychic apparatus' evolution. A representation of the fact that the form, and not the representation itself, may be inherited and whose existence could not be traced, although it would entail concrete effects. Archetypes are conceived by Jung as a mode of functioning through which living beings acquire a compass for survival in the world, a "behavioral pattern" with a merely biological substrate: "These ideas, forms and predispositions, although being unconscious, are not less active or alive, and, just like the instinct, pre-shape and influence the thoughts, feelings and acts of each psyche" (Jung, 1936, p. 73).

Thus, by locating these "primordial images" as the soul's substrate, Jung opens up the possibility of a set of archetypes among which we may find the archetype of the mother that serves as a basis of what he terms the maternal complex. The mother, in all its forms and representations, goes through culture, history, and mythology, both in the positive, creator and good-natured sense as in the negative aspect, which most of the times implies destruction, darkness, and death, also including the potential of magic, rebirth, and instinct.

Under these primordial images, the notion of mother may involve—for Jung—an extension of "the feminine instinct." Thus, the image of the *mater natura*, the mother goddess, is considered "the form that contains all that is living" (Jung, 1936, p. 94), and a way of reflecting on the various figures embodying maternity, as well as the difficulties sorted out by human history and its traditions to separate the feminine and the maternal, as if there was a maternal instinct in every woman, capable of organizing the maternal-filial relationship.

However, Jung shows a difference in regard to the maternal complex and its mainly unconscious basis between what this represents for the girl and the boy. While for the latter, the mother is symbolic per se, for the girl the mother becomes symbolic only over the course of psychic evolution. The need to go through certain psychic evolution to achieve a coherent definition of the mother figure entails the existence of various impediments that will undoubtedly be present in the relationship of a woman with her children (and with her own mother). The results of this impediment can be seen in what other authors call *maternal ravage*.

A CULTURE THAT CLUTTERS INSTINCT

The great debate on instincts and their differentiation or limits with concepts like will and motivation was also resumed by Lacan, especially in the relationship of what allegedly was an instinct ordering the relationship between a mother and her children. Lacan only returned to this idea throughout his teaching to prove that nothing in the world was less natural than maternity.

From the beginning, Lacan's teaching pointed out the importance of the symbolic order over human biology, stressing that the maternal instinct in mammals ends after the weaning process, whereas in human beings, both weaning and the so-called maternal feelings are regulated by dominant cultural conditions (Lacan, 2012).

In an attempt to break away from the idea of an instinct regulating the parental function, Lacan strives to assert that the feelings of paternity, maternity, and fraternity as we know them today are the result of cultural postulates that have marked the development of the family life, thus showing the power of cultural instances over the natural ones when a human family is set up, as well as in other social phenomena related to human beings.

Language introduces an anomaly in the human being, which involves giving up the natural order to access the symbolic order. This symbolic order undermines the instinctive forces through culture, language, the laws, and the symbols governing a specific society. Based on such anomaly put into operation by language, something is lost forever for the speaking being. Complete satisfaction becomes impossible; there are glimpses of satisfaction that always point toward lack. In this way, the subject is divided into the living being and the subject of jouissance.

Far from the natural order as a result of language, sexuality, and, consequently, maternity, lose their natural and instinctive character. "There is no sexual relationship" is the aphorism used by Lacan to account for the discrepancy between speaking beings and the impossibility of an encounter. In the light of this gap, certain *semblants* are articulated for us to believe in the possibility of an encounter with the other; among them are love, desire, and maternity.

Marie-Hélène Brousse (1993) highlights the abysmal distance between maternity and the biological act, proposing that "there is only a denatured mother," thus emphasizing that the phallic signifier goes through maternity and, with this, consent to a sacrifice of jouissance, castration. If this sacrifice of jouissance against the object-child is required, it is to the extent that, in many occasions, the child may crystallize itself as fetish-object, so a mother-child relationship not mediated by the phallic signifier cannot help but be fatal.

This idea would be developed by Lacan in his Seminar IV, in which he is against the "idea of a harmonic object which, given its nature, consumes the subject–object relationship" (Lacan, 1996). The phallic logic mediates the relationship with the object. This relationship, imaginary par excellence and for which the prototype is the mother–child relationship, cannot be dual. Even if this first relationship may have the illusory character of completeness or, as some post-Freudians called it, a symbiotic character, this cannot be understood without a phallic element establishing a triad, making symbolic that which runs the risk of staying imaginary.

Classically, psychoanalysts—following Freud's footsteps—understood the entrance of the infant into the symbolic register through the presence–absence binary, exemplified by Freud with his comments to the Fort-Da game of his grandson, Ernst:

> He was, however, on good terms with his parents and their one servant-girl, and tributes were paid to his being a "good boy." He did not disturb his parents at night, he conscientiously obeyed orders not to touch certain things or go into certain rooms, and above all he never cried when his mother left him for a few hours. At the same time, he was greatly attached to his mother, who had not only fed him herself but had also looked after him without any outside help. This good little boy, however, had an occasional disturbing habit of taking any small objects he could get hold of and throwing them away from him into a corner, under the bed, and so on, so that hunting for his toys and picking them

> up was often quite a business. As he did this he gave vent to a loud, long-drawn-out "O-O-O-O," accompanied by an expression of interest and satisfaction. His mother and the writer of the present account were agreed in thinking that this was not a mere interjection but represented the German word "fort" ["gone"]. I eventually realized that it was a game and that the only use he made of any of his toys was to play "gone" with them. One day I made an observation that confirmed my view. The child had a wooden reel with a piece of string tied round it. It never occurred to him to pull it along the floor behind him, for instance, and play at its being a carriage. What he did was to hold the reel by the string and very skillfully throw it over the edge of his curtained cot, so that it disappeared into it, at the same time uttering his expressive "O-O-O-O." He then pulled the reel out of the cot again by the string and hailed its reappearance with a joyful "da" ["there"]. This, then, was the complete game-disappearance and return. As a rule one only witnessed its first act, which was repeated untiringly as a game in itself, though there is no doubt that the greater pleasure was attached to the second act. (Freud, 1920, pp. 8–9)

It is the mother's desire for something beyond the child, the one that provokes such ups and downs, as Freud discovered while observing his little grandson, the essential condition to catapult the child into the symbolic register. It is the switching between absence and presence, that first "no" as necessary for the following "yes."

Nevertheless, it is worth mentioning that the symbol appears earlier in development as the iconic gesture of the other's desire. It is not uncommon to observe a six-month-old baby adopting mannerisms from his surroundings. A family member is always coughing, so the baby coughs when he/she is in their presence; while another one breathes loudly, so does the baby exhale loudly in his presence; another one blinks when making eye contact and the baby blinks in response, thus drawing his attention and desire. These are clear examples of what Laplanche calls generalized seduction, or the transmission of primary unconscious elements from a generation to another (Laplanche, 1987).

> That every infant—and so every person—begins life being given what he [Laplanche] calls "messages" by the parents (at first by the mother) that are beyond comprehension. These messages are not exclusively, or even predominantly verbal; they may be gestural, olfactory, tonal and so on. And they are enigmatic in a double sense. The parents themselves don't understand them—or even know about them—because they are unconscious. And the child cannot understand them because his powers of so-called understanding are so undeveloped, and because they are puzzling. What the child is able to "translate," in Laplanche's key word, he may be able to include, but the residue—which he intimates is always the larger share—constitutes an unconscious of "foreign bodies." (Phillips, 2013, p. 394)

Just as the grandmother knows not why she always coughs, the father has forgotten the reason he runs his fingers through his hair, and the grandfather overlooks his meaning of blinking. Such gestural movements, be they hand or body motions, transmit from family to child and back meaningful currency divorced from concretely specific definitions, as an ancient coin whose engravings time has eroded, passed in silence from hand to hand (Lacan, 2006b). In this way, gestural symbols are inherited, and through these the infant becomes immersed into a body language, a language of identification, demonstration, and absorption of primary symbols.

Thus, we can highlight the difference between the use of the sway of an object metaphorically representing the presence-absence of the main caregiver and the access this movement provides to the symbolic register, as Freud and Lacan conceived it and, on the other hand, the capture of individual gestures in a primary narcissistic process (Moncayo, 2008) that resembles a hunter of the parent's love and desire through "mirroring" (Fonagy, Gergely, Jurist, & Target, 2002) and the mirror stage (Lacan, 2006a; Verhaeghe & Vanheule, 2005). In his second topography of the mind, where Freud (1923) developed the concepts of id, ego, and super-ego, Freud defined primary narcissism as a primordial state prior to the formation of the ego, the prototype of which would be intra-uterine life. It remains unclear what would be narcissistic about this state given that there is no rudiment of a differentiated ego-representation that could be cathected or loved. Thus, this conception of primary narcissism differs from the earlier view where primary narcissism represented the first form of ego representations and secondary narcissism was a regressive and pathological return to the primary narcissism of early childhood. In this second view of primary narcissism, the principal characteristic of primary narcissism is not a first form of ego representation or an absence of a relationship to an object but a lack of differentiation or the presence of a fusion between subject and object, self and other. Primary narcissism, is only narcissistic in the sense that it is characterized by an absence of a differentiated and conscious relationship to the external environment. This could not be otherwise given that the primary objects in the infant's world represent the environment and these have not yet been differentiated from the ego. Differentiation has to wait until identification of the primary objects takes place. The first perceptual identity with the object constitutes the first part-representation of the ego but where the latter has not yet differentiated from the former (Moncayo, 2008).

Because the painful call to resolve tension emerges in the newborn's body, the flight reaction solves nothing; even if psychomotor development permitted the usual flight reaction, one cannot flee from oneself. Without the developmental resources necessary to neutralize the suffering on his own, the baby cries and the caregiver neutralizes the somatic tension through some appropriately "specific action," all the while giving communicative value to the baby's cry (Freud, 1895). The "interactive contingency," characteristic of early life interactions between infant and caregiver—with their rhythms of approach, encounter, avoidance, emotional harmony—develop into the future patterns for all later intersubjective relationships (Beebe & Lachmann, 2014).

Furthermore, that the interactions and interventions by the caregiver are nearly always accompanied by words, "motherese," or other symbolic acts provides one of the paths for the formation of the Other—the treasury of signifiers. "From the very beginning the somatic pressure (and its release) acquires an intersubjective dimension, marking the point at which the transition from the somatic to the psychical takes place" (Verhaege & Vanheule 2005). By closely studying mother child interactions, with the importance of emotional mirroring and interactive contingency on the one hand, and the accompanying presence of reassuring speech, one can grasp that language becomes an instrument for the regulation of emotion.

ABOUT THE REACTIVATED RAVAGE

The Nahuas talked about a divine veil covering the pregnancy process, as though the invocation of divinity covered the narcissistic crisis accompanying pregnancy and that, in Monique Bydlowski's words (2001), provides gestation with a particular *psychic transparency* during which the child has a double status, present in the mother's body and concerns and, at the same time, absent from the material reality. Such *psychic transparency* is characterized by a change in the woman's psychism which evokes ravages from adolescence, situated between dependency and rebellion. Bydlowski observes the significant tendency for pregnant women to reminisce about the past (especially those experiencing their first maternity process), as well as a withdrawal in which the psychic world would prioritize the external objects invested so far.

In this vein, Lemoine-Luccioni (1982) stresses that the phases highlighted by Freud in his narcissism analysis are also observed during pregnancy and the postpartum; here we retain the libido's narcissistic withdrawal and the paranoid delusions of grandeur that will accompany the pregnant woman, especially at the end of pregnancy. During pregnancy, the libido, previously directed toward the objects, is withdrawn to the ego; the fetus comes to fulfill the structural lack Freud spoke so much about, with its movements and responses to stimuli, it is clear that the creation delirium cannot help but be intensified. At this point, the generative power of the mother becomes so evident that Karen Horney's contribution on the greatness of the feminine and the potentiality of "womb envy" can be more easily understood (Horney, 1926 & 1932).

According to Helen Deutsch (1971), pregnancy produces a formidable disturbance of libidinal economy, leading the woman on a search for all the libidinal tendencies that had been abandoned before pregnancy. In this intensification of the drives, Deutsch finds the origins of the various psychical disorders of puerperium. For its part, Winnicott (1992) compares the mechanisms that are activated during pregnancy with the schizoid episode; a transition state necessary to sensitize the mother-to-be, allowing her to adapt to the infant's needs; however, such *ordinary maternal insanity* could erase itself, giving rise to an *extraordinary maternal insanity*.

This *extraordinary maternal insanity* has been studied since the beginning of the nineteenth century. In the 1850s, Louis-Victor Marcé became particularly interested in this issue on his *Treatise on Insanity of Pregnant and Postpartum women and Nursemaids*, a historical text re-edited in 2002 which inspired the beginnings of perinatal psychiatry (Marcé, 2002). In the twentieth century, consequences of the interwar period such as the postwar depression, and the forced migrations of the second Great War brought maternal-child matters back into the spotlight.

Many authors have studied this problem from the psychoanalytic perspective; hypotheses are diverse, but we can establish the great weight given to hostility and homosexuality as the source of puerperal psychotic disorders.

Zilboorg (1929) highlights the masculine identification and the wide sexual discrepancies of these women, as severe penis envy and sadistic tendencies toward men. The latter, according to the author, leaves the stamp of its particularity on the woman's relations. In such cases, maternal demands cause a state of stress; even leading to delirious confusion in some woman. Birth is conceived as a nodal point in the woman's sexual conflict, the agent of a psychosis.

As Frumkes (1934) points out, psychosis can be explained based on a strong unresolved incestuous drive, a great frigidity marked by a close bond with the father, and certain schizoid tendencies that get in the way of maternity.

At the Cassel Hospital (Main, 1958), it was reported that both these women's femininity and spontaneity were inhibited, implying a sexual immaturity potentially extending to frigidity. Brew and Seidenber (1950), as well as Douglas (1956) interpret attempts to destroy the infant, which take place both through infanticide and delirium, as a symbolic reaction to the inherent homosexuality in these women.

Despite the broad conceptual variations between all these theories, they share as a nodal point the central issue of feminine sexuality which, as women become mothers, turns more elusive and enigmatic. The fact that many theories point to latent homosexuality as a potential response to puerperal disorders is undoubtedly an attempt to name something that escapes and is structurally at the nexus of femininity and maternity. We should remember that, according to Freud (1908), the bisexual predisposition would be more closely related to woman (Diamond, 2009), of a deeper strength, and this would be a consequence of the first pre-Oedipal period; a period in which the connection between girl and mother is of crucial importance for her feminine becoming. However, once "womb envy" and "vaginal father" fantasies are explored, the statements that claim that women are more likely to have bisexual preferences may become more questionable (Lorand, 1939; Knafo & Moscovitz, 2018).

In this vein, Jacques-Alain Miller (2015) points out that, for a feminine subject, a child lies in the limits of her narcissism, and demands a construction between how she would be as a mother and how she was as a daughter. In his lecture on "The feminine" Freud carefully approaches how, as some women become mothers, they are redefined through the identification with their own mother. Under the impression of one's own maternity, an identification with her own mother may be revived, an identification against which the woman had been rebelling until marriage, and she may attract all the libido at hand to herself, in a way that the repetition compulsion may replicate the miserable marriage of the parents (Freud, 1920).

Furthermore, Freud (1933) observes the absolute difference between woman and mother found in the fantasies and sexual choices of his obsessive patients; and he includes the mother-woman schism in his theory, insisting that the woman can only access absolute satisfaction when she becomes a mother. As such, it is impossible to imagine a parallelism between masculine and feminine development, it is from this Other place associated with the adhesive, pre-Oedipal identification with the mother that becomes elucidated, a decisive phase that grounds the sexual development of the girl, her future femininity, and prepares for the acquisition of those qualities with which she would later fulfill her role in the sexual function and manage her inappreciable social performance (Freud, 1933). This first link to the tender character is one of the great obstacles to think about the Oedipus complex in the same way as it had been formulated for boys.

Ravage, the unsolvable dilemma in the mother–daughter relationship, can be understood as a demand intensified from its impossibility of fulfillment. The daughter demands the mother a substance, an insignia that guides her and based on which she could define herself as woman. The frustrating revelation that the mother does not seem able to give such an insignia, to transmit such a definition to the daughter—without the daughter surrendering herself and stepping off the path towards individuation—constitutes the driving force that encourages the girl to identify with her father. An identification that clearly needs to fall in order to be able to reach something beyond the Oedipus, a place not fully governed by the phallus (Wintrebert, 2015). If The Woman does not exist, the unary trait that could support the woman does not exist either and, therefore, there is no complete and coherent response to sexuality that can be inherited, transmitted; the mother is structurally in debt to her daughter and in this area, silence reigns (Hamann, 2014). Both silence and certain enigmatic signifiers passed on from mother to daughter may raise unanswered questions, aiming at an endless demand, toward ravage. In the light of such silence or sea of enigmatic signifiers, one of the more life-giving releases is undoubtedly an invention that is able to name something, which will be conditioned to an Oedipal moment during which the father may be called to temper such relationship.

The first Freudian attempts to explain the impasses and *aporias* of the feminine stance are formalized by Lacan, especially in his last teaching. For him, only the feminine side of the sexuation board allows for the access to the Other jouissance, a jouissance beyond the phallic metaphor. Woman and mother are on opposite sides of the table of sexuation; women relate to Other jouissance, while the mother's jouissance is of the phallic order. This way, the woman and the mother are figures whose relationship is undoubtedly tense: whereas the woman is the Other of desire, the mother would be the Other of demand.

The phallic signifier is not enough to fully account for this Other jouissance inherent to the feminine stance and will be a key aspect when Lacan considers Graves' White Goddess:

> How to know if, as Robert Graves puts it, the Father himself, the eternal father of us all, is not one Name among others of the White Goddess, the one that according to him gets lost in the night of the times, because she is the Different one, the forever other in her enjoyment—like those forms of the infinite whose enumeration we only start when we know that she is the one who will suspend us. (Lacan, 2001, p. 561–63, Spring awakening)

Lacan takes this infinite figure to rechristen the Name-of-the-Father as another face of the White Goddess, goddess of limitless jouissance, and completely dissociated from the maternal role. A year later, in 1975, in one of his conversations held in North American Universities, Lacan relates the divine manifestations of Tyche—those possible when creative openness to life's spontaneity reveals a healthy absence of superego ideals and repetition compulsion. Speaking on atheism, he suggests the following: "Atheism is the disease of the belief in God, believing that God does not intervene in the World. But God intervenes all the time, for example, in the form of a woman." (Lacan, 1975a).

In this way, differentiating the woman and mother on the basis of jouissance, Lacan establishes that the transition to maternity involves giving up on some part of feminine jouissance, that inscribed beyond the phallic signifier, this providing the condition for the Desire of the Mother to not be fully satisfied in her progeny.

If Freud considers the child as the fetish object par excellence, Lacan believes that this issue revolves around the idea that the woman as a mother should not find her feminine jouissance in the child as object. In maternity, the jouissance of a phallic position evoking castration can be found, a position characterized by the Father's law. If Lacan can assert that the woman does not exist, insofar as she embodies the difference, the otherness for all, but especially for herself; a different case is that of the mother figure, "the mother is one and all" (Miller, 2015). There are mothers and that does not condone them from the risk of their position; paraphrasing Sartre, everything goes well as long as the mother does not take herself to be the apotheosis of motherhood. The child is conceived by Lacan as a mechanism to shutter the woman's jouissance; the obturation of that jouissance sometimes turns her into another one, sometimes absent from herself (Lacan, 1975b).

Maternity involves a topological paradox, as Miquel Bassols explains, alluding to what is written about Gide's youth: [maternity is like] "going through a space without crossing it"; in "the figure of woman before becoming a mother [. . .] something of the mother's phallic position forms a gap" (Bassols, 2015, p. 77). According to Eric Laurent, maternity represents a point of no turning back, in which the so-called Name-of-the-Father is doubled, in the hope that a law may bring order to the mother–children relationship (Laurent, 2004). Maternity forces the subject to build a response, which is always individual, to the enigma of the sexual encounter, the enigma of femininity; in other words, maternity entails inventing solutions to the silence in which the maternal ravage was founded in pre-Oedipal times. When the response to the enigma of femininity cannot be provided through symbolic means (with all the symptoms involved), we can evoke other *sinthomes* or *suppletions* to compensate the absence of a response capable of opening up the abyss, madness.

Maternity positions the subject against a body event, understood as a remainder of the order to what is impossible to know: "a lack of knowledge in facing the knowledge we do not want to know" (Soria-Escalante, Orozco-Guzmán, López-Peñaloza, & Sigales Ruiz, 2014), a remainder that also remains impossible to be named. Such events leave indelible traces. We can understand maternity as one of the names for castration, one that leaves a mark on the body, makes a cut in history and even sometimes leads to a subversion in life. In the presence of such an event, we always need a singular and subjective way of stitching the narcissistic wound of birth.

The marks left by Lacan's last teaching are essential to understanding puerperal psychic disorders. Over the years, the well-known aphorism "he who wants to does not go mad" became "everyone is delirious"; we could add: even mothers. This second articulation between delirium and neurosis does not erase the particularity of psychosis as a structure. It is rather a new clinical practice of the continuous, a clinical practice that allows for conceiving variations in the knotting between the Imaginary, Symbolic, and Real registers, as an organizational arrangement with regard to jouissance disturbances. Where the Oedipal symptom or phantasm is absent, another solution can be built to make up for such fault.

This continuum results in a clinical practice of the real that invites the analyst to isolate, regulate, and name the jouissance modalities and thus be able to acknowledge the subject's anchoring points, features required to externalize and account for the unbearable jouissance. Such an approach to clinical practice makes way for a place in which interpretations and cuts may delimit the unspeakable, emphasizing the liveliness of the being, thus reducing the mortiferous jouissance. Maternities cannot be separated from their pain and subjectivity, and they must not and cannot be narrowed to a purely biological act for which the discourse of science would offer a straightforward answer for all cases.

Rather than a valid generalization for all women, psychoanalysis proposes listening to each one of them, individually. At the point where maternity becomes a symptom, the unnamable bursts in, waiting for its designation. At such point of disagreement between the reality and the ideal, our analytical listening should be our compass. Only through interrogating that real that sometimes arises with maternity, will we be able to build a clinical practice, one by one, that could distance itself sufficiently from the fictions and illusions of what would constitute the signifier of mothers. There exist a nigh-limitless, ever-branching series of mothers, each different from the other, with her own phantasms or deliriums giving nuance and uniqueness to their motherhood, with motherhood and maternal love defined as including the loving, the hating, the ambivalence, and defenses against, and the symptoms—conscious or not—of maternity and pregnancy.

REFERENCES

Alcántar-Rojas, B. (2000). Miquizpan. El momento del parto, un momento de muerte. Prácticas alrededor del embarazo y parto entre nahuas y mayas del Posclásico. *Estudios Mesoamericanos, 2*, 37–48.

Bassols, M. (2015). Feminidad y autorización del analista. *Bitácora Lacaniana, 4*, 69–84.

Beebe, B. & Lachmann, F. M. (2014). The origins of attachment: infant research and adult treatment. New York: Routledge.

Brew, M., & Seidenberg, R. (1950). Psychotic Reactions Associated with Pregnancy and Childbirth. *The Journal of Nervous and Mental Disease, 111*(5), 408–423.

Brousse, M-H. (1993). Femme ou mère. *La Cause Freudienne, 24*, 30–33.

Bydlowski, M. (2001). Le regard intérieur de la femme enceinte, transparence psychique et représentation de l'objet interne. *Devenir, 13*(2), 41. http://doi.org/10.3917/dev.012.0041.

De Castro, F., Place, J. M., Villalobos, A., & Allen-Leigh, B. (2015). Sintomatología depresiva materna en México: prevalencia nacional, atención y perfiles poblacionales de riesgo. *Salud Pública de México, 57*(2), 144–154. Retrieved from http://www.scielo.org.mx/scielo.php?script=sci_arttext&pid=S0036-36342015000200009.

Deutsch, H. (1971). *The Psychology of Women Vol 1*. New York, NY: Grune & Stratton.

Diamond, L. (2009). *Sexual Fluidity: Understanding Women's Love and Desire.* Cambridge, MA: Harvard University Press.
Douglas, G. (1956). Psychotic mothers. *The Lancet, 270*(6908), 124–25.
Fonagy, P., Gergely, G., Jurist, E. L., & Target, M. (2002). *Affect Regulation, Mentalization, and the Development of the Self.* New York: Other Press. Retrieved from http://www.apadivisions.org/division-39/publications/reviews/affect.aspx.
Freud, S. (1908). Las fantasías histéricas y su relación con la bisexualidad. In *Obreas Completas, IX (1906-1908)*, pp. 137–147. Buenos Aires: Amorrortu Editores.
Freud, S. (1895). Sobre la justificación de separar de la neurastenia un determinado síndrome en calidad de «neurosis de angustia». In *Obras Completas, III (1895 [1894])*, pp. 85–116. Buenos Aires: Amorrortu Editores.
Freud, S. (1911). Formulaciones sobre los dos principios del acaecer psíquico. In *Obras Completas, XII (1911)*, pp. 217–32. Buenos Aires: Amorrortu Editores.
Freud, S. (1915a). Trabajos sobre metapsicología. In *Obras Completas, XIV (1915)*, pp. 99–104. Buenos Aires: Amorrortu Editores.
Freud, S. (1915b). Pulsiones y destinos de pulsión. In *Obras Completas, XIV (1915)*, pp. 105–34. Buenos Aires: Amorrortu Editores.
Freud, S. (1915c). Lo inconsciente. In *Obras Completas, XIV (1915)*, pp. 153–214. Buenos Aires: Amorrortu Editores.
Freud S. (1920). *Beyond the Pleasure Principle*. New York: Dover Publications inc.
Freud, S. (1923). El yo y el ello. In *Obras Completas, XIX (1923)*, pp. 1-66. Buenos Aires: Amorrortu Editores.
Freud, S. (1926). Inhibición, síntoma y angustia. In *Obras Completas, XX (1925–1926)*, pp. 71–161. Buenos Aires: Amorrortu Editores.
Freud, S. (1933). *Nuevas Conferencias de Introducción al Psicooanálisis*. 33° conferencia. La feminidad. In *Obras Completas, XXII (1932–1933)*, pp. 104–25. Buenos Aires: Amorrortu Editores.
Frumkes, G. (1934). Mental disorders relates to childbirth. *The Journal of Nervous and Mental Disease*, *79*(5), 540–52.
Hamann, M. (2014). Estrago. *Boletín Eva-Lilith, 3*.
Horney, K. (1926). The flight from womanhood: The masculinity-complex in women, as viewed by men and by women. *The International Journal of Psychoanalysis, 7*, 324–39.
Horney, K. (1932). The dread of woman. *The International Journal of Psychoanalysis, 13*, 348–60.
Juárez, J. (2017, August 28). Una epidemia de cesáreas innecesarias en México. (J. P. van Wouwe, Ed.) *The New York Times*. http://doi.org/10.1371/journal.pone.0172623.
Jung, C. (1991). The concept of the collective unconscious. In *The Archetypes and the Collective Unconscious*. London: Routledge (Original work pubished 1936).
Knafo, D. & Moscovitz, S. (2018). Contemporary Freudian approaches. In *Introduction to Contemporary Psychoanalysis: Defining Terms and Building Bridges*. Oxford, UK: Routledge.
Lacan, J. (1975a). Conférences et Entretiens dans des universités nord-américaines. *Scilicet, 6/7*, 32–37.
Lacan, J. (1975b). *Le séminaire de Jacques Lacan. Livre XX: Encore (1972–1973)*. Paris: Seuil.
Lacan, J. (1996). El Seminario. Libro IV. *La Relación de Objeto. (1956–1957)*. Buenos Aires: Paidós.
Lacan, J. (2006a). The mirror stage as formative of the I function as revealed in psychoanalytic experience. In *Écrits* (pp. 75–81). New York: Norton & Company (Original work published 1949).
Lacan, J. (2006b). The subversion of the subject and the dialectic of desire. In *Écrits* (pp. 209–51). New York: Norton & Company (Original work published 1957).
Lacan, J. (2012). Los complejos familiares en la formación del individuo. In *Otros Escritos*. Buenos Aires: Paidós.
Laplanche, J. (1987). *Nuevos fundamentos para el psicoanálisis*. Buenos Aires: Amorrortu.
Laurent, E. (2004). L'amour fou d'une mère. In *L'amour dans les psychoses*. Paris: Seuil.

Lemoine-Luccioni, E. (1982). *La partición de las mujeres*. Buenos Aires: Amorrortu Editores.
Lorand, S. (1939). Contribution to the problem of vaginal orgasm. *International Journal of Psychoanalysis*. 20(3/4):432–38.
Main, T. (1958). Mothers with children in a psychiatric hospital. *The Lancet*, *272*(7051), 845–47. http://doi.org/10.1016/S0140-6736(58)90393-3.
Marcé, L.-V. (2002). *Traité pratique de la folie des femmes enceintes, des nouvelles accouchées et des nourrices. (1858)*. Paris: L'Harmattan.
Martell, L. K. (2001). Heading toward the new normal: A contemporary postpartum experience. *Journal of Obstetric, Gynecologic & Neonatal Nursing*, *30*(5), 496–506. http://doi.org/10.1111/J.1552-6909.2001.TB01569.X.
Miller, J. (2015). Mèrefemme. *La Cause Du Désir : Revue de Psychanalyse*, *89*, 178. Retrieved from https://www.cairn.info/revue-la-cause-du-desir-2015-1-p-115.htm.
Moncayo, R. (2008). *Evolving Lacanian Perspectives for Clinical Psychoanalysis. On Narcissism, Sexuation, and the Phases of Analysis in Contemporary Culture*. London: Karnak Books Ltd.
Phillips, A. (2013). Narcissism, for and against. In *One Way and Another: New and Selected Essays*. London: Hamish Hamilton.
Quezada, N. (1977). Creencias tradicionales sobre el embarazo y parto. *Anales de Antropología*, *14*(1), 307–26.
Quezada, N. (1996). *Amor Y Magia Amorosa Entre Los Aztecas. Supervivencia en el México colonial*. México: Universidad Nacional Autónoma de México.
Sahagún, (Fray) Bernardino de. (2013). *Historia general de las cosas de Nueva España*. México: Porrúa.
Soria-Escalante, H., Orozco-Guzmán, M., López-Peñaloza, J., Sigales Ruiz, S. « Condiciones violentas de duelo y pérdida: un enfoque psicoanalítico ». *Pensamiento Psicológico,* 12 (2), 2014, 79–95.
UNICEF México. (n.d.). La lactancia materna puede salvar la vida a millones de niños y niñas y prevenir enfermedades graves: UNICEF. Retrieved June 13, 2018, from https://www.unicef.org/mexico/spanish/noticias_29440.htm.
Verhaeghe, P., & Vanheule, S. (2005). Actual neurosis and PTSD: The impact of the Other. *Psychoanalytic Psychology*, *22*(4), 493–507. http://doi.org/10.1037/0736-9735.22.4.493.
Voces Feministas. (2017). México: 2.9 millones de mujeres entre los 15 y 49 años sufrieron violencia obstétrica. Retrieved June 13, 2018, from https://vocesfeministas.com/2017/08/30/mexico-29-millones-mujeres-15-49-sufrieron-violencia-obstetrica/.
Winnicott, D. (1992). La préoccupation maternelle primaire (1956). In *De la pédiatrie à la psychanalyse*. Paris: Payot.
Wintrebert, D. (2015). Un ravage mère-fille. In É. Leclerc-Razavet, G. Haberberg, & D. Wintrebert (Eds.), *L'enfant et la féminité de sa mère* (pp. 21–27). Paris: L'Harmatts.
Zilboorg, G. (1929). The dynamics of schizophrenic reactions related to pregnancy and childbirth. *American Journal of Psychiatry*, *8*(4), 744–66.

Chapter Six

The Sanguinary Dimension of Jealousy

Pain, Grief, and Unbending Certainty

Mario Orozco Guzmán

THE MOURNING OF JEALOUSY: AN UNTAMABLE PASSION CONTROLS US

Jealous passion involves a cultural history traversed by fratricidal struggles and the chronicle of "subjective suffering" (Freud, 1920), demonstrates various modulations and undulations in Freud's clinical monitoring. Normal jealousy is situated in the first stratum, or first wave, of the affective jealousy state (Freud, 1921–1922a). It is a union made of mourning, the pain for the lost object, and for the narcissistic affront, where it can be distinguished from another. It is normal for the subject to experience jealousy within the plot and drama of the Oedipus complex. It is a jealousy "of competence" (Freud, 1921–1922a), of bisexuality and ambivalence, of double rivalry and duplicity of pain—mourning. A man on one hand experiences *Schmerz* (Freud, 1921–1922b), pain for the woman he loves and hatred for his competitors, and on the other hand, *Trauer*, a feeling of mourning in relation to the man unconsciously loved and hated regarding the woman in a competitive condition for his love. It evokes a feeling of pain for losing the loved woman and the experience of mourning for losing the object of homosexual choice. Competitors are hated; however, loved objects, in their condition of loss, can either produce pain or mourning. Does this subtle difference suggest anything?

To a certain extent, it appears that it has something to do with the dimension of loss being conscious or unconscious. This difference frames the opposition in mourning-melancholia according to Freud. If it is inscribed in the conscious plane it could predominantly perhaps be considered pain in the face of loss. Pain appears in Freud's discourse as one of the first economic issues since the Project for a Scientific Psychology. As an experience, in the following document it will oppose the experience of satisfaction—an epistolary testimony of clinical findings—like in *The Interpretation of Dreams* (Freud, 1900). Excessive amounts of arousal that come from the outside penetrate the screen memories. This excessive arousal breaks into the psychic system and increases tension producing a feeling of displeasure. In such circumstances, there is a tendency to discharge and a facilitation between it and an image-memory of the object that produces pain (Freud, 1895). When this image is reinvested as "hostile," the person certainly feels displeasure, but the feeling is not as painful as it was originally. It does not fulfill the stimulation increase. For Freud (1900), this creation of pain is characterized as a dreadful experience against something external. Freud advised that the psychic apparatus does not show, in cases of painful stimulation, a tendency to invest the perception or memory of the impression occurs. What is reiterated is a tendency of flight and isolation. This isolation that the psychic apparatus easily and regularly performs with respect to what was once painful gives us the model and the first example of psychic repression (Freud, 1900). This suggests that the dimension of pain in jealousy conditions an experience of hostility and terror. The sources of pain, which are the agents, make the subject live in a state of derangement when they are present. The loved one and the hated rival are inserted in the experience of pain of jealousy, thereby becoming hostile objects that they would like to exclude from perception and memory. They constitute of terrifying presences that are best avoided. In contrast, mourning is inscribed in an inconceivable love for the consciousness, a homosexual love. You love who you should hate and hate or compete with whom you should love. In this case, the status of the object has slipped through a transformation in the opposite of the affection at play. The love that he feels toward the woman hurts him. That pain transforms her into a stranger, an enemy. The hatred against the rival hurts and it can turn us into strangers from what we love the most. Mourning affects deeply the ego because it is unaware to what degree the rival has replaced the loved woman in a libidinous supremacy.

Psychoanalysis discovered that if the human being is capable of eroticizing pain in the driving impulses of sadism and masochism, it is in the same measure, in which it is subjected, that it covers it with meaning. Pain enters into the dynamics of the libido as part of the psychic resistances known as shame and disgust (Freud, 1905). Pain as a conditioner of satisfaction indicates the presence of violence and cruelty in erotic life. It brings meaning to pleasure while making it feasible. When Freud suggests that pain makes its agent a hostile and terrifying presence, he is already subjectivizing to a great extent. There is pain in the experience of jealousy because it insinuates the terror that inspires us to lose the loved one. That insinuation of terror is already the subjective balance of pain, or subjective stigma:

> In fact, when the threat of loss is suggested to one of the objects considered irreplaceable, what emerges is anguish and it arises in the self. If, however, one of the objects is forced to disappear suddenly, without previous threat, it is pain that is imposed, and emanates from the id. I have to suffer pain in the id, if I brutally lose the loved person (mourning), their love (abandonment), the love I feel for the image of myself (humiliation), or even the integrity of my body. Mourning, abandonment, humiliation, and mutilation are the four circumstances that, suddenly, trigger psychological pain or the pain of love. (Nasio, 1999, pp. 45–46)[1]

Mourning, abandonment, humiliation, and mutilation develop as modalities of subjectivity of the pain of losing the loved one from the experience of jealousy. This passion is something that is suffered, it carries these meanings in which both the "self-love" (Freud, 1921), narcissistic condition, like the body, suffer a shock so violently painful or painfully violent that it appears as a deep perforation.

It is suggestive of what Spinoza (1984) had defined and treated jealousy in a very interesting way, as a condition:

> Hate toward something loved combined with Envy is called Jealousy, and thus Jealousy is nothing more than a fluctuation of the born soul, in which there is both Hate and Love, accompanied by the idea of another one that inspires Envy in us. Furthermore, such Hate toward something loved is greater in proportion to the Joy that one who feels Jealousy was accustomed to being affected by the Love that the beloved thing experienced towards him, and also in proportion to the feeling that he was affected in relation to the one who imagines is connected to the beloved thing, since he imagines it affecting Pleasure, which he hates; and also because he is forced to connect the image of the beloved with the image of the one he hates. (pp. 151–152)[2]

It is worth highlighting the convergence of Freud–Spinoza in this participation of ambivalence of affective fluctuation in the passion of jealousy. What fluctuates in the soul of the jealous subject is the sense of loss produced by another that makes us hate the loved thing. According to Spinoza (1984), in fact, the jealous person is suffering from mourning because he is a saddened lover when he assumes that *the loved woman gives herself to another*. Spinoza is forceful in bringing the dimension of ghosts into the drama of jealousy. The jealous individual feels a decrease in appetite, something inherent to mourning, assuming that his loved woman gives herself to another. It also reduces the esteem and respect that the loved woman may deserve, being forced to connect the image of the beloved with the shameful parts and the excretions of another, feeling an aversion toward her (Spinoza, 1984). That beloved one, who was once a source of pleasure, becomes a reason for repudiation. The pleasurable excrescences shared with this beloved are now repugnant since another intrudes his own secretions. In the body of this loved woman are shameful parts and excretions of two men. An aberrant confluence of humors. According to Héritier (1994), the discourse on humors of the body is always inscribed in the set of representations appropriate to a society, which varies from one society to another according to the means of observation it has, but which never ceases to be rational. It is an ideological set of relationships of meaning that increasingly underlies social relationships.

It is this meeting of humors that is a cause for disgust, leading to an ineludible homosexual bond. Hence, it produces pain as the beloved causes this disgusting encounter. Freud, in a strict sense, would speak more of pain than mourning, as mourning would only occur by imagining the unconsciously loved man rendered and lost before the hated woman. Attacks of jealousy echo those on self-love and also the beloved thing. On the other hand, attacks of hatred invoke thoughts of something extremely degrading.

Spinoza's proposals, which have led us to a loathsome encounter of fluids, open the door to the relationship between jealousy and homosexuality, a relationship that Freud will emphasize especially in the third level or layer of jealousy. However, the extent that there is an atrocious and painful shock of self-love has already been predicted from the first modality. It would be extremely important to learn how the ego recovers from this *narzisstischen Kränkung* (Freud, 1921–1922b), narcissistic affront, which implies losing and giving up on the beloved object. This loss offends the ego, aggravates the subject's self-love, and experiences the anti-stimulus protection inflicting a shock to the body, the jolt of pain. It is a situation of loss where mourning may have a melancholic impact because it is meant as a loss that is situated at the level of the exalted and idealized unity of the self. That is, we could be pointing out a loss that is lethal to the ego in encouraging its own loss. As Gallimberti (2011) emphasizes, he or she who is caught in the vortex of jealousy loses not only the loved person, but also him or herself, sinking into these feelings of anger, pain, exclusion, indignation, and offense that inexorably accompany the decline of self-esteem.

Jealousy is part of in the collective imagination of projection in the second stratum and wave that Freud reveals of his clinical spectrum. The subject attributes his repressed inclinations to infidelity, or indeed, his own unfaithful adventures, to his loving partner. But Freud (1921–1922b) allocates a mechanism that will then be exclusive of a perversion like fetishism to account for how the subject gets rid of tendencies toward infidelity: a *Verleugnung*. Through this process of refuting these inclinations or actions, the subject is far from being censored and judged by them. It is the other who has them and holds them in a vehement and reliable way. This process of *Verleugnung* implies that a part of the ego knows something that concerns its desire but is far from accepting its responsibility; it adjudicates to the other. The other is mainly at fault toward the subject, both in the sense of moral failure as well as in the ethical sense of openness to desire. In this manner, the subject presents himself as flawless and relentless before the loved one, to whom he does not cease to face his fault as something that makes him a saddened victim of the beloved's deceit and betrayal. The projection had been established not simply as a defense mechanism from Totem and Taboo. It can be said that are three moments in processing the experience of something that produces displeasure: an evacuative moment, specific allocation, and designation of its causal status. In the first instance, Freud (1913) refers to this release of unconscious hostility directed against someone who has died. There, the taboo of the dead is constituted. The evil leaves and is assigned to the dead man who becomes an evil and persecutory spirit. But the projection does not always intervene in processing internal conflicts such as that of ambivalence toward another. It also determines *the configuration of our outer world*; this causes the construction of a world where the origin of evil can be located and designated. This imaginary construction from the ego that projects its misfortune allows a first situation of desire. According to Lacan (1981), at the origin, before language, desire only exists on the single plane of the imaginary relationship of the specular stage. It exists when projected, alienated in the other. The tension it provokes has no escape. That is, as Hegel teaches it has no other way out than the destruction of the other. Projection is a narcissistic mechanism that assigns desire to the other and designates it as the virtual origin of desire. That is why, in the jealousy of projection, the loving companion, who die *Treue schuldig ist* (Freud, 1921–1922b), is in debt of fidelity and is found guilty of infidelity by virtue of the projection of his own propensities and alleged unfaithful actions. In this manner, the origin of evil, the desire for infidelity, stems from the other who appears as the bearer of guilt from the beginning. The asymmetry is evident: it is the other who must be faithful and, as she does not respond to this demand, it is understood and justified besieging her with suspicion. The mechanism of projection immunizes and creates a screen regarding the responsibility of desire. Gallimberti (2011) indicates how in couples with asymmetrical condition "according to certain rules of sexual or social value, jealousy is not seriously considered"[3] (p. 143). The person deceived is a source of ridicule, an object of the ridiculous picture nicknamed a "cuckold," not so much bypassing or undermining the person's pain, but making it a reason for enjoyment. However, those who claim to be deceived, in order to better conceal their deceptions, or in fact intention, arrogate to themselves an authentic moral caution, consecrate an ideal place of innocence, which even protects self-love in an exalted way.

Freud indicates how culture allows propensities for infidelity to find recreational possibilities without removal-allocation and designation of evil. A married woman is allowed a certain display of seduction and coquetry and the husband separates his "Don Juan" tendencies. They are allowed a certain seduction game insofar as it constitutes a scenario of dissatisfaction. The culture fosters a hysterical standard since the promoted libidinal appetite is only allowed to be satiated in the self-object (Freud, 1921–1922a). That is, the desire projected out of the fidelity owed must remain unsatisfied. The jealous individual, as Freud asserts, does not accept this cultural permissibility. For him, there is no reversibility of desire. Thrown from his narcissistic domain by his loving partner, there is no way to contain him or make him return. For the jealous individual at the projective level, a world has already been configured where the loving companion is unfaithful for making herself desired by someone other than him. Instead, as Freud (1921–1922b) warns, flirtation is a measure of *Versicherung gegen wirkliche Untraue*, of security against true infidelity; it is considered a sign of authentic infidelity. Therefore, Freud recommends not questioning the "material" that supports the accusation of infidelity. What is aspired is an urge that this material receives *einer anderen Einschätzung*, another assessment. That is, under this suggestion of clinical positioning, we would ensure that the subject can assess and appreciate this material, from another perspective that is not of narcissistic order and accommodation, as under this assessment, the "I" ends up liberated, exonerated of all evil. The lack of the other, of the beloved, covers his own fault, and provides the perfect alibi to be flawless and relentless in his critical evaluation. To accuse the other, to drastically blame him, is a way of complying with the Freudian idea that "there is no innocence in the origin, there is an imperfection"[4] (Sibony, 1998, p. 154). However, there is a bias present in the statement. If someone can presume to be innocent, it is the subject's ego in its narcissistic order. The burden of fault falls primarily and preferentially on the other.

This relatively unfeeling attitude of the jealous in the projective stratum already adjoins or creates a connection with the delirious one. However, for Freud (1921–1922b) it is surmountable to discover the unconscious phantasmal base. The delirious jealousy, third stratum, and wave of the passionate subsurface, also springs from the repression of inadmissible inclinations. Only in this case, it is about jealousy that derives from a *vergorenen homosexualität*, fermented homosexuality, which makes us evoke that confluence of fluids, of humors and excretions, suggested by Spinoza in the affection of jealousy. Evacuation-allocation-designation consume an operation that leads to the convincing belief that the competitor is really the object of a supreme love interest by the loved woman. The Schreber case leads Freud (1911, 1913) to consider the variants of subjective position before the *Zumutung der homosexuellen Wunschphantasie, den Mann zu lieben*, the demand of the fantasy of homosexual desire, to love the male. Faced with what is asked, which could appear condemning, a variant of subjective position is an attitude of contradiction but with imputation. The subject denies loving the man who seems to be his rival against the woman he loves, claiming that it is she who loves this eventual opponent. Freud suggests that alcohol plays an important role in these cases; it not only dispels the restrictions of moral order but also serves as a meeting place of libidinal temptation between men. It is a scenario where the jealous alcoholic seeks refuge as a victim of the deceptions of his beloved wife. He is absolutely sure that she is a whore as long as she gives herself to all *den Männer, die er zu lieben versucht ist*, all men, to whom he is tempted to love. These temptations of homosexual love, in their tempestuous flow, are those that are placed in the condition of fermentation. The ferment, the enzyme, which damages self-love, which aggravates it, is this phantom-incitement of male love, which seems to set up this shameful union of secretions between men through the woman he feels jealous about.

The delirious jealousy in women also contains this aspect of suspicion in relation to "all die Frauen," all women, who are to his liking. It highlights this excessive character of "all men" or "all women," which Freud refers to a much accentuated incidence of narcissism, which is correlative, as Freud (1905) had shown in some notes of his *Three Essays*, on homosexual preference. Here, projection does not play any role since the romantic preference, in the case of the jealous man, of his beloved woman by men—or of a man in particular—or of a jealous woman, of her beloved man by other women—or of one in particular—is something that is embodied and that *bleibt eine Angelegenheit der äussern Wahrnehmung*, remains a matter of external perception. It can be said that this romantic preference is evident in itself. It is so categorically objectified and materialized that it only confirms the deception that appears as a premise. This is what Lacan (1990) refers to when he mentions the certainty in psychosis where a delirious person, in his jealous conviction is exempt from any real reference. Normal jealousy refuses to enter into this forceful scheme of certainty. They are made of questions and doubts. Delirious jealousy does not cast conjectures or speculations. They trace the lack of doubt of the unconscious system (Freud, 1915a) but support a certainty coupled with accurate denial—properties not integrated into the unconscious system. People who are loved by their loved ones turn out to be, for these women, figures that could refer to a very specific moment of homosexual libidinal fixation, which makes them especially able to be *zur realen Liebe ungeeignete Personen* (Freud, 1921–1922b), people unfit for real love. That is, only appropriate for an ideal love. In this way, a woman would surprisingly love and honor an elderly woman, a maid, a caregiver. In these images it expresses an *Auffrischung Kung*, renewal of the mother or competing sisters. One can see the inadequate nature of the beloved's choice and the reason for competitive struggle.

Love and jealousy appear reciprocally needed in the commotion of passion: "If love has a cost, jealousy is the compensation. The two pans of the balance are well-balanced. Because if love is a powerful emotional force, jealousy is the social counterpoint of this force"[5] (Gallimberti, 2011, p. 144). Jealousy opens the narrow dual path of love. They open it to a tertiary condition, to the social dimension. According to Barthes (2009), as if jealousy came from that simple passage of the self to him, from an imaginary discourse (saturated with the other) to a discourse of the Other. The third person acquires superb relief, monopolizing a disproportionate interest beyond a relationship of imaginary identification. The third person is a regulatory and stabilizing agency of the jealous-loving passion. In this aspect, Freud (1910) proposes specific typologies of love in men. He unveils a type of libidinal choice where jealousy is installed as a sine qua non condition. It refers to men who feel a passion called *Dirnenliebe*, love for whores. Jealousy fully values these women. Just as jealousy manages to devalue the beloved woman by reducing her to the degrading place of a "whore," they also overvalue a woman who could be someone else's. It appears that jealousy provides such a heightened enjoyment to their love affair that it seems impossible to break the bond. They do not experience jealousy in relation to the person with whom these women can have a commitment such as marriage. They feel comfortable in this position of sharing the loved person with this other. Jealousy may rather appear in relation to some newcomer, some stranger, who can thrill and excite the beloved woman. There are then two references of the third person in this dilemma of love. That is, there is a third person in the legitimate possession that allows encouragement of desire, which would be placed in a jealous condition, and another third person that could signify the loss of possession and love position, and only then it would be a promoter of jealousy in the subject. Women in this condition, who show these *Zügen* traits, represent for these type of men a compelling reason for an excessive and exclusive passion to the extent where a faithfulness that they can hardly fulfill is fervently imposed. However, for Freud, this type of *Liebesverhältnis*, love affair, is part of a repetitive circuit in an extensive serial substitution. That is to say, this amorous passion thus hatched, with this conjunction of features, is part of a repetition compulsion that is renewed despite the impression that each amorous effervescence is *das genaue Abbild der anderen*, the exact copy of another. The amorous series, however, diversifies in its repetitive circuit; it is refreshed in each situation implying components of hatred and jealousy in its tertiary order. The case of Vera Renczi, addressed later, will set the standard to account for this approach to the repetitive seriation of jealousy in its criminal derivations.

THE INSTIGATING ELEMENT OF JEALOUSY. FROM DREAM TO MYTH

Freud (1900) unveils the oedipal drama and its jealousy plot based on the death dreams of loved ones in *The Interpretation of Dreams*. He notices how the desire for death is embedded in the condition of rivalry with respect to the romantic claim. According to Freud, things are presented as if from very early on, a sexual preference was opened, as if the boy saw in the father and the girl in the mother competitors in love, whose disappearance would bring them advantages.

This implies that the death of the father or the mother would be an advantage for the ego of the boy or girl who long to be preferred by their mother or father. The desire to outdo parents in preference carries a death wish. Competitors, involved in normal jealousy, are a true "hindrance" as they seem to oppose the aspiration of desires directed at the parent of the opposite sex, as Freud proposes in this text. Preferences can reproduce the preference that parents have over one of their children. According to Freud (1900), it is the rule that preference is already imposed on the parents themselves; a natural impulse ensures that the man praises his little girl and the mother favors the boy, while both, where the charm of sex does not cloud their judgment, strive in educating their children with rigor.

With their preferences, parents impose and instigate the first situations of jealousy among the children. They make them compete with each other and hinder one another in preferential aspiration. One could take advantage of the ambiguity and suggest that parents also compete among themselves for the preferential love of all or one of their children. The instigators of jealousy become jealous of each other and keep an eye on their preference. Being jealous of their preference as a narcissistic distinction precisely fills fraternal relationships with tension and competence.

Myths provide an account of how the first competitions and fraternal struggles are instilled and installed. Fraternal atavistic quarrels are mainly between brothers. We will account for them because they allow us to address their instigating element. That is, where the woman is located as an opposing element, the power of her love as Lacan (1999) would say. To illustrate this primordial and competitive condition of jealousy leading to a lethal outcome, it is inevitable that we stumble upon the legend of Cain and Abel. As in all myths, there are different versions. The fraternal dispute derived, according to one version, by God's preference regarding Abel's offering, implying an initial preference for Abel. According to Graves and Patai (2009), God looked favorably upon Abel and his offering, but he did not look favorably on Cain and his oblation, for which Cain was greatly irritated and his face was downcast. God contributes to Cain's despondency, the narcissistic debacle of pain and mourning in Cain, by directing a more favorable, preferential gaze toward Abel. Another version refers to a dispute around the land distributed among the brothers. An unequal distribution because all land was assigned to Cain, while the animals were assigned to Abel; hence, the difference in the type of offerings that are given to God. They supposedly agreed to respect their property. However, Abel broke this agreement by having his flocks trample Cain's land. He could have considered this action as similar to Abel having trampled upon him, even if he had promised that his animals would not damage his farm. To this, Cain responds by picking up a weapon and pursuing him "vengeful all over the mountains and valleys until he reached him and killed him" (Graves and Patai, 2009, p. 112). If it is mentioned that it is a vengeful act, we could infer that Abel's infraction would have had a deadly meaning and scope for Cain.

Another version refers to a competition regarding their mother Eve's love, she is considered legendarily as "first Eve," the object of Adam's rejection. This would have been motivated by the deep feeling of disgust that Adam felt in seeing the way God created his supposed companion using materials such as bones, muscles, blood, secretions, and strands of hair in some places (Graves and Patai, 2009). When this woman, thus made by God, stands before Adam, with "all her beauty," it provokes "profound disgust" in him. This emotional barrier (Freud, 1905) is an obstacle in the path open to pleasure. Therefore, he alludes to the women's genitals with her "strands of hair." Freud himself (1929–1930) indicated the unattractive impression of genitals. The woman's hairy genitals, an important unsightly detail, have a true ethical effect as they provoke in Adam the intense disgust, making him feel that God failed. The children would then have disputed this woman-mother repudiated by the father. Another version speculates that the fratricide occurred because of another loving choice. This version includes in its development the presence of twin sisters in the birth and in the romantic preferences of the brothers Cain and Abel. In this version, Adam is warned and cautioned by the law of interdiction of incest as makes Eve aware that each brother must take the twin sister of the other—a kind of fraternal exchange of women. Thus, Cain would take Qelimat, twin sister of Abel, and he would take Cain's twin called Lebhudha. Here, Adam introduces an ethical challenge to an aesthetic appetite. According to Freud (1921–1930), Cain wanted to marry his own twin sister, who was more beautiful, though Adam warned him that this would be incest and had each of the brothers make offerings to God before taking the wife that had been assigned to them. When Cain's offering was rejected, Satan induced him to kill Abel for the sake of Lebhudha.

What good would it bring to Lebhudha the assassination of her alleged owner, Abel? Does it offer an incestuous good when the competitor is eliminated as an element that marks the prohibition? Although it can also be said in this case, as in a version indicated above, it is about the transgression of an agreement. The aesthetic element, Lebhudha's beauty, appears to impose itself on the ethical element of the agreement between parents and children. The primordial murder of the brother carries with it the incitement of incestuous pretension.

The compulsion to repeat, in the serialization of ambivalence, is something that embeds jealousy since Cain and Abel, both in the ground pierced with pain as in the "fraternal mourning" (Assoun, 2000). This suggests confrontation and the experience of loss. Before birth, God had already sentenced not only the division between the twin sons of Isaac and Rebekah but also their confrontation and downfall. Destiny was sealed for Esau and Jacob. The sentence of a destiny cannot be raised without invoking the desire of the Other. As Esau committed crimes, such as homicide, rape, sodomy, and theft, Isaac was condemned by God to blindness (Graves and Patai, 2009). Jacob, however, would rob him and make his brother lose the blessing of his dying father. He robbed at the behest of his mother Rebekah. Esau had already sold his offspring to his brother in exchange for a plate of lentils. It is also said that Jacob would have demanded a significant amount of gold. From the mythical perspective, Jacob's brotherly love that takes advantage of his brother's hunger has been questioned, and instead the "exemplary love" that Esau had for his brother Jacob has been praised. The loss of the offspring had to have had divine approval, just as the theft of the blessing was supported by his mother. The theft of the blessing implies trickery on the mother's part. Although, in fact, after having purchased the offspring from his brother, Jacob would have acquired the right to a paternal blessing. What is noteworthy is that Cain's act was about to be repeated because of this double impersonation, according to Esau's bragging. According to Lacan (2003) it is a real illustration of how fate plays the fraternal dynasty that establishes, before any conflict, the heir or usurper's place.

Jacob usurps the heir's place and ignites the conflict with his brother Esau days before the mourning of the death of their father Isaac. Esau, in a vindictive desire, attempts to kill his brother Jacob. It should be emphasized that, to a great degree, Esau had allowed himself to be stripped of his preferential position as heir before his father. He lost privileges from his father; he is saddened because his mother didn't stop showing her preference for his brother Jacob—a preference that makes her participate in the deception for acquiring the blessing. We witness how some kind of hero is constituted in the figure of Jacob, who gains a place of power, on the threshold of his father's death, counting on his mother's favors. It is possible to observe this affective compound of jealousy comprised of pain and mourning.

Not being preferred by a mother, who is determined to support her favorite son as an alleged substitute father, hurts and is a reason to grieve. The hero's precedent was most likely offered by the youngest son, the mother's favorite, whom she had protected from paternal jealousy and had become the father's successor in the times of the primordial mob (Freud, 1921).

This maternal figure provides protection from the father's jealousy but not from fraternal jealousy. It could also be said that she supports and instigates it. In the Jacob–Esau drama, the deceived turns out to be the father because of Rebekah's fickle preference over one of her children: "What is blessed is also the mother's will, and apparently Jacob never asks for anything that she does not encourage him to do. The secret servitude of the hero is recognized" (Assoun, 2000, p. 145). Behind the hero's feat is the power of the mother's "uncontrolled law" (Lacan, 1999). The power of her will that throws prerogatives on a certain son instead of another or others.

As well in the case of Joseph a romantic preference is found, in this case from the father, Jacob, in relation to the lineage conceived. This preference will foster fraternal jealousy and shape the violence that "takes root in injustice, this acute form of absence"[6] (Sibony, 1998, p. 143). Joseph complains to his father about the evils that his brothers undertake and that they make him return home complaining at any given time, and "Jacob believed him because he loved him more than all his other children because he was Rachel's firstborn son and the closest to him, both in character and physicality" (Graves and Patai, 2009, p. 309). The preference is already implanted in the domestic bond based on the narcissistic father–son identification. What infuriates his brothers so much are Joseph's dreams where he predicts that he will have them under his control and power—something similar to God's prediction regarding the submission that Jacob would impose on his brother Esau. Joseph has been preferred by this father, who believes what he tells him more than his other children. The brothers carry out their fatal project against their hated brother Joseph. Jacob lived deceived, grieved and mourned for a son who had not died. His other children wanted to make him believe that he died devoured by a ferocious animal. Joseph vainly showed his promising future in the dreams he told, but also his shrewdness in interpreting them. He held the power of privileged knowledge and also a powerful prior knowledge due to the preference of paternal love. This criminal design associated with an experience of jealousy made regrets reappear among the brothers, who knew they did not have the preference of paternal love and privileged powers. Joseph made them look careless, in a condition of scarcity and soon subject to his rule—approximately what Jacob does to Esau. Joseph's pride was so great that he predicted, through a dream with remarkable narcissistic scope, a future where not only his brothers would offer him obedience but also his parents: the youngest child is undoubtedly in the process of seizing the paternal reign and crossing its transgressing limit (Assoun, 2000). The youngest son threaten to go over the limit, taking the father's place. It is perhaps a parricidal trance. The narcissistic coat that this father had provided to his son Joseph as a privilege, and which was stowed upon him lying tinged with his blood, could in turn leave him naked and castrated. Joseph's boasts, typical of this imaginary, aggressive, and specular condition, which Lacan (2003) reveals, in the relationship between the small partners, also imply seduction and despotism. The heir has tyrannical aspirations in his position to usurp even his father's place.

The preferences granted engender this sense of injustice where fratricidal violence is found. Freud (1921) indicated that there were artificial groups such as the Church and the army supported by the illusion of a leader who "equally loves all individuals in the masses. Everything depends on that illusion" (p. 90). From that illusion of equitable love, from love that does not make distinctions, all those who make up this group depend on each other, and the idea depends on an undifferentiated homogenous whole. This gullible love also sustains the family as an artificial, institutional mass. Parents should not differentiate between children; they should not prefer one over the others. But it can be seen that fratricidal struggles are a consequence of this unequal distribution of love from one of the parents or of a divine figure. Jealousy accounts for an authentic narcissistic perforation:

> The radical *entre-deux* effect where the distribution between oneself and the Other harms itself and is harmful. Jealousy, a narcissistic wound due to another's presence escapes us because perhaps he has taken our place or because one would like to take his place, completely retaining ours . . . Violence of the "first distribution" impossible. Especially when it is the "first" place that is being distributed.[7] (Sibony, 1998, p. 62)

Fathers and gods in mythical narration, and fathers who set themselves up in the role of gods, distribute the first place, assign the first place, the love preference, inflicting narcissistic wounds. Jealousy is instigated by the gesture of making the inequitable distribution of love known. The illusion of love that presumably does not make distinctions is broken.

A mythical condition of jealous envy is instigated by the serpent of Eden in Genesis. Before the jealous conflict between Cain and Abel prompted by God and his preferences, this "disguised Satan" appears (Graves and Patai, 2009), seducing Eve and convincing her to eat the fruit that would allow her to gain knowledge on good and evil. He urges her to covet divine knowledge and Eve is encouraged to equate herself with God, to possess God's wisdom. She is urged to want what the Other has, to be jealous of that sovereign good:

> Even in the story of Eve pulling off the fruit and rejecting the ban, it can be said that she wants to be like God (the word used by the Serpent) but, in more clinical terms, it means that she is jealous, and although jealousy is in the place of the other and possesses the object, it does not appease her; her narcissistic wound is radical. In other words, her identity failure, essential in the process of her evolution, is not allowed to be fulfilled in this manner. The impossible

> distribution, of oneself or the other, also implies being unable to stand the difference—which would allow, for example, to desire the same object, but not in the same way.[8] (Sibony, 1998, p. 172)

In a clinical testimony, a woman indicates that she cannot stand the difference between her and another woman to whom her romantic partner has given what he supposedly did not want to give to her. Jealousy puts her in a condition that is extremely disgraceful and ominous, but there is no way to cover her narcissistic failure. Another woman has been preferred by this romantic partner. Certain features in the other are portentously indubitable signs to determine preference. The other woman possesses the ideal attributes of preference, the attributes that break the illusion of the romantic partner's fidelity. Romantic preference establishes a phallic concession that indicates a fundamental privilege.

These attributes that mark the exalted preference are ones that arise envious greed in Jacqueline de Bellefort regarding Linnet Ridgeway in the famous Agatha Christie novel (2004), *Death on the Nile*. Jacqueline contrived the image of Linnet based on a striking ideal: "But you are a queen, Linnet. You have always been that. Sa Majesté la reine Linette, Linette la blonde. And I am the queen's favorite one. The maid of honor she trusts" (p. 14). Jacqueline sets out to kill the queen and took her place at a crucial point in time, at the very moment when she "intended to steal my Simon from me. It is true! I do not think she wavered a minute. I was her friend, but that did not matter to her. She was just crazy about Simon" (Christie, 2004, p. 265). Jacqueline is warned by her friend of the best that she has. The narcissistic failure, the painful perforation in Jacqueline is not filled, it does not settle, not even after having heard from Simon that he did not want anyone but her. However, it appears as if Simon wanted something more. It is, above all, about the money of the queen and Jacqueline, consequently metonymic, she wanted what her beloved and idolized Simon wants, making seen a fickle sense of his passion: "He wants things as a child wants them" (Christie, 2004, p. 264). This is how Jacqueline is involved in the homicidal plan of someone "who she loved beyond reason, beyond any moral and piety" (p. 266). For Simon's love, the love of this child, the love of what this child wants, Jacqueline calms the waters and is prepared for anything, as Freud (1921) stated, in the blindness of love, one becomes a criminal without remorse. Getting rid of Linnet, Jacqueline went from being the queen's favorite to being the queen with everything, and that set of attributes of narcissistic luster that Joanna Southwood, another character caught in envious greed toward this kind of goddess, exceedingly proclaimed, "You know, Linnet? I really envy you. You have everything you want. You are only twenty years old and the absolute owner of your actions, with a pile of money, beauty, and perfect health" (Christie, 2004, p. 10). Linnet represents the embodied exaltation of fullness. She models the dominating women that Simon Doyle despises. The ideal figure to combine both jealousy and envy in a whirlwind: "envy is jealousy: the subject thinks that what she lacks, the other has taken, and she wants to be in the place of this other—to take it upon herself and return it at will, its object"[9] (Sibony, 1998, p. 172). This is what Jacqueline thought about the majestic Linnet; she thought Linnet had what she needed. In fact, Linnet will have in Simon Doyle what Jacqueline lacks, since Linnet has precisely stolen what she loved most in this world (Christie, 2004), his radiant phallus. The criminal act undertaken by Jacqueline and her idolized Simon Doyle can perhaps be conceived as instigated by the same victim and her vast narcissistic domains. This act can then be expressed as an effort to narcissistically restore phallic control.

THE HOMICIDAL VIOLENCE OF IDEAL ZEAL AND JEALOUSY: VERA RENCZI

Jealous passion can lead to the reality of completing the act: "Controlled by hateful passion, the jealous person loses all critical reasoning, fails to distinguish reality, and blinded by spite, risks falling into aggressive, even criminal, uncontrollable acts"[10] (Lauru, 2015, p. 91). The passion of hate converges with that of love, says Lacan (1981), on this dead-end road where one aspires to "capture the other in himself" (p. 401). Jealous passion made of love and hate supposes imaginary labyrinths where the lover and the beloved are lost, where their differences are lost. It encapsulates the loss of the true otherness of the captured other, trapped in passion. Almudena Grandes (2015) says in one of her stories that passion carefully chooses its victims, and only confers power upon those who have previously been able to deny themselves in order to give themselves completely to others. In the case of Vera Renczi, jealous passion will make her choose her victims carefully and grant her the power to demand the complete surrender and capture of the other to affirm herself. Passion with deadly implications in a serial record is what we find in Vera Renczi, known as the "mysterious hunter" (Durigon, 2015, p. 300). Hunting targets for Vera, born toward the end of the nineteenth century or the beginning of the twentieth, were men whom she first carefully seduces and then kills with arsenic. Hunting for unfaithful men, or unfaithfulness grasped in captured men. It was from a very young age of fifteen that she took on this type of hunting without necessarily having this tragic outcome. In principle, she attracted men of different ages and socioeconomic status but she did not kill them. The deadly series began with her first husband, a wealthy banker named Karl Schick, who was thirty years older than Vera. It is said that it had been an arranged marriage. That is, as if it were an actual business started and run by the father's wishes. Giddens

(2000) indicates how this type of contract marriage can be found in premodern Europe in terms of economic circumstances and the preservation of the privilege of social distinction.

It is precisely business and economic interests that are inscribed in the passionate flow of a woman who was said to possess a "pressing need for a male protective image" (p. 300). Based on this, her romantic choice would be marked by the virtual anaclitic path of libidinal choice. In this case, the image of a protective father, as Freud (1914) points out, gives her a channel for her demanded love. The father was heavily involved in businesses, which made him travel constantly. Perhaps the "compelling" need for protection could also refer to how the father set out on those trips. Vera belonged to an aristocratic family from Romania, which was in decline. She was beautiful and rich and some sexual liberties were attributed to her: "At certain times and places, in aristocratic strata, women were sufficiently liberated from the demands of reproduction and routine work, to be able to procure independent sexual pleasure" (Giddens, 2000, p. 45). Vera Renczi took pleasure in exercising sexual enjoyment fixed in the confines of the death of her romantic partner and as compensation for suppressing her freedom in the conjugal transaction that reduced her to the status of an object of mercantile exchange. Sara F. Matthews-Grieco (2005) notes how in the Former European System, conditions prevailed where "the woman's body and her eventual beauty continued to be a fundamental resource, exploited in the market of marriage or commercial sex"[11] (p. 207). She adds that "except in the highest ranks of aristocracy"[12] (p. 195), sexual freedom was a privilege for men and chastity was required for women. It can also be said that the husbands' adultery was considered a relatively normal event. Vera exemplifies such aristocratic exception where the rules of the marriage game could be reversed. That is, sexual freedom rights for women and demands of fidelity for men.

It is said that before turning three years old, a "tragedy" (Durigon, 2015) occurred in Vera's life. Her mother's death cast a shadow and knocked down a promise of "lifelong happiness" from having beauty and money as her supposed guaranteed resource to explore and exploit. It is death that comes to intervene as a third element in relation with the mother, an interjection that can be bloody as it untimely speeds up a collapse of narcissism called primordial by Dolto (2008), which is constituted by the base image that sustains the experience of continuity of the being at the body level in spite of its transformations and space-time transfers. This continuity of being is woven from the fundamental relationships of body-to-body contact with the maternal figure. We refer to relationships of coexistence and body co-belonging that forge a feeling of existence of a human being, which ties their body to narcissism and to the image of the fundamental other embedded in the mother. Therefore, the fact of losing this tie or anchor of fundamental narcissism could have damaged Vera's base image that, as Dolto (2005) points out, cannot occur without a representation immediately arising, a ghost, that threatens life itself. Vera grew up with a base image of narcissistic trust, in herself and in the unstable other. It is perhaps this that invites us to understand the dimension of that tragedy that Vera had from losing her mother. Vera cannot do anything for her mother nor can her mother do anything facing the advent of death. The imaginary perspective of narcissism is shattered. According to Derrida (2000), I can give everything to the other, except for immortality, except to die for her to the point of dying in her place and, thus, freeing her from her own death. As Freud (1914) indicated, children can provide many reasons for narcissistic satisfaction to parents. Death should bow before the majesty of babies, before the majesty of their narcissism. In imaginary reciprocity, children may think that death must respect their parents and be subject to the omnipotence of parents. However, death does not respect anything. It has no respect for the narcissism of the overturned omnipotence of children on parents or of parents on children.

If death commands, is it to the extent that "she" became preferable, a motive of preference for this dying mother? Would Vera be jealous of that death that took her mother from her? It should be noted that losing the mother, in Vera's case, is accompanied by losing money and possessing the house ostentatiously sheltering the line of nobility. Only beauty will remain as a resource to explore and exploit in its full potential. Another possible loss that could be inferred would be the distance between her and her father, whom she adored, for business reasons. Due to economic interests and business matters, the father, symbol of loving protection, moves away from his daughter. And to exacerbate this loss and distance, her father will subsequently have Vera admitted in an institution specially destined for aristocratic girls. It is unknown whether the instigating element of jealousy has been devised under the figure of this tertiary component of the mother's death, the father's business, and the business trips. It was already known that Vera's series of love affairs ended badly due to "her possessive and jealous nature," which, for her, it was revealed that her partner was currently inevitably a cause for suspicion if he did not spend "all his free time with her, as she assumed that if he was not besides her he would be cheating on her with another woman" (Durigon, 2015, pp. 300–301). This other woman would be of enormous social relevance, "a refined lady," or of a degrading status, "a vulgar prostitute." This presence of another woman, who will take her place as a romantic preference, is outlined in an ominous horizon of hostility and terror. To what extent does death appear on that horizon? This helps to remember in Freud's *The Interpretation of Dreams* (1900), the revealing the presence of death under the dreamlike embellishment of the trip. He recalls that, for the child, who is otherwise spared from scenes of suffering that precede death, "being dead" is synonymous with "being far away," not disturbing survivors anymore. Nothing changes how the absence occurs, whether it is by travel, abandonment, separation, or death.

The trip, like death in the mother's case, signifies a causal factor of a loved one's absence, and the absence of being loved by the other—a deadly factor that may resignify the mother's loss. The father seems to prefer traveling over being with his daughter, whereas the mother, in her omnipotent whim, could have preferred dying than living with her. Death and travel are metaphorically linked and possibly reflect instigating elements of jealousy for Vera.

Similar to her father, the banker whom Vera married at the age of sixteen had to constantly leave Vera for business they had established, a wine cellar. Not even having a child prevented her husband from persisting in distancing himself from her. When she gave birth, it appeared that her suspicions of infidelity were dissipating. However, her certainty settles in with the determination of the fatal act, as the man kept working extremely hard, she became more convinced of his unfaithfulness. She became a very possessive woman and created scenes if her husband simply looked at another woman. Karl's gaze at another woman was full of resounding and forceful meaning. It is precisely indicated the year it happened, 1920, and the time of day it happened, but not the exact day when Vera's facial expression turned neutral. "We are unaware what that means, except it was at that time when Vera thought about the conspiracy of her husband's various imaginary lovers, until something in her mind snapped. Vera decided to chastise him so he would never cheat on her again. 'I could not endure another day of jealousy'" (Durigon, 2015, p. 302). What is it that truly breaks in this circumstance? Is it the unattainable image of the husband as a renewed, serial figure of her beloved father? Severely chastising someone is what a parent does to punish their child that has done wrong. Criminal poisoning is triggered by a sense of punishment for another crime: infidelity. To avoid being exposed to further deception, in this case to stop Karl from looking at any other woman besides her, the act must be definitive. The crime of infidelity is unforgivable, as it causes a painful, narcissistic burial. It deserves a lethal punishment.

It is possible to distinguish that Vera's hatred does not point to conspiratorial women. Based on her growing certainty, it could be any woman. If there is anything regarding fermented homosexuality, to which Freud refers, it would be understood as the imaginary union that Spinoza suggests with the shameful parts and excretions of the other woman through her "beloved thing." It appears that Karl could have fully looked at any woman. Hatred, in that assemblage of ambivalence or the soul's fluctuation to which Spinoza refers, is concentrated and primed in this man whose increasing work made Vera's suspicions absolutely imperious, thus culminating in absolute conviction. This man had failed her; he had insulted her in his narcissism, perhaps like her father by virtue of his business trips—the businesses and trips that distance Vera from her father, her husband and from a privileged place of preference. It could signify the experience of parental separation as abandonment, considering that those terms define her condition when she tried to report and explain her husband's disappearance. This man had committed the most unforgivable error, an error that is punishable by death. On observing her neutral expression, Vera explained that at the time of the crime she apparently felt indifferent. It also suggests a kind of momentary neutralization of her sex and perhaps her sexual passion. We could argue that at the very moment when Vera was about to kill her unfaithful partners, she appeared sexually indifferent, "as if, and it would be tempting to think about it, before death, sexual difference is no longer found: this would be the last horizon, namely the end of sexual difference. This would be a being-until-death" (Derrida, 2000, p. 50).

Néstor Durigon (2015) presents a biographical characterization of a woman where two crucial moments of jealousy can be traced, one of doubt and the other of atrocious conviction regarding deception. Didier Lauru (2015) proposes something similar in the dramatic sequence of *Othello*, by William Shakespeare (1991). Othello refuses to succumb to the jealousy that Iago astutely wanted to insinuate and instigate. He felt no jealousy even though Desdemona's beauty and certain virtues were praised and suspected nothing. In fact, even devaluing his own merits did not make him doubt or fear deception from Desdemona. He gave the impression of being positioned as someone who was forced to reject jealousy (Barthes, 2009). It is certainly clear that once a person doubts, the soul's state is irrevocably set (Shakespeare, 1991). This is what Iago intended: to plant the seed of doubt. He was aware that for Othello, this requires the irremissible provision of evidence, and that Othello would urgently ask for it. "Let me see, or at least, try it in such a way, that the test does not leave a bolt of doubt, or woe to your life!" (p. 398). However, Othello was already filled with doubt and was torn between believing and doubting his wife's honesty or between believing and doubting Iago's word. In such torture, Othello desperately yearned certainty: "I would like to be completely convinced!" (p. 399). Conviction overcomes all doubt in the fourth act, as suggested by Lauru (2015), since Iago affirmed that Othello's ignorant jealousy (Shakespeare, 1991) is constituted in interpreting the behavior of Cassio, Desdemona's supposed lover: "Othello has forged the security of having been deceived"[13] (Lauru, 2015, p. 92). This security is what made him insult his wife by calling her a whore. It is the same security, the arduous certainty that lead to the homicidal act. An obvious narcissistic component was detected in these extreme positions of jealousy:

> In Othello's case, as is the case of many pathologically jealous people, his goal was to appropriate the other, to make her love him, no matter what the cost.

> The jealous man is not aware of the transformation of reality and denies all that may agree with his certainty: the other deceives him. In his blindness, he comes to hate the object of his love to the point of destroying and killing her in reality.[14] (p. 95)

Othello needed what he feared most: the certainty of deception, which is reflected in his role as an agent interpreting reality; that is, as a tireless promoter of its distortion.

Similar to Othello, Vera was as certain of her husband's infidelity. However, this rigid conviction will become her criminal pivot. She did not make claims to justify her act. She did not need to claim anything because in principle, there is no recognition of the criminal act. According to the biographer, she meets the conventional mourning demands, although her husband's death has not yet been made public. As it has been pointed out, Vera talked about abandonment not only from her spouse but also from her son. She then adds that both died in a traffic accident. It is striking that Vera's mourning appeared before the declaration of her husband's death. Vera soon remarried Joseph Renczi, a rich man, a little older than her and stamps with his name, by virtue of the law of partnership, a symbolic identity. The biographer informs us of a similarity between Vera and this man: beauty and availability of lovers, which offers and illustrates, on this occasion, a way of choosing a narcissistic object. Marriage does not prevent Joseph from pursuing his love affairs. Vera reused arsenic as an instrument of punishment. It is explained how Vera, in a sadistic type of bravery, took great pain to look after him during his prolonged agony because of the poison. More than caring for Joseph, she seemed to morbidly take care, to savor the deleterious effects on his body. The series continues its repetitive course as Vera pointed out that Joseph's untimely disappearance is also due to abandonment. It turns into aggression of the other, under the image of abandonment, which was a violent act insidiously exercised by her against this other. In the future, Vera does not remarry but she devoted herself to hunting men and keeping their bodies at home as real trophies. Catching another in the passionate convergence of love–hate, she constitutes a kind of leitmotiv at all costs.

As a result of this fascinating hunt, she attracts all kinds of romantic characters to her house. It seemed to make no difference whether they were rich or poor, boisterous or quiet. The diversity in romantic contingency, together with her certainty, made her observe the sign of infidelity in their empty gazes (Durigon, 2015). Her certainty is so dominant that it filled the void of the gaze and gave it an absolute complete meaning. Not having this security, it could be said that Vera exempted herself from the pain and grief that this brutal attack of jealousy would imply: Vera always remained firm in her belief that fidelity was fundamental in a relationship; therefore, she believed that she could not be held responsible if a man broke this rule. The roots of her problem lay very deep, and they clung to the firm belief that she could not trust anyone. Her low self-esteem became increasingly dangerous as she progressed into adulthood.

We could return to projective jealousy to understand something of criminal irresponsibility, based on the route: evacuation-assignment-designation of the temptation or the unfaithful act. The belief remains firm. It is the other who always deceives, and this deception is observed when he does not look at her. Infidelity is an absolute masculine issue rather than feminine. However, it is a matter of glance that gaze painfully at infamous stares. Vera does not question her own possible infidelity; she doesn't even question her infidelity in relation to possible homosexual fantasies. Women are presumably not responsible for men's infidelity. Infidelity, in this case, is something that corresponds to an ideal of a fundamentally narcissistic person. Freud (1915–1917b) pointed out that mourning does not have to be the result of losing a loved one, it could also be from "an abstraction that takes its place, like homeland, freedom, an ideal, etc." (p. 241). With an abstraction like homeland or freedom, a subject may be willing to risk his life and take on a fight to death. Fidelity may very well correspond to an idealized abstraction, a blissful idea, which performs the same function as a loved one. Vera seems unwilling to lose this ideal of fidelity, which is invested in worth and narcissistic significance. It also possesses the nature of a rule, something that should order relationships between the sexes. It probably is something that should order life or bring order to life. It is then an ideal of inter-human legislation. It is a kind of narcissistic imagination of something that belongs to the symbolic sphere. She is not responsible for the man's unfaithfulness but assumes the responsibility of teaching a lesson to those who announce their willingness for infidelity; although she only subtly catches this announcement and she will, without a doubt, not wait for what she already knows is happening.

The biographer informs us that Vera's hunts continued her "happy dance" by getting rid of unfaithful men after seducing them. However, one of the men she met in her hunts was a banker, like her first husband. She precisely chose a married person who would succumb to the fault configured in infidelity to enter into an affair with her. The wife in question succeeds in chasing her husband to Vera's house. Her husband does not return, and she decided to report him as a missing person. They visited Vera's residence and soon to discover the thirty-five coffins with the name and age of each man that Vera murdered after carefully pouring arsenic into their food and drinks. Vera did not immediately admit her criminal act but she pointed out that it would be "friends and family who have taken care of me" (Durigon, 2015, p. 305). Little is told in Vera Renczi's biography of family ties. In fact, nothing is known about what happens to her father after she was admitted into the hospital at the age of fifteen. It could be questioned how much Vera felt cared for and protected by her father. Would the claim or complaint of abandonment that Vera uses in a deceitful way to account for the disappearance of her first husband be a message addressed to her father? Although, neither her father nor any of her relatives are invoked by the biographer. Vera confessed to her crimes and justified them as "she felt that they were cheating on her with other women, or that they began to lose interest in her. In any case, it could mean that they abandoned her, and she wanted to prevent it" (p. 305). As soon as she perceived that sign of deception and realized they were losing interest in her, she then felt irretrievably lost: "The other has no value in her eyes; he only shows her fascination for her own jealous love. Hating himself, the jealous man runs to his loss in spite of himself. When losing the other, he becomes lost at the same time"[15] (Lauru, 2015, p. 95). Keeping the corpses drives away and conjures up the experience of loss. As a true expert in hunting, Vera kept all her preys tagged, like a well-differentiated collection. She had not abandoned an uncertain destiny for her preys. It's been predicted that just as she put them in the coffin is just as she hunted them. That is why corpses are found in different states of decomposition and putrefaction. She preserved the corpses of the men hunted in different conditions of organic degradation, beyond the dignity of the burial (Lacan, 2003) and of the symbolism of funerals. Strictly, these men "could no longer betray her" or be unfaithful toward her. Preserving her lovers' corpses maintains the reality of the rule of fidelity to her until death. She killed because she knew that these men, including her son, would leave her for another woman at any time. "Vera did not kill any man for profit, revenge, or simple emotion; she did so because she saw them as the source of all her unhappiness" (Lacan, 2003, p. 306). We could agree with the biographer's statement if we leave the father out of the issue, if the father is not questioned in relation to the fidelity issue.

Based on such questioning regarding the ideal of fidelity as the foundation of happiness that we refer to how Descartes (1999) addresses the issue of jealousy. It promptly articulates desire and fear in the following manner: "they are some kind of fear, which refers to the desire to preserve the possession of goods" (p. 179). We hold to these goods in such high esteem that the thought of losing it frightens us and makes us wonder what could cause its loss. The good that Vera holds in high esteem is fidelity. She may have more esteem for it than for herself. Descartes points out that there is an honest dimension in this passion. In this manner, a captain jealously watches over a territory. An honest woman guards jealously her honor, to not appear suspicious. According to Descartes, jealous passion can be reprehensible when someone cannot get away from their good for fear of it being stolen. This is what happens with the miser and his economic assets. Jealousy has a lot of greed. The love of the jealous person is not a "good kind" of love insofar as it makes him distrust his wife. It makes us believe that in reality it is not her whom he loves "but only the good that he imagines she alone possesses, and he would not be afraid of losing that good if he thought he was unworthy of it, or that his wife was unfaithful to him" (p. 180). Vera did not love these eventual lovers, she loved "fidelity" as the supreme good, which refers to the absolute possession. According to Lachaud (2000), jealousy pushes a woman to be on the side of the Other not barred with madness attacks, but whatever the sex, jealousy is a demand to be the One, someone irreplaceable for the other, what is already an imaginary position of aggregation, an annulment of the otherness, an aspiration toward the ONE, toward The woman.

There is no otherness, there cannot be any, for someone like Vera, who erected as the only one, in the only jealous guardian of fidelity. No man turns out to be worthy of her as the Other unbarred and fierce defender of fidelity.

Ever since she was a child, Vera showed signs of this attitude of absolute possession and greed of her property. Her father questioned her on one occasion about poisoning a dog that had been given to her. She claimed to have heard her neighbors talk about killing her dog for barking so much the night before. Thus, with her act, she prevented others from doing it—suppressing these others from performing the fatal act. Her father insisted on questioning her about the need to kill the dog. She pointed out she did it "because I do not want my dog to belong to anyone else" (Durigon, 2015, p. 307). Instead of questioning this position of absolute possession, her father punished her by severely hitting her, chastening her, "to teach her to control her jealousy" (p. 307). With that gesture, it seems that it could have pushed her to accentuate her jealousy to the point of becoming a sovereign defender of everything she considered hers, as her precious good. And she not only considered the men she married and hunted to be hers, but she also conceived the rule of fidelity as her own. According to Lachaud (2000), the jealous person reveals the radical impossibility of symbolizing fidelity; failure arises from the despair engendered by her earliest childhood experience. The object is potentially always present . . . jealousy never lacks a subject, even when what produces it is not initially available. Thus, the subject is completely correct in being jealous. They will always be correct. The other is unfaithful to the exact extent that he swears his fidelity.

Vera was always right. Her speech was never wrong. Failure was what was noticed in the other unfaithful and shown as a true signal or truth according to Vera.

There is no place for mourning; there is no place for the hole in reality that communicates the loss of a highly esteemed or highly treasured ideal as a supreme good. Freud (1915–1917a) affirmed that the subject could oppose an extreme and intense *Sträuben*, resistance, to the loss that examining reality exposes. This resistance leads to a *Abwendung von der Realität*, distancing from reality and to a *Festhalten des Objekts*, retention of the object, through a *Wunsch psychose halluzinatorische*, hallucinatory psychosis of desire. The object has not left. On the contrary, the object is firmly attached to the subject. Vera did not accept the urge of the reality test in terms of assuming that her ideal of fidelity had been lost or is an imaginary illusion. In fact, she clings tenaciously to her ideal abstraction from the moment her father manifests the desire for something other than herself—his business trips.

According to Lachaud (2000), regarding love relationships, not only is the man married to the phallus, as Lacan specified, but so is the woman. The jealous love of women, the fact that they are jealous of everything, of other women, football, television, bridge, makes the man believe that he is married to her and that the phallus is common property, an indispensable supplement for the partner.

Vera's jealousy seemed to be triggered by her marked lack of control when her first husband goes out on business trips with greater diligence or pressing nature, just like her father did after her mother's death. The business trips of her father, whose name is not specified by the biographer (we would say that there is no name-of-the-father), would create a feeling of abandonment and loss, of bloody usurpation of an alleged romantic preference position.

We are unaware about the circumstances of Vera's mother's death, but we can guess that losing her mother at such an early age marks a blunt and painful narcissistic affront in relation to her position that what she possesses cannot belong to anyone else. Death soon possessed her mother. Then, another figurative mode of death, regarded in this case as travel, would possess and capture her father. Death and business trips inflict a narcissistic wound and are a factor of affliction for her. They would have stripped her of an illusion of full and omnipotent totality with her mother and father. They would have removed the illusion of fidelity as an absolute sense of belonging. However, Vera rebels; she is strongly opposed to this lack of possession and loss. To maintain the illusion of the ideal of fidelity and not lose it, it is indispensable and imperative to provoke the loss of the unfaithful. Vera mourned, even before the disappearance of Karl Schick, her first husband, instead of admitting the loss and grieving the loss of the abstract ideal of fidelity. She sent these unfaithful men, who seem to jeopardize their perennial commitment to this ideal, to hell, with this majestic good which they enjoy.

However, the father who questioned the aggressive act of his little daughter is not questioned or accused by her of abandonment or anything that involves him in his repeated criminal behavior. In this manner, we could capture an eventual "weight of blindness that influences the image of the 'hero with such a sweet smile,'"[16] (Brun 2013, p. 27), of the innocent-looking father. This heroic image of the father seems to be preserved or cared for insofar as there is no trace of blame on him. Vera would rather give the impression of identifying with a severely intransigent and punitive father because she stands as a heroine who defends the idea or ideal of fidelity as a supreme cause. Men, in contrast, will soon be accused of infidelity at the very moment when Vera notices the fatal signal, the hollow look on their face. She, not being whole, should fill that void, be the only one for the beloved. There is no reflection or imaginary reference in that look. These men are unfaithful from the moment they do not look at her or stop looking at her—or admiring her. However, it should be emphasized that Vera's very look is full of such certainties that the empty gaze of the hunted companion comes only to confirm and prove it absolutely: "By swirling around the idea of betrayal, the thought undergoes a real and true shock, until the threshold of paranoid delirium arises, in which the most innocent and insignificant events are interpreted as irrefutable proof that justify the suspicions of the jealous one"[17] (Gallimberti, 2011, p. 140). Yahweh, the God of the Jews, like Vera, was extremely attentive and angry at the manifestations of infidelity. He was jealous of that infidelity and was extremely jealous of his people willing to worship other gods. Above all, it is from the book of Exodus that he appears as a God so jealous that he seems determined to exterminate his people in the desert by virtue of their constant disobedience. It is this desire for extermination that is sustained as a tireless, unwavering desire to end infidelity by eliminating those who commit it. The jealous and uncompromising anger that dominates God with regard to the unfaithful, whom he insists on punishing in a dismal way, could be an ideal model for Vera. As long as her criminal act does not imply any guilt, she may believe that she not only has the right but it is also her duty to fulfill it. We would perhaps be faced with imperative enjoyment, anchored in the extermination of the unfaithful, of those who act against his ideal abstraction and put them in danger of losing it.

In the biography, what stands out the most is that it does not mention what happens to the father. After this businessman arranges his daughter's marriage, we do not find out more about him in the summarized account. He reappears toward the end, in the scene where he questions his daughter about the murder of the beloved dog. One could wonder to what extent his daughter's alleged response that she could not allow her dog to be someone else's makes him distance himself from her, to the point where he hospitalizes her. It is certain that she was the only one who could decide the fate, and particularly, the fatal destiny, of her dog. For her, being the owner of someone implies owning them to the ultimate consequences, appropriating their life and death, as Freud (1915b) suggests in relation to the oral-cannibalistic stage. Voracious or devouring love, impregnated with ambivalence and narcissism, insofar as it is compatible with the suppression of the existence of the object as something separate. In fact, Gallimberti talks about "sentimental cannibalism"[18] (p. 142) to refer to this ostensible devouring desire that betrays the jealous possessiveness and that ends in homicide insofar as it is clearly proposed that the beloved cannot and should not exist separately from the lover.

We should conclude by affirming that, for Vera, it is about sacrificing the unfaithful, specifically one by one, to save the ideal abstraction of fidelity, in its universality. To not lose this fidelity in its status of ideal perfection, we should lose men. She intends to lose them by seducing them and making them consume the fateful drink. Already a seductive trick, in Baudrillard's terms (1992), she summons the power of the feminine or the feminine power of a "decentered erogeneity, diffuse versatility of enjoyment and transfiguration of the whole body by desire"[19] (p. 21). A world of infinite possibilities of enjoyment promises this figure whose seduction combines some signs in his evil use. She has these men who "were unable to flee, dazzled by a sorceress" under her spell and paralyzing domain (Durigon, 2015, p. 305). Her enjoyment in preserving an elevated ideal results from a supreme power. As Lacan stated (2001), because her enjoyment radically lies in the Other, the woman has much more of a relationship with God than everything in the ancient speculation following the path of what is manifestly articulated only as the good in man. It could then be speculated that there was some mysticism in this serial killer insofar as she considers and glimpses an enjoyment that is beyond the phallic realm, even pleasure, in death. Her commitment to fidelity was radical and to death. She was extremely faithful to fidelity, a fidelity that involves sacrifice. Derrida (2000) recalls, "I cannot answer the call, the request, the obligation, or even the love of another, without sacrificing another, others" (p. 70). Thus, in the state of degradation and decomposition, the bodies of these fallible, unfaithful men are erected as dissected evidence of the fulfillment of a supreme duty. In this manner, she commemorates the definitive power of her lesson and allowed her to take over, in her captivating image of unity, without failure. An image of ecstatic fullness that results ineffable, as Lacan (1971) would suggest of mystical experience. However, something could be said about a place that Vera fantasies for her ideal of fidelity, from God's place, according to Vázquez (1992) beyond the increasing fury of men. Beyond human fury is the fury of God, the punishing fury of someone like Vera. In fact, Vera practices these furious acts not because it inspires an appetite for revenge but an ecstatic sense of exercising good, assuming the role of a father jealous of justice. As the Duke of Ferrara mentions in Lope de Vega's work (1999), *El castigo sin venganza*: "I will be a father and not a husband,/ giving holy justice/ to a sin without shame/ a punishment without revenge" (p. 243). That is why it is of least importance if Vera's real existence is proven or not, as suggested by Durigon. We care about her life as a legend, the legend-fiction of a woman who defends fidelity as if it was a heroic act. Brother William of Baskerville, in the novel *El nombre de la rosa*, by Umberto Eco (1993), indicates that a similarity has been found between the weaknesses of the wicked and the saints: jealousy.

The deadly zeal of fidelity requires a legend, like that of Vera Renczi, to testify that not only malevolence and holiness enter into the passionate fluctuation of the soul, expounded by Spinoza, but in a squeezing and ferocious knotting. There is a legend of a woman who is passionately committed to punishing evil by administering death as a sovereign good.

NOTES

1. The translation from Spanish to English is mine.
2. Translation to English is mine
3. selon des règles détermines de valeur sexuelle ou sociale, la jalousie n'est pas pris sérieusement en considération.
4. Il n'y a pas d'innocence à l'origine, il y a du manqué.
5. Si l'amour a un cout, la jalousie en est le dédommagement. Les deux plateaux de la balance s'équilibrent ici. Car si l'amour est une puissante force émotionnelle, la jalousie est le contrepoint social de cette force.
6. prendracine dans l'injustice, cette forme aiguedumanqué.
7. Effet d'entre-deux radical ou le partage entre soi et l'Autre se faire mal et fait mal. Jalousie, blessure narcissique due au fait qu'il y a de l'autre, qu'il nous échappe, qu'il a peut-être pris notre part, qu'on voudrait prendre sa place, tout en gardant la notre . . . Violence du "premier" partage impossible. Surtout quand c'est la "premier" place qu'il s'agit de partager. Translation is mine.
8. Même dans le mythe d'Eve arrachant le fruit et bravant l'interdit, on peut dire qu'elle est jalouse, et le jaloux a beau être a la place de l'autre et détenir comme lui l'objet, celane l'apaise pas, sa blessure narcissique est radicale; en d'autres termes, sa faille identitaire, essentielle au processus de son devenir ne se laisse pas combler ainsi. Le partage impossible, de soi ou de l'autre, c'est aussi ne pas pouvoir supporter la différence—qui permettrait par exemple de désirer le même objet, mais pas de la même façon.
9. L'envie est jalousie: le sujet pense que ce qui lui manque, l'autre le lui a pris, et il v eu têtre a la place de cet autre—pour se le prendre a lui-même et se le rendre a volonté, son objet.
10. Dominé par sa passion haineuse, le jaloux perd tout sens critique, ne parvient plus à discriminer la réalité et, aveuglé par son dépit, risque de se laisser aller à des passages à l'acte agressifs, voire criminels, incontrôlables. (All French to Spanish translations are mine).
11. Le corps d'une femme et son éventuelle beauté demeuraient toujours un capital fondamental, exploite sur le marche du mariage ou sur celui du sexe commercial.
12. sauf dans les plus hautes rangs de l'aristocratie.
13. Othello s'est forgé l'assurance d'avoir été trompé.
14. Car chez Othello, comme pour de nombreux jaloux pathologiques, le but visé est de s'approprier l'autre, de se faire aimer de lui, à n'importe quel prix. Le jaloux n'a pas conscience de la transformation de la réalité et dénie tout ce qui vient à l'encontre de sa certitude : l'autre le trompe. Dans son aveuglement, il ne vient à haïr son objet d'amour au point de le détruire et de le tuer dans la réalité.
15. L'autre n'a plus aucune valeur à ses yeux, seule compte sa fascination pour son propre amour jaloux. En se haïssant lui-même, le jaloux court a sa perte malgré lui. En perdant l'autre, il se perd au même instant.
16. le poids de l'aventeuglement qui pese sur l'image du "heros au sourir si doux"
17. A force de tournoyer autour de l'idée de trahison, la pensée subit un véritable et réel bouleversement, jusqu' a effleurer le seuil du délire paranoïaque, dans lequel les évènements les plus innocents et les plus insignifiants son interprétées comme des preuves irréfutables venant justifier absolument les soupçons du jaloux.
18. "Sentimental cannibalism."
19. érogénéité décentrée, polyvalence diffuse de la jouissance et transfiguration de tout les corps par le désir.

REFERENCES

Assoun, P.-L. (2000). *Lecciones psicoanalíticas sobre hermanos y hermanas*. Buenos Aires: Nueva Visión.
Barthes, R. (2009). *Fragmentos de un discurso amoroso*. México: Siglo XXI.
Baudrillard, J. (1992). *De la séduction*. Paris: Denoël
Brun, D. (2013). *L'insidieuse malfaisance du père*. Paris: Odile Jacob.
Christie, A. (2004). *Muerte en el Nilo*. Barcelona: Molino.
Derrida, J. (2000). *Dar la muerte*. Barcelona: Paidós.
Descartes, R. (1999). *Tratado de las pasiones*. Barcelona: RBA.
De Vega, L. (1999). *El castigo sin venganza*. Barcelona: Folio.
Dolto, F. (2008). *La imagen incosnciente del cuerpo*. Buenos Aires: Paidós.
Durigon, N. (2015). *Asesinas seriales*. Buenos Aires: Ediciones B.
Eco, U. (1993). *El Nombre de la Rosa*. Barcelona: RBA.
Freud, S. (1895). Proyecto de psicología para neurólogos. In J. Strachey (Ed.), Etcheverry, J. L. (Trans.), 2006, *Obras Completas de Sigmund Freud* (2nd ed. Vol. I). pp. 323–465, Buenos Aires: Amorrortu.
Freud, S. (1900). La interpretación de los sueños. In J. Strachey (Ed.), Etcheverry, J. L. (Trans.), 2006, *Obras Completas de Sigmund Freud* (2nd ed., Vol. IV) pp. 1–670. Buenos Aires: Amorrortu.
Freud, S. (1905). Tres ensayos de teoría sexual. In J. Strachey (Ed.), Etcheverry, J. L. (Trans.), 2006, *Obras Completas de Sigmund Freud* (2nd ed., Vol. VII), pp. 109–223. Buenos Aires: Amorrortu.
Freud, S. (1910). Über einen besonderen Typus der Objektwahl beim Manne. In M. Bonaparte & A. Freud (Eds.), 1999, *Sigmund Freud Gesammelte Werke* (5th ed., Vol. VIII). Frankfurt am Main: S. Fischer Verlag.
Freud, S. (1911). Psychoanalytische Bemerkungen über einen autobiographisch beschriebenen Fall von Paranoia. In M. Bonaparte & A. Freud (Eds.), 1999, *Sigmund Freud Gesammelte Werke* (5th ed., Vol. VIII). Frankfurt am Main: S. Fischer Verlag.
Freud, S. (1913). Tótem y Tabú. In J. Strachey (Ed.), Etcheverry, J. L. (Trans.), 2006, *Obras Completas de Sigmund Freud* (2nd ed., Vol. XIII), pp. 1–164. Buenos Aires: Amorrortu.
Freud, S. (1914). Introducción del Narcisismo. In J. Strachey (Ed.), Etcheverry, J. L. (Trans.), 2006, *Obras Completas de Sigmund Freud* (2nd ed., Vol. XIV), pp. 65–98. Buenos Aires: Amorrortu.
Freud, S. (1915a). Lo inconsciente. In J. Strachey (Ed.), Etcheverry, J. L. (Trans.), 2006, *Obras Completas de Sigmund Freud* (2nd ed., Vol. XIV), pp. 253–214. Buenos Aires: Amorrortu.
Freud, S. (1915b). Pulsiones y destinos de pulsión. In J. Strachey (Ed.), Etcheverry, J. L. (Trans.), 2006, *Obras Completas de Sigmund Freud* (2nd ed., Vol. XIV), pp. 105–134. Buenos Aires: Amorrortu.
Freud, S. (1915–1917a). Trauer und Melancholie. In M. Bonaparte & A. Freud (Eds.), 1999, *Sigmund Freud Gesammelte Werke* (5th ed., Vol. X). Frankfut am Main: S. Fischer Verlag.
Freud, S. (1915–1917b). Duelo y Melancolía. In J. Strachey (Ed.), Etcheverry, J. L. (Trans.), 2006, *Obras Completas de Sigmund Freud Complete Works* (2nd ed., Vol. XIV) pp. 235–256. Buenos Aires: Amorrortu.
Freud, S. (1920). Más allá del principio de placer. In J. Strachey (Ed.), Etcheverry, J. L. (Trans.), 2006, *Obras Completas de Sigmund Freud* (2nd ed., Vol. XVIII) pp. 1–62. Buenos Aires: Amorrortu.
Freud, S. (1921). Psicología de las masas y análisis del yo. In J. Strachey (Ed.), Etcheverry, J. L. (Trans.), 2006, *Obras completes de Sigmund Freud* (2nd ed., Vol. XVIII), pp. 63–136. Buenos Aires: Amorrortu.
Freud, S. (1921–1922a). Sobre algunos mecanismos neuróticos en los celos, la paranoia y la homosexualidad. In J. Strachey (Ed.), Etcheverry, J. L. (Trans.), 2006, *Obras Completas de Sigmund Freud* (2nd ed., Vol. XVIII), pp. 213–226. Buenos Aires: Amorrortu.
Freud, S. (1921–1922b). Über einige neurotische Mechanismen bei Eifersucht, Paranoia und Homosexualität. In M. Bonaparte & A. Freud (Eds.), 1999, *Sigmund Freud Gesammelte Werk*, (5th ed., Vol. XIII)., Frankfut am Main: S. Fischer Verlag.

Freud, S. (1929–1930). El malestar en la cultura. In J. Strachey (Ed.), Etcheverry, J. L. (Trans.), 2006, *Obras Completas de Sigmund Freud* (2nd ed., Vol. XXI), pp. 57–140. Buenos Aires: Amorrortu.

Gallimberti, U. (2011) *Qu'est-ce que l'amour?* Paris: Payot.

Giddens, A. (2000) *La transformación de la intimidad. Sexualidad, amor y erotismo en las sociedades modernas.* Madrid: Cátedra.

Grandes, A. (2015). *Modelos de mujer.* Mexico: Tusquets.

Graves, R. & Patai, R. (2009). *Los mitos hebreos.* Madrid: Alianza.

Héritier, F. (1994) *Les deux soeurs et leur mère*. Paris: Odile Jacob.

Lacan, J. (1971). *D'un discours qui ne serait pas du semblant. Leçon du 20 janvier*. Unpublished.

Lacan, J. (1981). *Los escritos técnicos de Freud.* Buenos Aires: Paidós.

Lacan, J. (1990). *Seminario 3, Las Psicosis*. Buenos Aires: Paidós.

Lacan, J. (1999). *Formaciones de lo inconsciente.* Buenos Aires: Paidós.

Lacan, J. (2001). *Aún.* Buenos Aires: Paidós.

Lacan, J. (2003). *La familia.* Barcelona: Argonauta.

Lachaud, D. (2000). *Celos. Un estudio psicoanalítico de su diversidad.* Buenos Aires: Nueva Visión.

Lauru, D. (2015). *De la haine de soi à la haine de l'autre*. Paris: Albin Michel.

Matthews-Grieco, S. L. (2005). Corps et sexualité d'Ancien Régime. En A. Corbin, J. J. Courtine y G. Vigarello, *Histoire du corps*, 1. Paris: Seuil.

Nasio, J. D. (1999). *El libro del amor y del dolor.* Barcelona: Gedisa.

Shakespeare, W. (1991). *Shakespeare Complete Works, II.* México: Aguilar

Sibony, D. (1998). *Violence.* Paris: Seuil.

Spinoza, B. (1984). *Ética.* Madrid: Sarpe.

Vázquez, P. (1992). Dios. En *Mística, poesía española.* Barcelona: Mitre.

Chapter Seven

Grief, Rêve, and Son-Au-Dela

Carolina Koretzky

IMPRISONED MEANING AND PARADOXICAL SUFFERING

It is always a subjective suffering that leads a subject, at a specific moment in their life, to knock on the door of a psychoanalyst. Sometimes it is the insistence of an enigmatic symptom bearing a message, an imprisoned meaning that escapes conscious knowledge, and for which the cure will be sought to deliver. This is the case in which misunderstanding of the symptom calls for decryption and the effects of truth occur. This insistence on the symptom, this side "that doesn't stop" despite the suffering provoked, indicates a point of paradoxical satisfaction. However, the arrival of a subject to an analyst can also occur as the result of a traumatic encounter, one that makes the subject distressed and unresponsive when faced with a continuing void. Trauma is, first of all, an unforeseen, senseless event, a break-in that leaves the subject petrified, without a response. Afterward, despite the passing of time, trauma as a "foreign body" continues to produce effects such as anxiety, inhibitions, nightmares, and motor disorders (Freud and Breuer, 1895).

Such event opens a hole in all the meanings of reality. On encountering this, the network of meanings available to each individual cannot support the meaning of this unforeseen event. There is no protocol, no training manual, and no ready-made solution. The responses within the unique elaboration to this breach that is created by bad encounters, which each subject can give in its own solitude, are irremediable. In the clinical work, for some subjects, the loss of a loved one may also be in the form of an unexpected intrusion, leaving the subject distraught.

For Freud, the consequences of a traumatic encounter are not different from the acute moments of a painful mourning. In his famous *Studies on Hysteria*, Freud said that the very nature of psychological trauma means the exclusion of any possible reaction, for example, when a loved one seems irreplaceable (Freud and Breuer, 1895).

Three years after the death of his father, Freud published *The Interpretation of Dreams*, a major work in the birth of psychoanalysis, which laid the foundations for the constitution of the psychical system in 1899. In the preface to the second edition, Freud writes, "[This book] has proved to me to be a fragment of my self-analysis, my reaction to my father's death, and therefore to the most significant event, the most radical loss in a man's life" (Freud, 1899, p. 18).

MOURNING AND THE IRREPLACEABLE

The term "irreplaceable" that Freud refers to in the preface was the issue of a significant debate concerning mourning. In the 1917 text "Mourning and Melancholia," a central text but with some controversy, Freud addressed the issue of melancholia from the viewpoint of mourning, where the reconciliation of melancholia and mourning seems justified by the overall picture of these two states (Freud, 1917). If the loss of a loved one and the loss of an idol is the triggering circumstance, in the case of melancholia, it is in place of a temporary state of mourning. The same circumstance triggers mourning and melancholia and, likewise, the same psychic state, what he calls "a profoundly painful depression, a suspension of interest in the outside world, the loss of the capacity to love, the inhibition of all activity and the diminishment of a sense of self-esteem," (Freud, 1917, pp. 146–147), but with one exception; in a melancholic state, this decrease in the sense of self-esteem would be accompanied by what is lacking in mourning, the low in self-esteem, self-regarding feelings, and self-reproaches, which could lead to the extreme of an expectation of retribution. This clinical indication is valuable in separating the two clinical conditions. The controversy originates from Freud's question on what is then, the work of mourning (Freud, 1917). He replies, "I don't think there's anything that will be forced to portray it this way; the test of reality has shown that the beloved object no longer exists and dictates the requirement to remove all libido from the ties that hold it to that object" (Freud, 1917, p. 147).[1]

However, Freud notes that although the testing of reality shows the loved object no longer exists, the connection of the libido to the lost object is not immediately detached; the subject does not willingly abandon a libido position (Freud, 1917). The culmination of this "rebellion" to detachment can reach as far as the complete diversion of reality and a tendency to maintain the object with a hallucinatory psychosis of desire. Nevertheless, Freud concludes that, usually, the work of mourning is carried out in detail, and even if reality always takes precedence over denial of loss or hallucination of the object, the existence of the lost object continues psychically. As Roland Barthes (2009) said so well, the mourning, therefore, weighs between the "certainty of the definitive" (p. 105) and the outbursts, whether dreamed or not, of the presence of being lost. "Mourning: I have learned that it is immutable and sporadic: it does not wear, because it is not continuous" (p. 124).

Even if the detachment from the libido to the object is not simple or immediate, the question of the irreplaceability of the lost object can still be explored in this text by Freud. Indeed, one might wonder, beyond the cases of pathological mourning or melancholic psychosis, whether the so-called normal mourning theory of Freud gives rise to an ideal (Delecroix and Forest, 2015). The path in which reality would demand to free the libido attached to the lost object, and place that libido on a new object, could imply an ideal of cure.

Regarding this debate between the substitutability and the irreplaceability in mourning, it must be noted that, after the death of Freud's daughter, these words were echoed in a 1929 letter to Binswanger. Freud acknowledges that this type of "acute mourning" will remain inconsolable without ever finding a substitute. Freud wrote this is the only way we can perpetuate the love, the same love we do not want to give up to.

This is precisely where Lacan's advances become precious and enable us to think of mourning in terms of an elusive remnant. This remnant is no less present; remains that are the presence of an object that does not resolve to disappear with the disappeared.

Let us take the example of Roland Barthes' 2009 *Mourning Diary*, which he began writing the day after his mother's death. It is not a fictional work; it contains 330 sheets of writing, which he kept for almost two years. Eric Marty (2010) notes the strange task that Barthes engaged in, as he calls "Diary" an exercise in writing at the extreme opposite of the "tell it all" nature of a diary. On the contrary, the underuse of the blank page—the date, two-three lines—is a profoundly fragmentary writing, "is the expression *à la lettre* to the impossibility of saying everything" (Marty, 2010) on the event. In addition, we have Mallarmé's experience in a newspaper after the death of his son Anatole, published under the title *Pour un tombeau d'Anatole*. This text is also composed of fragments and abruptly intertwined verses. Barthes incessantly pointed out this fragmentation as the product of a contradiction, even a profound incompatibility of mourning and story (Compagnon, 2013). For Barthes (2009), the work of mourning can only be accomplished by writing: "eager to put me in the book on the Photo, that is, to integrate my suffering into a writing, . . . believing . . . that writing dialects seizures" (p. 114); "no doubt I will be wrong until I write something from her (*Photo*, or something else)" (p. 227).

In a few sentences in this document, it is striking how Barthes, through his writing, gets around the object at stake in connection to his mother, "strangely, her voice that I knew so well, which is said to be the very grain of remembrance ('the dear inflexion'), I do not hear. It is like the localized deafness" (Barthes, 2009, p. 24). Thus, Barthes values the presence of his mother's voice as what emerges with all its strength in the silence of his disappearance. Although his mother's voice is lost, the "localized deafness" that Barthes hears is no less an object presented by its absence. His mother's voice seems to have had a prominent place in the economy of his desire. The pain and the suffering associated with mourning were often shown following the encounter with this object. Thus, the deceptive appearance of his mother's voice would present his radical loss. As Samoyault (2015) claims, "sometimes he cries in front of his friends, but most often it takes place at his home, on his way home, when his heard a servant saying '*voila*' with the inflexions that his mother had in her voice" (p. 641). These outbursts of the presence of the missing being appear in the form of an object—in this case, the inflection of her voice—which resounds in silence. The loved one disappears, and yet what has been lost in that loss takes center stage in the daily life of the subject.

But Lacan went one step further—from the suffering of the one who was lost, to what has been lost, to the object that I am to the lost one. These advances are directly related to his conceptualization of small object *a*. In this quest for the place of the object in mourning, at the seminar on *Le Désir et son Interprétation*, we find the detailed analysis of a dream by Freud, then repeated and commented on by Lacan. This dream is about loss—it is the dream of a thread that just lost its father—that explicitly refers to the use of fantasy. In the straight line of our commentary, Lacan proposes to approach the analysis of this dream by the object and not by the Freudian method, by working around the signifiers of the dream (Miller, 2014).

THE DREAM OF THE DEAD FATHER IN THE LIGHT OF THE OEDIPUS COMPLEX

Freud (1899) introduces this dream into chapter 6 of *The Interpretation of Dreams*, a fundamental chapter titled "The Dream-Work." Due to its frequency, Freud grouped dreams about dead people in a separate category within a set he called "absurd dreams." A few years later, Freud echoed this same dream in the article *Formulations on the Two Principles of Mental Functioning* (1911), where he examines nothing less than the report of what the subject maintains regarding what is called reality.

In this dream, the son (i.e., the dreamer) sees his father in his dream. His father has just died, as a consequence of a long-lasting illness, during which he suffered immensely. The subject sees his father appearing in front of him in his dream, and feels a deep pain, which is manifested by the thought that his father is not aware of his own death. According to Freud, it is certainly absurd that one does not understand if one does not add that he had died "according to his wishes." So, he did not know that he had died as per his wishes. Freud delivers two levels of deciphering: the first level starts with the rejected phrase "according to his wishes." The son had wished for his father's death, so that he would not have to see him suffering staying on his deathbed; hence, the father did not know that he had died "in accordance with the son's wishes," one might say, accompanied by a divisive effect in the son at the hard root. But Freud does not stop there and directs our attention to the presence in the dream of a child's desire where the *son's desire of his father's death* is not an altruistic desire but a child's desire. The father had already died (hence, the imperfection of the "he didn't know") and this happens in the past and does not relate to present-day illness; the father had already died in accordance with the oedipal wish.

"According to his wishes," this is the repressed phrase that in his description gives this absurd image, therefore, absurdity is the hallmark of repression. Like all dreams, the absurd dream, "which does not differentiate between the desire and the dream," reveals that the unconsciousness does not respond to the principle of contradiction. In the country of primary processes, we circulate with the "neurotic currency"[2] (Freud, 1915). Thus, by restoring the unconscious vow and the phrases that are suppressed by censorship, all the absurdity is dispelled and the dream becomes intelligible. Freud (1911) treats this dream with signifier evaluation and not with "wishful thinking," an expression that Lacan completely rejects and can be translated as "taking the desires as if they were realities" and thus answering pious wishes. To imagine that the subject has such a dream of seeing his father alive is a "false way" because these dreamlike encounters do not seem to bring any satisfaction.

However, it is important to emphasize that, above all, Freud deals with the problem (that this dream raises) by the signifier and brings an eminently Oedipal interpretation (Lacan, 2013) behind this thought, sustained by the love of the father (death could shorten the suffering and agony of the father), there is the wish for infant death. The text of the dream in its entirety would read that the father had died (according to the dreamer's wish), and did not know (that this was the dreamer's wish).

MOVING BEYOND: FROM MEANING TO FANTASY

In his lecture, Lacan (2013, p. 115) proposes table 7.1.

Lacan opens two paths in his lecture; on the one hand, he will not start from the meaning but from the touch—from that *pain*—which invades the thread from the thought that he (i.e., the father) did not know he was dead.

On the subject side		*On the father side*
Pain that he was dead		he did not know that he was dead
	according to his wish	

On the other hand, he is particularly interested in the *imperfect* time of knowing.

Pain as an expression of affect, according to Freud (1915), is that of the unconsciousness that cannot be repressed. The affects are unknown and displaced, it is uncontrolled, it drifts (Lacan, 2004). Except in the case of anguish, which is an exception, what is unknown in the posting is its source, namely, the true representation to which it is attached. This pain disorder, therefore, refers to something that is not well known about the subject. Without this reference to the deceptive element of affect, we quickly fall into the common sense that naturally links pain to loss. Thus Lacan provides a new perspective when he indicates the central impact of this dream, the pain, which is not related to the depiction of the father who is unaware of his death; this is a false link and a lure. Basically, it is a pain that has the function of masking something about it, keeping out the subject of the "pain of existence." Therefore, we find a key sentence that illuminates the presence of this affect in the dream. According to Lacan (2013), the pain of existence when the desire is no longer present, if it was experienced by someone, it was no doubt experienced by the person who is far from being a stranger to the subject, namely his father, but what is certain, at least, is that the person knew it. The meaning of this pain, we will never know whether the person who experienced it in the real order knew or did not, but what is notable is that the subject does not know that what he is assuming is, in fact, that pain.

From this sentence, we can deduce Lacan's thesis; when facing the father in his dream, the subject is enduring pain while completely ignoring what he is taking on. Lacan substitutes the pain related to the loss or agony of the father, or even the guilt for the wishes of death, instead, with the pain of existence. It is the pain that passes through the last words of the tragedy of Oedipus, the ultimate cry of the King of Thebes, "mé phûnai"; it is better not to be born. As if in this last cry, this pain resounds in its entirety when the desire to sustain existence is no longer present; if it is to have such a destiny (the murderer of the father who committed incest was hunted and banished from Thebes), it would have been better not to have been born. This pain of existence is not that of the suffering of the illness or death of the father, but that which the subject feels in the dream, this pain is close, in the experience, to that pain of life when nothing else dwells in it except that very existence, and that everything, in the excess of suffering, tends to abolish that indelible term which is the desire to live. (Lacan, 2013).

The subject ignores the pain he is taking on. Ignorance—we know that it is an essential passion for Lacan (2013)—appears in the very formula of the dream, "he did not know," the signifiers that form this formula are caught up in their materiality rather than in their meaning. "He did not know," who is "he"? The father, according to the son, did not know his son could carry such wishes! But the "he" is also the son; he knows well that the father has suffered a great deal, but there is something he does not know, there is something he cannot see at all, from where he stands. It is that, the pain of his father, he assumes it without knowing it.

The question is why does he not realize that he is taking on the pain of his father? Lacan believes that the son places ignorance before him (his own) but he places it in the character of the father—the father does not know. It is imperative that he maintains this ignorance in order not to know that it is better not to be born (Lacan, 2013). It is imperative that the son does not know that it would be better not to be born, because if there is nothing at the end of life but the pain of existence, it is better to assume the pain on the other, who always speaks, like me, the dreamer, I continue speaking (Lacan, 2013).

This is precisely where Lacan tackles the question of image, the other, and the fantasy because the burning question is regarding the purpose of the father's appearance in the dream. Nothing else, says Lacan, than to say that he, the subject, is not dead, since he can suffer in place of the dead. This dream corresponds to the dream's quest for support, a support that the image comes to fill with its function as a veil and mask.

The evocation, according to Lacan (2013), which includes the ancient rites of the dead and the function of the necrotic that brings the "shadow" of death into the circle of incantation, allows him to pinpoint this kind of dream with the astonishing expression of the "phantom of dream," the phantom of the dreamer because the loved one is no longer there to speak the truth in his heart. The phantom in question is a structured scenario in which Lacan makes the oedipal interpretation (infant death wish) a mask of what is deeper in the structure of desire. The father-based interpretation is a myth that shapes the desire beyond the Oedipus.

Jacques-Alain Miller (2014) underlines the radical change of Seminar VI in which the Oedipus is not the only solution of desire, it is only its standard form; it is pathogenic; it does not exhaust the destiny of desire. As proposed by Lacan (2013), he does not treat this dream by the signifier but by the object because it is the field of desire that is of the relation of articulation of the subject to the object. This object is neither a natural object in the sense of the biological nor the object of knowledge which traverses all the philosophical tradition. This object that structures and causes the desire of the subject is the correlate of that "point of panic"[3] which has caused it to disappear because it can have no other sign of the subject than the sign of his abolition

(Lacan, 2013). In this lecture, the phantom—which correlates a subject with the object that structures his desire—is the suture facing the point of panic, and therefore the father is not responsible. Lacan states that the subject is barred, annulled, abolished, by the action of the signifier, finds its support in the other, which is what, for the subject speaking, defines the object as such. Thus, following the confrontation of the subject with death, the appearance of the dead father in the dream becomes this imaginary support, this veil that "makes the mortal sense fall." The imaginary fixation (petit *a* du phantom, father) made of oedipal rivalry is a shield that serves as protection for the son because, through the figure of the father as rival, it is the dreamer who wins the game; he knows something that the father does not know, through which the subject does not feel himself directly invaded, engulfed, by what opens to him of pure and simple bliss, of direct confrontation with the anguish of death. The paradox is revealed because, thanks to the shield, the dreamer remains ignorant where precisely he believes he knows what the father ignores! The shield allows him to remain ignorant of a reality that is not in the order of the oedipal castration.

This reading of the dream of the dead father, proposed by Lacan, can only be done if the question of loss is addressed beyond the Oedipus Complex. To read the father's place in the dream like a veil, a shield against reality is to make the father's place an elucidation of knowing about a loss. A wishful thinking of knowledge that serves to maintain an ignorance, which, beyond the father, concerns the confines of our existence as talking and mortal beings.

This reading of Lacan portrays a perspective that goes from the father and the oedipal castration to the castration that can be called "originary," which touches our subjection to a signifier chain that has founded us as beings of language. In this way, mourning constitutes "a savage and transitory crossing of the S(A) barred" (Adam, 2017, p. 54). The castration is not the father's loss, but the effect of language that makes us exist only in a constant and eternal metonymy that is precisely the foundation of our desire.

THIS OBJECT THAT CAUSES OUR DESIRE

In mourning, there is something that cannot be named despite the detailed and precise enumeration of what has been lost in a disappearance. Of course, in mourning, as Freud (1917) stated, it authenticates the actual loss, piece by piece, sign by sign, until exhaustion. When it is done, it is finished. But Lacan (2001) wonders what does it mean if this object was a petit *a*, an object of desire? What have we lost in the very loss of our loved one? Lacan's progress around the object will lead one to think that the question is certainly that of *what* has been lost in the loss itself but above all to be able to pinpoint what is the object that I am to be disappeared. Thus, we mourn someone only when we can say "I was his lack" (Lacan, 2001). The work of mourning will be less to enumerate the traits of the disappeared invested libidinally than to perceive the object that I was myself for the object as the cause of his desire. The assumption of the lack that I was for the disappeared, dissolves what comes back to the subject in terms of guilt: I have failed in my task. The Freudian motto that compels a second time to consume the loss of the object from a detailed recollection of what was experienced with the deceased is reinstated because, for Lacan (2004), it is indeed a matter of restoring the link, but rather with the true object of the relationship, the masked object, the object *petit a*. As in the dream of the dead father that we have just examined, the pain of loss will continue as long as the desire is suspended in the narcissistic image, that is, the foundation of love. Lacan, on the other hand, proposes a course of care that is guided by a distinction between i (*a*) and, this time, not as an object of desire (phantom of a dream in the dream of the dead father) but as a cause that has been able to cause a desire for bereavement. It is at the cost of the emergence of these irreducible and irreplaceable remains that the bereaved may return to the path of desire. As in the case of anxiety, analytical work in moments of mourning allows access to an object beyond love, to an object that is coated in love. Psychoanalysis does not propose to solve sadness or to heal loss, but to obtain by the associative work under transference, a gain of knowledge. This knowledge concerns nothing less than what, in loss and lack, has been able to cause and sustain the desire of a subject.

NOTES

1. Barthes' discourse translation from French to English by the Editor
2. Freud recalls in 1911 that the most confusing character of unconscious repressed processes, to which researchers become accustomed only by overcoming great repugnances, is that in these processes the test of reality is not valid, the reality of thought is equivalent to the external reality, the desire for its fulfillment, to the event; this flows directly from the domination of the old principle of pleasure. . . . that we never allow ourselves to be drawn into introducing the standard of reality into repressed psychic formations; the value of fantasies in symptom formation would be underestimated . . . . We have an obligation to use the currency in the country we are exploring—in our case, the neurotic currency (p. 142).
3. On the "panic point" we refer to the enlightening reading by Jacques-Alain Miller, "Une introduction à la lecture du Séminaire VI," in La Cause du désir, n°86, Navarin éditeur, 2014, pp. 62–72.

REFERENCES

Adam, R. (2017). Défaire le deuil. In *La Cause du désir*, n°96, Navarin Editeur.

Barthes, R. (2009). *Journal de deuil.* Paris: Seuil/IMEC.

Compagnon, A. (2013). Écrire le deuil. *Acta fabula, Let's Proust again! 14*(2), Retrieved from: http://www.fabula.org/acta/document7574.php.

Delecroix, V. & Forest, P. (2015). *Le deuil. Entre le chagrin et le néant*. Paris: Gallimard
Freud, S. & Breuer, J. (1895). Le Mécanisme psychique de phénomènes hystériques. In *Etudes sur l'hystérie*, Paris: PUF.
Freud, S. (1899). *L'Interprétation du rêve.* Paris, France: PUF.
Freud, S. (1911). Formulations sur les deux principes of the Cours des evenements psychiques, in *Résultats, idées, problèmes*, I, 1984, Paris: PUF.
Freud, S. (1915). Le Réfoulement, in *Métapsychologie* (1968) Paris: Gallimard.
Freud, S. (1917). Deuil et mélancolie. In *Métapsychologie*, 1968, Paris: Gallimard.
Freud, S. (1929). *Correspondance 1873-1939* (1966). Paris: Gallimard.
Lacan, J. (2001). *Le Transfert. Le Séminaire, Livre VIII.* Paris, France: Le Seuil.
Lacan, J. (2004). *L'angoisse. Le Séminaire, Livre X.* Paris, France: Le Seuil.
Lacan, J. (2013). *Le désir et son interprétation. Le Séminaire, Livre X.* France: La Martinère.
Marty, E. (2010). *Roland Barthes. La littérature et le droit à la mort.* Paris: Seuil.
Miller, J. (2014). Une introduction à la lecture du Séminaire VI, in *La Cause du désir*. Paris: Navarin éditeur
Samoyault, T. (2015) *Roland Barthes.* Paris, France: Seuil

Chapter Eight

On the Unconscious as Faith in Hidden Meaning at the Twilight of Analysis

David Hafner

Dreams are fragmented and fragmenting; we find in them the most blatant paradoxes, where impossible is nothing. Resisting realist knowledge in favor of elaborating our truer motivations, they reveal us as moral relativists, showing the idiosyncratic fundamentalism grounding our ethics. In the realm of *Nyx*, we depict ourselves as we are (Freud, 1900). Freudian psychoanalysis rests on a few fundamental discoveries. In addition to the above-mentioned nature of dreams, they include but are not limited to the notion that life is fundamentally suffering, with many humans choosing partial blindness over conflictual truth, that the human condition involves unresolvable otherness, that though language distorts thought, it rarely if ever depicts with precision a given qualia such as a dreaming experience (Gleitman & Papafragou, 2010), and that the endless variety of symptoms found in the psychoanalysis are singular responses to underlying painful conditions of humanity (Hill, 2001). "The phenomenology of the psyche is so colorful, so variegated in form and meaning, that we cannot possibly reflect all its riches in *one* mirror. Nor in our description of it can we embrace the whole, but must be content to shed light only on single parts of the total phenomena" (Jung, 1975, p. 85). Through the self-analysis of his dreams, Freud established that the unconscious constitutes an immutable aspect of human psychology. To communicate the obstinate persistence of unconscious patterns Freud encountered, he alluded to the spirits of Homer's *Odyssey*, the shades of Erebus who drink sacrificial blood and wine libations to return to the land of the living and offer wisdom (Orozco, 2011). These shades, as the unconscious in Freud's works, are indestructible; unconscious desire never exhausts itself. Perhaps unconscious representations are only perceptible when they are attached to conscious associations, the kind of associations we stumble upon in free association, drawn up through excitation or desire,[1] but in Freudian metapsychology, the unconscious remains forever active. To climb out of the cave of shadows, though tricky, is momentarily possible; but to avoid backsliding into the hall of mirrors, there's the rub. It follows that if everyone's crazy, it's because all discourses are defenses against the underlying unpleasantness, and we construct these because we perceive the true state of things to be unbearable.

In his *Traumdeutung*, Freud lists three kinds of primary processes characteristic of unconscious thought: displacement, condensation, and transposition.[2] Freud found indirect evidence for the work of condensation based on the extensive dream thoughts and associations relative to the limited dream content. Though critics might contend that dream associations after the fact have no necessary relation to dream production, that they only appear secondarily, Freud affirms their presence at the genesis of the dream through their otherwise inexplicable significance in dream interpretation.

> It is no doubt true that some trains of thought arise for the first time during the analysis. But one can convince oneself in all such cases that these new connections are only set up between thoughts which were already linked in some other way in the dream thoughts. The new connections are, as it were, loop-lines or short-circuits, made possible by the existence of other and deeper-lying connecting paths. It must be allowed that the great bulk of the thoughts which are revealed in analysis were already active during the process of forming the dream; for, after working through a string of thoughts which seem to have no connection with the formation of a dream, one suddenly comes upon one which is represented in its content and is indispensable for its interpretation, but which could not have been reached except by this particular line of approach. (Freud, 1900, pp. 280–81)

Freud thus invoked the concept of condensation as involving the possibility that an entire chain of associations might be concentrated in a single symbolic element, or as an composite image of two ideas, for example his Uncle Joseph and his colleague R. Displacement involves the relocation of an emotional value from the relevant idea, to some other dream element; the emotion might suppressed or embellished in hyperbole, or even represented through antinomy. In Freud's theory dream displacement is the principal means of encryption, of the application of the influence of internal censorship. Hence, "Dream-displacement and dream-condensation are the two governing factors to whose activity we may in essence ascribe the form assumed by dreams" (Freud, 1900, p. 308).

Transposition and deformation, along with description and depiction are discussed in the following subsection of Freud's magnum opus, where he considers the prerequisites of representability. For their potential use in dream content, relational or abstract ideas require transformation into idiomatic expressions or other symbolic forms susceptible to being represented pictorially.[3] One finds these symbolic encryptions, as well as allusional rebus and pictograms, in the ciphered dreams we analyze. And of course there is the very relevant observation that the dreaming experience cannot justifiably be reduced to the dream telling; at the very least we transcribe from dream image to storytelling, if not from language to image during the dream experience. Lacan closely follows Freud's pathbreaking notion that dreaming involves two moments or operations: "having the dream, and interpreting it." Having the dream consists in transforming symbolic elements into images, and dream interpretation involves the symmetrical transformation of dream imagery into language.

> There are two operations—having the dream, and interpreting it. Interpreting is an operation in which we intervene. But don't forget that in the majority of cases, we also intervene in the first. In an analysis, we intervene not only in that we interpret the dream of the subject—if indeed we do interpret it—but, on account of our already being, as analyst, in the life of the subject, we are already in his dream . . .
>
> iS—imagining the symbol, putting the symbolic discourse into a figurative form, namely the dream.
>
> sI—symbolizing the image, making a dream-interpretation. (Lacan, 1991, p. 152)

Of particular interest is Lacan's perception that countertransference structurally comes before the transference dream. Even when one keeps in mind that all dreams are transference dreams, insofar as they are narrated in transference, the real analyst's impingement and the impressions he leaves contribute to the dream experience of the patient, in addition to whatever transference or projection may be in play.

Bion (2005), meanwhile, further differentiates between dream meaning as the consciously wished communication and the dream's interpretation related to sensorial data, observes that the essence of a dreaming experience is in its emotional experience. In Bion's theory, the core of the dream remains an emotional experience related to sensation, it is only after meeting certain conditions of representability that the abstract emotional state takes on the form of symbolic elements.

> We have now arrived at this position: the core of the dream is not the manifest content, but the emotional experience; the sense data pertaining to this emotional experience are worked on by α-function, so that they are transformed into material suitable for unconscious waking thought, the dream-thoughts, and equally suitable for conscious submission to common sense. Freud clearly thought that this material was equally suitable for more than correlation with and by common sense, and attempted to apply to it the methods of scientific

> investigation, as if what I am calling α-elements lent themselves to that kind of procedure. This is to assume that the α-elements can be used for purposes other than simple correlation—one of the most rudimentary of scientific procedures. The manifest content, as it would be called if we were discussing dreams in Freud's terms, is a statement that these α-elements are constantly conjoined; that being so, it is in every way analogous to the selected fact, the function of which is to display the constant conjunction of elements characteristic of the paranoid-schizoid position, and some of which it has the property of showing to be related. We shall have to consider later how the manifest content of a dream (a narrativized collection of visual images) and a mathematical formulation such as an algebraic calculus can come to be fulfilling an apparently identical function when they are in every other respect so different from each other. I must point out only that the hypothesis, the word regarded as a hypothesis, and the manifest consent of a dream all share the characteristics of the selected fact in being able to bring coherence to facts previously known but not previously seen to be connected. Since the core of the problem that awaits solution is an emotional experience, we must make a distinction between this and the emotional experience that is secondary to a problem that awaits solution. We have hitherto supposed that every problem, of whatever kind, is, when reduced to its abstract basic elements, the task of finding the selected fact that harmonizes elements previously known by showing them as related to each other in a way that was not apparent before the discovery of the selected fact. This is a description that is so close to the description in Kleinian theory of the interplay between paranoid-schizoid and depressive positions that speculation must be aroused about the nature of this description, which is an example of a selected fact, and about the nature of the phenomenon to which it applies. Are there in fact elements? And if they are seen to be related to each other in a particular way, does this mean any more than that—the human mind being what it is—the individual from time to time has this experience of observing the harmonious inter-relatedness of these elements, whereas in fact there is no reason to suppose that any such relatedness exists? Elements and relatedness alike are aberrations of the observing instrument. (Bion, 2005, pp. 233–34)

Any psychoanalysis that is informed by advances in neurobiology must take into consideration that emotional states tend to be nonconscious and primary, and that cognition typically appears after the fact through rationalization. Extensive research by Antonio Damasio, Francois Ansermet, John Jost, and Leyens JP among others points in this direction. "It would follow, that the prime motivations from the point of view of the mental apparatus are changes in feeling states. While drives, needs, emotional forces arising from within the body are highly important in determining behavior from the point of view of psychological functioning they exert their effect through changes in feelings. The same is true for stimuli arising from the external world. This approach removes feelings from their conceptual tie to the instinctual drive alone and gives them a central position in psychoanalytic psychology" (Sandler, 1987, p. 296). Green's reflections on the representation of affect, consisting in a rewording of Bion's position, proffer one potential bridge between Lacan, Bion, and Sandler. "One always speaks of affect in terms of complement, of connotations. One says: there is representation and then one must not forget the affect that accompanies it. But what makes us so sure that the affect has this accompanying role? And why not think, on the contrary, *that the profound nature of the affect is to be a psychical event linked to a movement awaiting a form*?" (Green, 1999, p. 265). Formless affective/emotional tension—given form by the symbolic grammar of unconscious fantasies—are transcribed to the dream images as experienced by the dreamer; dream analysis consists in the ulterior retranslation of dream images to their symbolic subtitles, delineating if possible, the original formless tension in crescendo.

In a way, for the unanalyzed, those innocents of unfettered unconsciousness, the dream reveals destiny. If one never goes about deciphering one's dreams, leaves one's life unexamined, the dream could just as easily predict the future as tell of the past. But this is not a fixed future; or so we hope (Forrester, 1994). If one does analyze one's dreams through the artifice of a second; if one undertakes a training analysis (Freud, 1937), it is by modifying the status of the unconscious, by shifting its productions from oracular prophecies to symbolic semblance, until the grammar of unconscious fantasy appears. This occurs at the level of the dream interpretation, and also more generally at the level of psychoanalytic treatment. By saying, by giving voice to the patient's subjective history, we can modify memory, traumas, seductions, guilty transgressions, the unconscious insofar as it was historical, by using unconscious fantasy as a fulcrum. The fantasy rehistoricizes until it is revealed to be the biased creator of reality. It follows naturally that for the analysand, the dream will come to show neither the past, nor the future, but hidden desires, those amputated from his sense of being. This occurs regardless of whether or not the analysand refuses to believe in the possibility of coincidences.

A common path, though by no means the only, toward the conclusion of analysis involves:

1. the installation of faith in the analyst as knowing by one of several means,
2. the loosening of ego identifications through the accentuation of unconscious contradictions,
3. the shift of faith to the unconscious as subjective truth,
4. the enactment of the transference fantasies where the analyst incarnates the partial objects which inspire the patient's unconscious desire—often characterized by the sensation of not advancing at all,
5. the hallucinosis of said partial objects,

6. the appearance of those phrases and fragments of language imbued with personal significance and satisfaction which had remained hidden beneath the fantasy,
7. the disillusionment with the analyst who had been mistaken for the liminal object(s),
8. proud narcissistic reinvestment with accompanying euphoria,
9. a final transference of libido investment from the analytic setting to the open world with its opportunities. (Balint, 1936)

In such a process we can see ego ideals being traded for the unconscious as combinatory, then for transference fantasy, then for partial body objects, then for the meaningless inscriptions of language, and finally to the relativity of knowing this or that historization. That is to say, narration must be fictitious. In other words, narration is the externalization of unconscious fantasy which leads back to the referential delusion; to speak with others is to talk to oneself.

It is this confrontation with relativity, the hollowness—and corresponding wide open promise—of the true self, that led Lacan toward a definition of the unconscious as void of meaning. For the very last Lacan, the unconscious is nothing more than nonsense which suddenly erupts, disrupting the semblance of continuity. Once it can be reduced to sense, it has lost its otherness. It becomes simply another iteration of unconscious fantasy.[4] Lacan's last formulation of the unconscious has much in common with Matte-Blanco's infinite sets[5] and Bion's Origin.[6] "In such a theory, the end of analysis marks a satisfaction commensurate with the fall of the subject supposed to know and the hope that the unconscious, essentially, organizes itself through a syntax that would give meaning. The end of analysis implies a giving up on the search for the one true narrative; taking into account this dimension of lack [and of luck] while grasping the singular jouissance of the drive which orients us" (Hafner, 2017). In another idiom, one might say that psychoanalysis uses the illusion of transitional space, before revealing this illusory nature of the transitional and opening up onto the field of culture.

CLEAR OBJECT DREAMS

Though we typically understand dreams as unconscious formations, toward the end of analysis we come across another style of dream. Simply put, dreams at the end of analysis needn't be encrypted formations of the unconscious to be recounted in stream of consciousness; *they are the paradoxical statements of how partial objects relate*. As they become denser and more compact they reduce down to the grammar of unconscious fantasy. One dreamer sees a piece of meat in a frying pan moving and asks, "but how could it move, *c'est cuite*"? Or another, whose life was saved by analysis, dreams of walking through the valley of death with vultures circling overhead. Or another, dozing, waiting alone for the next session, sees a woman abruptly swoop down in front, grabbing his throat with her hand while commanding, "come." These dreams are not dreams for interpretation, they are transparent. They are without the anxiety of the refusal of subjective division. Candidly announcing the unconscious contradiction, they show the liminal object in all its paradoxical splendor. *Nous n'interprétons pas les oeuvres, ce sont elles qui nous interprètent.*

The presence of the partial object in the dream is not limited to dreams at the end of analysis. Often transference dreams of entering into analysis already point toward the partial object to be created. In fact this is how I understand Freud's observation of the dream navel.[7] Lacan followed Freud's lead when he theorized that the fantasy, and its object, show up when the signifying chain runs aground. At the precise moment when the words and signifiers founder, the partial objects and the subject's fantastical relation to such partial objects come to the fore (Guéguen, 1992). And so acting out and other dramatic symbolizations constitute to a great degree enactments of fundamental unconscious fantasies, even if such knowledge remains apparently closed off to both patient and analyst for some time. Consider the following dream near the beginning of analysis: "*I was in a foreign country, sightseeing. I wander among the many monuments and stone ruins and wonder how long it will take to see them all.*" The analyst interpreted, "*It's a dream about analysis. You are wondering how long you will dedicate to it.*" This interpretation is of course right; but we should not be distracted from the detail that these monuments are also anal objects.

This observation of the object as the dream navel—and it would seem clear the object fantasy functions as the navel for reality—permits us to blend dreaming and acting out. It is well known that in acting-out—so common in psychoanalytic experience when the patient's words, or the analyst's hearing do not elucidate the unconscious at play—there is a dramatic rendition of the unconscious fantasy; that the liminal object is called up where words failed. The unconscious enactment of acting out hides the traumatic object in plain sight. Think of the patient with little tolerance for the world's frustrating inertia, who whenever gripped by disappointment and anger, spits a blob of saliva. One can see this blob of spit as a proto-image of the object to be elucidated through free association. Eventually the patient would recall witnessing a childhood playground scene, in which a pre-teen boy skated up toward a girl only to spit on her hair and glide away as she screamed in disgust.

A MARVELOUS SHAPE-SHIFTING DREAM

Consider the following experience of analysis as narrated through dreams. A young man came to speak to, not necessarily with, a psychoanalyst. At the beginning, he didn't divulge any notable grievance. Instead the demand was formulated as a wish for training analysis, one to be undertaken after a bachelor's degree and a couple of years of extensive drug consumption, a mode of satisfaction that had progressively unplugged him from society, constructed a quasi-autistic bubble, and even led to an eventual diminution of language faculties. To speak had become difficult. In the absence of an explicit complaining symptom, the question of differential diagnosis was not evident. In this early period of therapy, he spoke a great deal of his mother, less of his father, and wasn't chasing after either sex. The first session, though scheduled, was missed.[8] One of the patient's molars had became infected a second time just the weekend before, and procrastinating as always, he wrote the day before to announce his absence; he would be visiting the dentist instead. The analyst responded imperially convoking the patient to another appointment. The second session, the first meeting, took place the day after the original. With the patient taciturn, averting his eyes, and speaking lethargically, the analyst decided to be direct, hoping to awaken something. "*Do you like boys or girls, are you a man or a woman, and why are you here?*" The patient responded, *"I like girls, I have a penis so logically I must be a man, and I am both bored and boring."* The first declaration of object choice was simple enough. The question of identity however shows itself to be more complicated; just as the symptom complaint reveals both active and passive roles. *Bore* alludes to the multiple facets of the partial object already announcing itself in the patient's speech. The analyst concentrated on a symptom of hypersomnolence and established a daily rhythm of sessions, five times a week.

He carries his great aunt's name Andromeda, in the form of the matronymic second name, Andre.[9] The general thematic narrative of the persecuted maiden resonates with relational symptoms of an initial presentation of incompetence followed by excellence, an interest in accomplishing tasks of the highest, impossible difficulty, and the tendency to await in silence until the other beckons.[10]

The preliminary interviews lasted for over a year, during this period, the young man manifested no inclination toward using the couch. On occasion he would miss one or two sessions, one or two weeks of sessions. He always paid for the missed sessions, a small price to remain in the clouds. Confronted with a patient with little to no interest in dialogue, you resort to silence and cunning. Once, after having been absent for a week or two, he comes back. Now, he has the beginnings of a beard, and this catches your eye since before he always shaved. He doesn't mention this. Does it have to do with sexual identity, modes of satisfaction, a sign of separation from the mother? Continuing the strategy of silence, you scratch your five o'clock shadow, flagrantly punctuating the patient's body without words.

During the first year of analysis, little apparent progress was made, the symptoms of hypersomnia, boredom, and listlessness continued unabated. The patient missed sessions regularly, and generally had little else to say than complain of his boredom. This unruffled hibernation continued for so long that the analyst eventually interpreted—through an act of nomination—calling the patient, *he who pretends to sleep*. This interpretation points toward the shared nature of the patient's sleeping through sessions, or in the waiting room, and his childhood tendency to lie in bed and pretend to be asleep when his parents came home late from work.

Consider the initial transference dream, nearly an ode to Freud's ideas of psychoanalysis as archaeology. "*In a foreign country, sightseeing. I wander among the many monuments and wonder how long it will take to see them all.*" In this early transference dream—of course all dreams in analysis are transference dreams insofar as they are transference enactments to and for the analyst—but here we find the Dramatis Personæ of the analysis: the dreamer, sight and seeing, foreignness, and the anal monument. Noteworthy is the absence of a second human figure.

DREAM OF A MINOTAUR'S LABYRINTH

After a year and a half of face-to-face sessions he finally asks you "*when will I be able to lie*[11] *down on the divan?*" You promptly end the session, saying next time. Sometime after, there is a nightmare of a Minotaur's labyrinth. He runs up and down winding subterranean stairs and hallways, fleeing a horned, cloven-footed being he names the demon of knowledge. It goes without saying that the Minotaur in the dream is part of the patient's mind, though we should admit this signifier does lie printed on the spine of a book facing the divan, so it is not without arbitrary countertransferential intrusion. The subterranean hallways could be understood as metaphors for entrails. This would permit understanding the horned Minotaur as a phallic symbol referencing sodomy, or a mortal chase threatening annihilation. In this second moment of analysis, there are many dreams of hordes, zombies climbing up out of the earth, plagues, death's representatives of all kinds, and the attempt to flee houses through underground passageways. The monuments are no longer the lifeless stones of another time, but castaway relics returning to undead life, much like the thirsty Homeric shades, those boundlessly expanding minions of Thanatos. These dreams offer the inverse punishment for early criminal fantasies, when after meandering through the dark convoluted passageways of the parents' workplace, the dreamer would install himself in the balcony and imagine fierce firefights.

CHAUTIGO

When after half a year, the patient began speaking French, the analyst marked this minimal sign of life with a "*Soudain tu parles français!*" and dream-play took on a multilingual nature. Dreaming that his lover has found the ideal apartment for the two of them, he narrates finding a "rundown looking brick building, but inside it is beautiful and spacious. Plus it is cheap. The address is on rue *chautigo*." The overwriting of words found in the nonsensical *chautigo* spawns a sort of condensation of three tongues. This neologism fits into the classic diachronic enunciation of language; it does not have the timelessness of some hallucinatory phenomena. A fairly clear demonstration of the replacement of one signifier with another in the signifying chain; one phoneme chosen from a list of alternate synchronous elements, to replace the initially expected syllable. Instead of con-tigo, one finds show, that which must always involve the gaze. Hidden next to the eye-catching *chautigo* are the less conspicuous cheap, looking, and two. *Cheap* comments on the paternal family's miserliness, their refusal to discard anything and the patient's willful disregard for questions of money. *Looking* points toward scopic satisfaction at play in the oedipal drama. Finally, as opposed to the inaugural transference dream, the dream involves more than one. The analyst treats these libidinally charged ideas through silent interpretation or even discrete psychodrama.

"Plus it was cheap" alludes to a discursive, broken-record effect which took place in this analysis. For a long moment, he always spoke, inexorably, of the question of money. He discussed having it, not having it, working for it, the slavery and prostitution of any employment, of saving, of squandering. Speech often flowed in contradictory circles around this insistent word, "money." One day while he speaks yet again of money, you take out a euro and let it fall loudly on your desk, you flip it in the air and hear it ring, and perhaps you spin it on your desk. Then you take out a banknote and begin to crinkle and crumple it. One after the other, you use the real objects to produce their characteristic rustle and ring, wordlessly interpreting his insistence on money. Suddenly a truth effect, he begins laughing; he stops speaking about money.

FATHER

The analysis advances in cycles, beginning again numerous times, before falling by the wayside, only to be taken up again; symptoms of inertia and a tendency to ignore what is known lead to a path of two steps forward one step back. As though the patient were procrastinating, making the analyst wait for the gift of meaningful speech, just as the child's bowels move with a regular rhythm. Each of these new hibernations and subsequent awakenings entails the beginning of a new phase of analysis. And yet, it is not a continuous progression without backsliding, he is always periodically missing sessions. A couple of years into the analysis, after having waited in the waiting room for hours, he left without seeing his analyst. He often did this frequently. Then, after the weekend, he returned to the consulting room with the following dream: "*I am in my analyst's waiting room; he enters and asks us who really needs a session today since he doesn't have much time. I say everything is going fairly well. Then it is nighttime and I am in his apartment, which seems more like a museum. He has a cello, a chess table, a poker table; all are interests that I share with him. He puts his hand on my shoulder and I feel as though I am his son.*"

The dream of shared possessions with the analyst is new and seemingly pertains to identification at the level of a doppelgänger, of semblance. Yet the question of time could be read as maliciousness directed toward the analyst, which would resonate with the imaginary identification through possessions. "*Once he is gone I will inherit.*" Though this reading does not take into account the rare fleeting dreams of identification with a young girl which would imply a more primal feminine identity and the father as being a forbidden sexual object. This preconscious feminine identification occurs at imaginary and symbolic levels. As a young child, the patient would role play the archetypal *demoiselle en détresse*, incarnating an iteration sharing his namesake. Jung and Lacan both theorize the subject's destiny as always exceeding, preexisting the person. The subject's destiny is supraindividual. One is subject to, we might even write subjugated by archetypal and symbolic constellations in existence prior to our conception.

> We have already discovered one way in which Jung manages nonetheless to accomplish such an alignment with postmodernism. This is through his spontaneous recourse to the phenomenology of the image. Another aspect of this phenomenological turn lies in his insistence that we must proceed in psychology from the outside in—and not from the inside out . . . We are reminded here of Husserl's shibboleth for phenomenological method: "To the things themselves!"—not to mention Heidegger's claim that human beings possess an essential being "outside" themselves. And we are put in mind as well of Lévi-Strauss's idea that the elementary structures of kinship exist outside—independently of voluntary actions of—the members of a given social grouping: *their objectivity is as "impersonal" (in Jung's term) as primordial images themselves. The structures of structuralism and the images of analytical psychology alike precede and prestructure the human persons who exist in their ambience and by their means*. The "outside" of such structures and such images is a very different outside from that which figures into early modern notions of sensory

> experience and its imitation in iconic signs. It belongs to a world or cosmos that tis the source of symbols, just as it is the origin of the psyche itself-indeed, of the objective psyche as Jung came to call it. To think in this post-modernist direction is not to eliminate the significance of the human subject and its nucleus, the ego. Jung even declares that "psyche is the greatest of all cosmic wonders and the *sina qua non* of the world as object," and that "the psyche is the world's pivot: not only is it the great condition for the existence of a world at all, it is also an intervention in the existing natural order, and no one can say with certainty where this intervention will finally end." To say this is not to return to a Romantic inflation of self; it is to remain resolutely postmodernist—but now with a final twist. The twist, familiar to Jungians, is that the objective psyche is a the same time a collective psyche, at once prepersonal and pluripersonal (or more exactly, omnipersonal). What is perhaps less familiar is that the operative premise of structural linguistics—a premise to which not only Lévi-Strauss but Jakobson, Barthes, Merleau-Ponty and Derrida [here one could also include Wittgenstein and Lacan; indeed their absence eludes understanding] also subscribe—is equally collective in character. (Casey, 2017, pp. 319–22)

MOTHER

In dreams, the figure of the woman typically appears as the white goddess with her many names: the goddess of the new moon, the night mare, *la belle dame sans merci.* As his time in treatment advances, he ceases dreaming of underground tunnels and hordes of undead and begins to dream instead of *Achlys*. He dreams of swimming beneath the surface of a frozen lake. In the distance a woman's corpse drifts in underwater currents like flotsam. As he approaches she precipitously turns her face toward him with a death stare, and he awakens from this nightmare in skittish fright. Other dreams of persecutory women follow, the nightmare invariably concerns the sudden appearance of terrifying presence, followed by paralytic inhibition upon waking, he doesn't move until his heart slows. The dream reveals two moments of the gaze, initially he stares fixedly at the floating corpse, as though shocked yet unable to avert his eyes; until suddenly she gazes back, catching him in her sight. The stillness transfers from the flotsam to the dreamer as he wakes paralyzed with fear. In this stage of analysis, he begins to observe the frequency with which he uses the signifier, "which," a word rich in homonyms and not without evoking the Shakespeare's Weird Sisters.

MARBLE

He dreams of a young boy asking his mother why he has a penis. She tells him it is so he can fly. He is doubtful. She steps up to an open window and the two float out with three balloons suspending them during their descent.

He asks why they are going down. She tells him he can fly as high as he wants. They begin to near the ground and the balloons pop. They fall onto a lawn. She touches her thigh and tells him she has a penis too. The dream stops.

Though the dream explicitly references the phallic mother, the latent dream content appears the next day as an abrupt recollection. The following day, arriving at the analyst's residence, he goes directly to the toilet before even passing through the waiting room. At this point he realizes that he often uses the doctor's toilet to relieve himself of the anal object, often prior to the session, and sometimes afterward, though if this ritual occurs afterward he is accompanied by anxiety. Suddenly an ancient memory returns. The baby boy is alone, taking a bath in his parents' bathroom. Playing in the water with a marble, he rubs it along his anus. The marble enters and in a moment of distressed anguish, he dreads the question what will he do!? He excretes the marble, relief. Then he sees, with surprise, feces coat the marble. He no longer plays with marbles.[12]

The partial object and the fixating memory have abruptly become conscious, but though the patient knows about this object, this memory, he does not yet know it truly; there has been no hallucinosis.

MOTHER ON THE STAIRS

As treatment continues, the patient continues relocating himself in relation to the mother. Another mother dream follows, though now there are two feminine figures, and the persecutory terror transforms into foreign guilt. In a bathroom discussing something he found with another, something that resembles a wasp [a phallic symbol linked to early dreams of poisonous stings as metaphors for insemination], for lack of a better memory. He tries to convince the other they should help in some way, but the other emphatically counsels against such action reminding him, "doesn't he know how vicious these things are, and what it will do if it catches them?" He flees and leaves the unlucky hunted to his own measures.

Walking down his street, he sees others setting up a trap on the far side. He knows there will be repercussions but does nothing to stop them. They flip a boat, using a pulley-system, onto some pedestrian. He turns up the stairs to his parent's house, wanting nothing to do with them.

At the top of the stairs waits a lady, perhaps a ghost? She asks if he knows of the betrayal of trust and the mistreatment of those coming from south of the border. He asserts that he had nothing to do with it. She replies, but you know who did. Yes, he answers, adding, but please don't make me tell you. She invites him to finish climbing the stone stairs and sit facing her.She begins to speak but then pauses to tell him that he must, "tell her to go away," someone else has climbed the stairs and arrived since they started talking. He turns to see his mother. He tells her to go away; she stays immobile. He shouts more emphatically, she turns back down the stairs.

Now he returns again and sees the woman with whom he's been speaking resembles his mother. They begin to talk again. At this point alarm wakes him.

A set of specific elements gradually become clear in the mist of absolute forgetfulness. One can see the scopic object, and its proximity to Medusean dread, to paralyzing shame. The anal object also reveals itself, both in the form of parasitic life which relates to anal excretion and in the spherical shape of *agalma* as translucent marble.

The signifier "ant" is worth our time do to its homophony with the "aunt" of the patient's namesake. On occasion, ants appear in patient's perceptual field in hallucinatory fashion. Even when the natural object exists in the shared perceptual reality, he regularly cannot resolve the doubt of whether the insect exists for everyone or whether it is a visual hallucination. For example, imagine the frustrated patient observing an endless stream of ants flowing from the Mediterranean garden outside through an air conditioning unit into his living room. He begins spraying them with pesticide, but when others complain about toxicity, he resorts to crushing them one by one with such determination that his roommates descend the stairs to see what is the matter. Momentarily distracted by her query, when he looks back to the ant cemetery to explain his ferocious behavior, he sees an ant, much larger than geometry and perspective should permit, climbing up his pants. He shakes it off, stunned by the odd experience. The roommate asks what's wrong, ignoring the hallucination, he complains about house space being insufficiently divided between inside and outside; the ants won't stay outside. We would be remiss not to add that this hallucinatory moment occurs during a house visit by another of his aunts.

Upon recounting associations to this hallucinatory experience, as though following free association chains of dream thoughts, the patient recalls the question, "*What, you got ants in your pants?!*" A quote heard in his father's voice. His father would often say this phrase when asking about the young patient's constant movement. The complaint of "ants in the pants" seems to have been directed against disturbing the other's tranquility, or at least the façade of tranquility found in unswerving daily repetition.

FAMILY OF FOUR

Upon waking the dreamer writes:

> *The four of my family are at some theater, sitting in the audience. As she so often does in real life, my mother offers me an article to read. The article*

discusses violence in the Middle East, something about refugees being victimized. When I got to the last paragraph, the author makes a joke about the potential idea of offering an incognito interview from some blacked-out room working from his computer and smartphone, as being a LacOedipian fantasy dream. I can't stop laughing. It's an obvious jab at the analyst who is always typing on his computer during the sessions.[13] *The plot of whatever we are watching involves violent people, hitmen perhaps in a murderous game of cat and mouse. One wishes to leave the city, and starts placing automatic weapons in a backpack. Upon seeing a bulletless gun left by another, he interprets it as saying the escape plan is a trap; to be a continuous refugee, escaping from nation culture and home, is to trap oneself in no man's land, to suffer wanderlust in endless deserts.*

Of particular importance seems to be the proximity, the juxtaposition of the analyst and the mother in the dream, with the mother sharing articles to be read which allude to the analyst. It would seem the transference begins to condense more and more upon a pre-oedipal maternal imago.

Moreover, it points to a defensive strategy of the patient, that of voiding the mind and presenting himself incognito, as though in this way he would escape the cat and mouse games humans play. He has mentioned that since a young age, he spontaneously perceives Pollockesque amorphous patterns on tiles and surfaces as portraying skulls, malevolent armored beings, and a hellish, yawning maw. He writes of his fear of presenting himself lest they eat his thoughts, his brain. The voidless interviewee can always shapeshift, adapting to mollify the others' hunger.[14] Nonetheless the dream announces the pointlessness of such a hermetic solution, the dreamer knows flight to the desert oases of narcissism offers nothing but a trap.

TOPOLOGY

Having begun to elaborate the partial objects in play, the voracious mouth, the anal monument, the maternal phallus, as well as some externally invested objects giving rise to identity as son, the dream analysis brings about a revelation in the patients perception of his family structure. Once again he dreams of speaking to a frightful woman, though this time it is a dream of origins.

Speaking with a woman, she asks if he knows the form of the universe. The conversation continues with her hinting that the form has changed in the past; does he remember when, she asks? He say it happened with the big bang; creation was the change, right? The other says no, that it changed more recently. "*L'univers change à la naissance de la sœŋk.*"[15] The universe changes at the birth of the five.

At that very moment he awakes, this instant of polyphony involves a kind of key signifier, a master keystone. At once he hears "five," "sun," and "son." As though a gong were sounded, his body is overrun with fright, with dread that accompanies the declaration. He jabbers and flounders; he hides himself behind his closed eyes so as not to see.

As the lingering dread dissipates, he begins to understand. He was born when his brother was five years old. The universe changes at the age of five when the second son is born. The universe does not only symbolically determines the unborn, the arrival of the newborn reforms the symbolic universe. A radical sense of lightness of being. Subjective history is not simply weathered, one actively contributes to it. Here we should add that though the patient never spoke openly of a sister, it not even being clear he had conscious knowledge of a female sibling, that we have reason to know his mother had a miscarriage; between the births of two brothers, the mother lost a daughter to spontaneous abortion. Had the sunken sister lived there would have been five in the family.

A dream of the real, which balances itself on the equivocity, on the polyphony of language. It is no longer the synchronic replacement, a deterministic universe in which one element may replace another, but the simultaneous superpositioning of various elements. The dream shifts the subject from a Laplacean universe to an Einsteinian one. As in previous dreams, the bearer of horror is a woman.

BOUCHONNÉE

If we can say the subject grappling with psychotic thought processes presents his unconscious as the wide open sky, it's quite simply because we receive his language productions as continually condensed and displaced. This would seem to be where the idea of schizographie comes from. We are born into a world whose sociocultural coordinates anticipate us, which often relates directly to the neurotic's individual myth. Such individual myths tend to relate to the fantasy life of the individual, to his unconscious fantasies and idiosyncratic drives. These unconscious fantasies, insofar as they remain unconscious, protect the individual from existing in what Lacan refers to as "continuous discourse"; for this reason the early Lacan of 1955 mentions, "It is a function of the ego that we do not have to perpetually listen to this articulation that organizes our actions like spoken actions."[16] Few hellscapes could be more horrific than the obligation to continually resignify every shift in the perceptual field by consciously cogitating it through language. Shortly after, Lacan points out that this difference between continual exposure to the verbalization of reality and the relative sanctuary offered by the contact barrier is the very postulate of the Freudian unconscious.

One day while speaking of clogged toilets and considering the stagnation of the therapeutic process, describing his motion as something that drifts endlessly in circles, which is not without convoking the mental image of the flushing toilet, the word *bouchonnée* makes itself heard. This lapsus, takes the place of bouché: from blocked, obstructed and overcast, to spoiled wine. This lapsus does not lead to a clear double entendre, and confronted with this abrupt shattering of meaning, the patient falls silent. Upon later reflection, it seems instead to produce an endless flight of homophonic variations on one subject. It provokes a sort of associational rampancy: *bouche aux nez, la bouffe, naysayer, slayer, la boue chaud ey, Booo! Shh! Nay!* Bouchonnée with its associative links to the mouth, ambrosial wine, orality, silence, and spoiled wine point toward the death drives' silent inertia, the internal scourge, and the speaking body's enclosing in on itself.

There is the real noise, which is not the same thing as the signifier, and then through a kind of decadence of hypothetical language function, the complete lexicon of interchangeable signifiers appears. One might argue our patient has already left the moment of the unconscious once he begins to attempt to justify his lapsus through reason. This is the primary message of later Lacan. And yet, one can observe how this expansive field of body phenomena flow outward from this focal point. *Bouchonnée* is not necessarily the name of this unconscious node, but it does appear as a representative, a spokesperson for this intersection. Eigen, following Winnicott's lead, describes the potential non-communication between language and unconscious in his usual elegant prose.

> Some struggle to get into or out of words. The idea of putting feelings into words is an odd locution. How does one do that? Can you picture it? Sometimes I think of drawing feelings from a well and pouring them, a little at a time, into buckets of words. Often we do the reverse. We try to fill the well with words. Instead of drawing from a deep and bottomless well, we pour words into it. We lower word buckets down, hoping to catch something, often coming up with more words. Some of these words are juicy enough, some dry. But we fear that what we pull up is what we put in, missing living water. (Eigen, 2009)

COME AND SEE

With regard to the dream mentioned at the beginning of the chapter, this dream appears late in analysis, and appears less as a classic dream with wish fulfillment distortion and more like a straightforward manifestation of unconscious fantasy. Dozing in the waiting room between sessions, after a first session in which it felt impossible to say anything worthwhile, he is seized by the following dream. A woman abruptly swoops down in front of him, she grabs his throat with her hand and commands, "*Come!*" He awakes immediately, the analyst opens the door and they goes to his next session of analysis.

Eureka. Suddenly speaking is easy. He speaks of his choice of silence. Youthful memories of his mother washing his foul mouth with soap, of his father rebuking him for shouting of shameful body functions, of a friend's parent demanding silence in carpool. Silence has become a character trait, as though one could only appreciate music in silence. This character trait has condensed with procrastination and superficial deference, narcissistic traits molded to gain mobility and confidence while maintaining absolute distance. Crossing the street, he never thinks twice of giving the right of way to the other, even after the other has offered him passage. But if you overrun or shatter his deference, he is suddenly harried. Losing his ritual dance which locates him in relation to the others. What is personality, character, if not our unconscious patterns?

ON SILENT INTERPRETATION

"Let there be light." This is how Lacan begins one of the final sessions of his 1980 seminar *Dissolution*, where he defines speech as a constraint, a shackle. "What the unconscious demonstrates above all is that *speech is obscurantist*" (Lacan, 1980). The very last Lacan finds himself very far from the proverb, the truth will set you free. The words themselves are obscurantist insofar as they offer no reliable link between sonority, orthography, and signification, insofar as any displacement of the speech's quilting point radically changes discursive meaning, reordering the acoustic chain into new words; since none of them, neither sonority, nor spelling, nor meaning belong to any complete or consistent system. Evidently, this is equally the case when referring to the analyst's speech. As always, the poet is a trailblazer.

Faced with the verb's impotence upon the obstinate real of the symptom, sometimes the analyst has no choice but silence.

In the series of silent interpretations, we could include the famous example of Lacan and Susanne Hommel, where Lacan wordlessly interpreted the homophonic equivocity of Susanne's speech. Though instead of employing the object, he placed the metaphor on the analysand's body. Susanne Hommel narrates the scene in a recent documentary, *Rendez-vous chez Lacan*. It took place in 1974, contemporaneous with Lacan's seminars *Les non-dupes errent* & *RSI*.

> I was born in Germany, in 1938. So I lived through the war years, with all the horrors and anguish, hunger after the war, the lies. That's why I always wanted to leave Germany. At one of my first sessions, I asked Lacan if I would ever be cured of this suffering. Saying it, I knew the answer. I'd had some sort of idea that analysis might remove the pain. Something in his look made me understand, "no that's something you'll cope with all your life." One day, in a session, I was talking about a dream I'd had. And I said, "I wake up every

> morning at 5 o'clock. At 5 o'clock, the Gestapo used to come get the Jews in their homes." Lacan lept up from his chair and came to me. He gently stroked my cheek. I understood "*geste à peau*"—skin gesture. He'd changed *Gestapo* into *geste à peau*. Such a tender gesture; it was extremely tender. That surprise did not diminish the pain, but it did transform it. Forty years later when I tell you about this gesture, I still have it on my cheek. It's a gesture that was an appeal to humanity. (Miller, 2011)

Lacan's interpretation resembles the upraised hand of Leonardo's *St. John the Baptist*, an index finger indicating the truth beyond the present, pointing toward a beyond representation. Yet the finger does not designate a truth of meaning, but the real of equivocity. This interpretation playing on equivocity alludes to the object and its concomitant fantasy hidden in plain sight in the ambiguity of language. This wordless interpretation, and yet not an interpretation outside of language, avoids enunciation by approaching the letter through a non-verbal sign. *These three examples differ despite their shared aphonia:* the first concerns an aspect of the analysand's presentation of which he never speaks (scratching 5 o'clock shadow), what has been scotomized from his discourse. The second draws the analysand's attention to an object (flipping coins and crumpling dollar bills) of preconscious fantasy by means of the object representative of the imagino-symbolic reality. In the third, the analyst inscribes equivocity onto the body of the analysand with a burst of nonsense. All are attempts to act directly on the phonological ambiguity without compromising the analyst's silence, but what they operate on could not be more different: identifications, objects of fantasy, the body. Miller describes the need to move from the restitution of historical meaning to the effects of meaning of the symbolic combinatory to the indexing of unrelated master signifiers where sometimes the interpretation becomes dulled in its intervention. Interpretation in reverse as interpretation of a post-interpretative age. It was about time. Interpretation, insofar as it is not aimed at meaning, has been necessary since the decade of resistance, that is to say the crisis of the analytic movement of the twenties.

The end of analysis, if it aims for the pass advocated by Lacanian schools, perseveres toward a maximal condensation of fantasy. Such a direction of treatment produces equivocal formulations, often consisting of nonsensical neologisms. Addressing the end of analysis, Lacan wrote first of identification with the symptom, then on traversing the fantasy. Both of these ideals of an end to analysis are interpretations of Freud's *Wo es war soll Ich warden.*[17] Concerning the end of the analysis and *Wo es war*, Éric Laurent affirms, "identification of a mode of enjoying is not an identification with a mode of enjoying." Naturally the patient enjoys his fantasy, or more exactly, fantasy functions as an apparatus for transforming jouissance into pleasure, into pathos. Successful analysis would imply the possibility of isolating this fantastical modality of enjoying; though not necessarily blindly identifying with it without perspective. The last period of the analysis highlights a transition from the effects of truths and meanings, to a proliferation of equivocation and lapses. The return to a real unconscious happens after a transmutation of the subject of the unconscious by the pivot of the transferential unconscious. But is equivocation, although it is the driving force of the psychoanalytic transmutation, the goal in itself of the end of the analysis? I'm not so sure. It seems to me that even if at the end of the analysis it is a question of crossing the fantasy, from a neologization of the singular language of the analysand to this limit point, as Miller elaborated it in the early eighties, that it is not at all toward equivocity that one strives at the end of analysis, but rather towards the unspeakable. It is said, since the word is the only weapon that the analyst has and the analysand both. But we must not be mistaken in believing that the subjective neologism elaborated in the past constitutes the last true truth of the subject. There is still some transference, formations of the unconscious, lapses. In the last period of his teaching, Lacan faces up to a progressive disillusionment with the word, hence the silent interpretations. Even if equivocity remained fundamental in his seminar *Encore* and the concurrent *L'étourdit*, Lacan already confided that equivocity and *lalangue* ran up against the impotence of modifying the *sinthome*. Perhaps even more stunning, one can see that conceptualizing the end of analysis through the discourse of the analyst instead of the master discourse implies a certain disentanglement from the subject supposed to know. The reverse of the Kierkegaardian *Vertrauensvorschuss*, in the psychoanalytic leap, it's a case of ridding oneself of the presumption that a supposedly knowledgeable other knows one's deepest truth. At the end, the analsyand does without analytic sessions in order to transmit what he knows, hoping it will pass. There is no guarantee whatsoever the analysand would be able to say what he must, nor that the analyst will be able to hear it. This deception, this disillusionment in the Other who would have been the guarantee of knowledge marks the exit from a Lacanian analysis. The end of Lacan's analysis with Loewenstein passed through stages of imaginary competition, deception, and finally unbeing.

> I think of the kind of faith which carries me now beyond all that, which almost makes me forget it; yes, it is composed of a capacity for forgetting which is a function of that precious audience of those who followed me—who would never have forgotten me, even if I had been alone in walking out—of what I am going to write for Rome, my report on the function of language in analysis, of the fact that I know better and better what is mine to say about an experience which I have only these last years been able to recognize and soley thereby truly to master.
>
> I hope to see you in London. Whatever happens, rest assured that you will encounter there a man more convinced of his duties and his destiny. Lagache

> will bring the file on the affair there: and you will see from it that it was not we who were engaging in the divisiveness.
> These pages were not written in order to add to that file—but in order to transmit to you, in the frank tone that our particular relationship allows us, the kind of living testimony without which a history cannot be written. No objectivity can be achieved in human matters without that subjective basis.
> That is why I am authorizing you to make use of it with whomever you believe capable of understanding it—and specifically Heinz Hartmann, to whom, moreover, I shall send a message.
> You know Loew, that if you come to France before or after the Congress, my wife and I will be happy if you come with your wife for the visit at our country house to which you have long been invited. I could tell you much more about what we are expecting from the future of our work. We have given ourselves over to it in a manner sufficiently wholehearted to find ourselves, in our relations with you, to be very tardy indeed.
> Rest assured, though, that our loyalty to your person remains unchanged. (Lacan, 1953, pp.64–65)

For Lacan, Loewenstein fell from his prior elevation, where he had possessed the power to reply to Lacan's demand for privileged knowledge, to that of an equal, a dear colleague, warmly awaited, but no longer the necessary fulcrum for Lacan's faith in his unconscious desire and his destiny. We find the words with which Freud thanks Fliess and describes his exit from analysis equally adequate. "I rejoice once again that eleven years ago I already realized that it was necessary for me to love you in order to enrich my life" (Freud, 1898).

This is the subtle finesse of psychoanalysis; the beauty of psychoanalysis resides in its ruse, by beginning with the master discourse, where the patient places himself as a slave before the omniscient doctor, the analytic discourse tricks him, luring him toward his own liberty. From a slave of the transference localizing knowledge in another master, the analysand becomes slave to his unconscious, to himself and no one else.

Over the course of this analysis there has been a temporal condensation of dreams. Toward the beginning of analysis the dreams were historical, novels of dream images, structured by the diachronic rules of language. Whereas at the end of analysis the dreams become more and more instantaneous, accenting the synchrony of thought. These instantaneous dreams accentuate the double-faced nature of the fantasy, indicating the object and its fantasy hidden in equivocity. Yet though the proliferous unconscious formations have been accentuated into these fundamental fantasies, have been moved about, the narcissistic foundation of his character remains as it was. I would wish to end this text with one of his poems:

Her name would have been,
Had her carriage not missed its path
By an abrupt detour
to its arrival.

An abandoned house,
Clinging to steep mountain face,
In tumultuous conversation.

O carpool passenger
Staring out the window,
Let's play a game.
Joyful child,
Who can be quiet for longer?

Is there nothing,
more than endless
halls of mirrors?
But as another said,
Mirrors in mirrors,
Hide secrets,
Always.

NOTES

1. "This struggle between the doctor and the patient, between intellect and instinctual life, between understanding and seeking to act, is played out almost exclusively in the phenomena of transference. It is on that field that the victory must be won—the victory whose expression is the permanent cure of the neurosis. It cannot be disputed that controlling the phenomena of transference presents the psycho-analyst with the greatest difficulties. But it should not be forgotten that it is precisely they that do us the inestimable service of making the patient's hidden and forgotten erotic impulses immediate and manifest. For when all is said and done, it is impossible *to* destroy anyone *in absentia* or *in effigie*" (Freud 1912, pp. 108).

2. "As is well known, the general framework of these rules of transformation is constituted by the processes of condensation (*Verdichtung*) and displacement (*Verschiebung*). On the other hand, transformations and their rules are to be ascribed to the field of activity of representation, which constitutes the foundation of subjective experience of dreams; in this way transformations can all be seen as leading back to the semantic variations on the German terms centered on the root word *Stellung* (hence *Darstellung* [presentation, exposition, description], *Vorstellung* [representation, depiction], *Entstellung* [deformation, transposition], etc.) and are subordinated to their verbal translatability—if it is true, and we take it to be so, that the foundation of language is constituted by verbal representations" (Corrao, F. (1994). "Narrative Transformations." Ed. Ammaniti, M. & Stern, M. In: Psychoanalysis and Development: Representations and Narratives. NYU Press.

3. "In the dreamwork a psychical force is operating which on the one hand strips the elements which have a high psychical value of their intensity, and on the other hand, by means of overdetermination, creates from elements of low psychical value new values, which afterwards find their way into the dream-content. If that is so, a transference and displacement of psychical intensities occurs in the process of dream-formation, and it is as a result of these that the difference between the text of the dream-content and that of the dream-thoughts comes about. [. . .] She was at the Opera. A Wagner opera was being performed. There were tables set out in the stalls, at which people were eating and drinking. In the middle of the stalls there was a high tower, which had a platform on top of it surrounded by an iron railing. High up at the top was the conductor, who had the features of Hans Richter. He kept running round the railing, and was perspiring violently; and from that position he was conducting the orchestra which was grouped about the base of the tower. I decided to take the tower in the stalls metaphorically. It

then emerged that the man whom she had wanted to see in Hans Richter's place towered high above the other members of the orchestra. [. . .] The foregoing discussion has led us at last to the discovery of a third factor [the two previous ones being condensation and displacement] whose share in the transformation of the dream-thoughts into the dream-content is not to be underrated: namely, considerations of representability in the peculiar psychical material of which dreams make use—for the most part, that is, representability in visual images" (Freud, 1900, p. 324, 356).

4. This is of course not Miller's opinion, as he places the unconscious in the realm of the collective and locates the subject's singularity in his sinthome.

5. "The symmetrical aspect of the bi-logical structures of our unconscious operates or thinks in a space of a higher number of dimensions than that of our perceptions and conscious thinking. This is the reason why we cannot be aware of it or, put in another way, this is the reason why it is unconscious for us; our lower-dimensional thinking cannot grasp it, just as a painted tray cannot be a recipient for real apples" (Matte-Blanco, 1988, p. 74).

6. "Psychoanalysis itself is just a stripe on the coat of the tiger. Ultimately, it may meet the Tiger—The Thing Itself, O" (Bion, 1990, p. 112).

7. There is often a passage in even the most thoroughly interpreted dream which has to be left obscure; this is because we become aware during the work of interpretation that at that point there is a tangle of dream-thoughts which cannot be unraveled and which moreover adds nothing to our knowledge of the content of the dream. This is the dream's navel, the spot where it reaches down into the unknown" (Freud, 1900), Insofar as we sometimes awaken from nightmares so we may continue sleeping, it follows that one's experience of waking life also contains a tangled obscure point, from which the experience of reality might unravel, reality's navel.

8. The first transference dream announces a voyage toward self-knowledge before the patient ever set foot in France. The dreamer uses a long strand of black hair to pass through a turnstile in an airport, as though the hair was a passport. During this dream some French words appear visually, as though written or *engraved*. This is this patient's first French dream, announcing the quest.

9. As the patient's identity has been disguised, and I have included no intimate details in this vignette, I am confident beyond any doubt that no one but the patient could recognize this history. Moreover, I wish to add that this description is not only inadequate, it leaves out significant details and so is not even precise. I am relying on it simply to illustrate a point.

10. At the bottom of all neurotic structures, we find a fundamental inconsistency of identification; though Freud initially linked hysteria—where ego identification with straw men appears to permit interrogating the essence of femininity—with bisexuality, following in Freud's footsteps, we consider this fundamental identificatory ambiguity as essential in all neuroses. The subject hesitates between multiple identity claims which are used as master signifiers in the founding act of identification, at the cost of using them in a nonsensical manner. The Lacan of Lituraterre this phenomena of the written body through the metaphor of master signifiers that cut into the opaque material of language and sense as a torrential rainfall carving gulleys and valleys into the earth.

11. One hears the underlying deceitfulness.

12. Early memory of marble insertion, momentary anxiety, excretion of marble covered in feces. Other memory of finding isolated roundworms in feces, before one day excreting a clump of them. An early fixation of anal jouissance. This must have occurred during early childhood, though historical reconstruction does lead to precise dates. Though the combination of the phallic mother, the marble, and roundworms point toward a castration fantasy, perhaps that term is inadequate, as the anxiety could be more appropriately described in relation to the brief loss of liminal space through the reintegration of the previously separate object.

13. Though one could also read into a reference of the enigma of who is the subject. The patient's mind as a blacked-out room, from which he authors his relations with the world, attempting to maintain an incognito presence in an inhospitable environment.

14. The prevalence of oral satisfaction and its persecutory inverse intertwines with the patient's arrival at and exit from analysis; a new flare up of an old dental infection preventing

the first session, and its reinfection [third time] and subsequent extraction were contemporaneous [nearly wrote *contemporous*] with the end of analysis.

15. As the interlocutor utters this word, there is an explosion of homophony and metonymic interconnections. The initial five (cinq) simultaneously says sank, but it also evokes son, sun, and back to the French soleil.

16. Lacan, J. (1993). *The Psychoses. The Seminar of Jacques Lacan, Book III, 1955–1956.* Trans. Russell Grigg. London: Routledge, pp. 112.

17. There where it was, must I become. In one of Lacan's readings, Freud's ethical maxim affirms a goal of reintegration and harmony, even reconciliation (*versöhnung*).

REFERENCES

Balint, M. (1936). The Final Goal of Psychoanalytic Treatment. In *Primary Love and Psychoanalytic Technique*. London: Karnac.

Bion, W. R. (1990). *A Memoir of the Future*. London: Karnac.

Bion, W. R. (2005). *Cogitations*. London: Karnac.

Casey, E. S. (2017). Jung and the postmodern condition. In: *C.G. Jung and the Humanities: Toward a Hermeneutics of Culture*, Ed. Karin Barnaby & Pellegrino D'Acierno. Princeton: Princeton University Press.

Corrao, F. (1994). Narrative Transformations. Ed. Ammaniti, M & Stern, M. In: *Psychoanalysis and Development: Representations and Narratives*. New York: NYU Press.

Eigen, M. (2011). *Contact with the Depths*. New York: Routledge.

Eigen, M. (2011). *Faith and Transformation. Eigen in Seoul, Vol. 2*. New York: Routledge.

Freud, S. (1900). Interpretation of Dreams. In: *Standard Edition of the Complete Psychological Works of Sigmund Freud*, Trans. & Ed. James Strachey. (Vol. 4). London: Hogarth Press.

Freud, S. (1912). The Dynamics of Transference. In: *Standard Edition of the Complete Psychological Works of Sigmund Freud*, Trans. & Ed. James Strachey. (Vol. 12). London: Hogarth Press.

Freud, S. (1937). Analysis Terminable and Interminable. In: *Standard edition of the Complete Psychological Works of Sigmund Freud*, Trans. & Ed. James Strachey. (Vol. 23). London: Hogarth Press.

Forrester, J. (1994). ". . . a perfect likeness of the past." In: *The Seductions of Psychoanalysis: Freud, Lacan & Derrida*. Cambridge University Press: Cambridge.

Forrester, J. (2016). *Thinking in Cases*. London: Polity.

Gleitman, L. & Papafragou, A. (2010). New Perspectives on Language and Thought. In: K. Holyoak and R. Morrison, eds. (in press), *Cambridge Handbook of Thinking and Reasoning*. 2nd ed. New York: Oxford University Press.

Guéguen, P. G. (1992). On Fantasy, Lacan, and Klein. *NFF* Spring/Fall, 6(1&2).

Green. (1999). *The Fabric of Affect in the Psychoanalytic Discourse*. New York: Routledge.

Hafner, D. (2017). An introduction to the transference unconscious. *Language and Psychoanalysis*. 6(1): 33-65.

Hafner, D. (2018). Building Castles Made of Pleasure. *Psychoanalytic Review*. 105(3).

Hill, P. H. F. (2001). *Using Lacanian Clinical Technique*. London: Press for the Habilitation of Psychoanalysis.

Jung, C. G. (1971). Introduction to Psychology and Literature. In: *CW 15: The Spirit in Man, Art, & Literature*. Princeton: Princeton University Press.

Jung, C. G. (1975). Psychology and Literature. In *The Sprit in Man, Art, and Literature*. R. F. C. Hull (Trans.). New Jersey: Princeton University Press.

Lacan, J. (1991). The Ego in Freud's Theory and in the Technique of Psychoanalysis. *The Seminar of Jacques Lacan, Book II, 1954–1955*. Trans. Sylvana Tomaselli. New York: Norton.

Lacan, J. (1993). *The Psychoses. The Seminar of Jacques Lacan, Book III, 1955–1956*. Trans. Russell Grigg. London: Routledge.

Lacan, J. (1980). Let There Be Light. *The Seminar of Jacques Lacan, Book XXVII, 1980*. Trans. David Hafner. [unpublished].

Laurent, E. (2010). La passe et les restes d'identification. *La Cause freudienne: Le désir du psychanalyste*. 76. décembre 2010, 44–49.

Matte-Blanco. (1980). *The Unconscious as Infinite Sets: An Essay in Bi-Logic*. New York: Routledge.

Matte-Blanco. (1988). *Thinking, Feeling, and Being: Clinical Reflections on the Fundamental Antinomy of Human Beings and World.* New York: Routledge.

Miller, G. (2011). Rendez-vous chez Lacan. [Motion Picture]. France: Editions Montparnasse.

Orozco, M. (2011). Apariciones espectrales de la sombra. Ed. Orozco, M. et al. In: *Configuraciones Psicoanalíticas Sobre Espectros y Fantasmas.* Mexico: Plaza y Valdes.

Sandler, J. (1972/1987). The Role of Affects in Psychoanalytic Theory. In: J. Sandler (ed.) *From Safety to Superego: Selected Papers of Joseph Sandler* (p. 285–297). New York: Guilford Press.

Index

About the Contributors

Hada Soria Escalante has a PhD in psychology from the Inter-Institutional Doctorate program in Psychology in Mexico (Padrón Nacional de Posgrados de Calidad, CONACYT). She is a clinical psychologist and psychoanalyst, member of Espacio Analítico Mexicano, an affiliate of Espace Analytique (France). She has coordinated and edited several editorial numbers on psychoanalysis, the last of which is the book *Narcisismo Infame: Reflexiones psicoanalíticas*, edited by Paidós, México. She is the founder and current director of the psychoanalytic journal *Décsir*, from Espacio Analítico Mexicano. She has been reviewer in international congress committees in psychology. She is a researcher belonging to the Sistema Nacional de Investigadores (Mexico), currently in charge of the "Laboratory on Psychoanalytic Theory and Clinic of the Subject and Culture," at the Universidad de Monterrey (Mexico), where she also teaches undergraduate and graduate courses, as well as providing clinical supervision. She has written in several books and journals of psychoanalysis. Her line of research focuses on the construction of subjectivity in contexts of death, loss, mourning, and violence; as well as the dialogue between psychoanalysis and other fields of research involving the subject.

Marilyn Charles is a psychologist and psychoanalyst at the Austen Riggs Center in Stockbridge, Massachusetts, affiliated with Harvard University, University of Monterrey (UDEM), Boston Graduate School of Psychoanalysis, and Chicago Center for Psychoanalysis. As co-chair of APCS and past president of APA Division 39 (Psychoanalysis), she promotes psychodynamic training, community involvement, outreach, and research. Interests include creativity, psychosis, resilience, and the intergenerational transmission of trauma. Books include: *Patterns: Building Blocks of Experience*, *Construct-*

ing Realities: Transformations through Myth and Metaphor, *Learning from Experience: A Guidebook for Clinicians*, *Working with Trauma: Lessons from Bion and Lacan*, and *Psychoanalysis and Literature: The Stories We Live*. Edited volumes: *Introduction to Contemporary Psychoanalysis*, *Fragments of Trauma and the Social Production of Suffering* (with Michael O'Loughlin), *The Importance of Play in Early Childhood Education: Psychoanalytic, Attachment, and Developmental Perspectives* (with Jill Bellinson), and *Women & Psychosis: Multidisciplinary Perspectives and Women and the Psychosocial Construction of Madness* (with Marie Brown).

Paola J. González Castro, PhD (2016); MA (2011) in human and social sciences with mention in psychoanalysis from the University of Paris 8, and BS (2007) in psychology, is a full-time professor at the University of Monterrey where she teaches courses on child development, clinical psychology, addiction, research methods and models, and clinical assessment. She has also supervised undergraduate and graduate internships and research programs as well as directed undergraduate theses. Her research focuses on vital events and its possible psychological impact on female young adults. She has presented at the World Congress on Menopause, World Association of Cultural Psychiatry, Journées de l'Ecole de la Cause Freudienne, Jornadas de la Nueva Escuela Lacaniana de la Ciudad de México, and published in reviews such as Acta Psiquiátrica y Psicológicade América Latina, Perinatología y Reproducción Humana and Climacteirc.

David Hafner is full professor and postgraduate coordinator of Psychoanalytic Psychotherapy at the University of Monterrey. He received his PhD (Summa Cum Laude) and MA from University of Paris 8 in 2016 and 2010, and his BA from the University of Chicago. A psychotherapist at Desarrollo en Movimiento A.C. drug rehabilitation center from 2015 to 2017, his current research focuses on differential diagnosis. He has published in *The Psychoanalytic Review*, *Language and Psychoanalysis*, *Critical Inquiry*, *Culture/Clinic: Applied Lacanian Psychoanalysis*, *(Re)-turn*, and *Revista Decsir*.

Carolina Koretzky is an Argentinian clinical psychologist and psychoanalyst, living in Paris, France. She is a member of L'École de la Cause Freudienne and the World Association of Psychoanalysis. She is a professor at the Department of Psychoanalysis (University of Paris 8) and at the Master in Lacanian Psychoanalytic Theory (National University of Córdoba). She is the author of the book *Le réveil: Une élucidation psychanalytique*, soon to be translated to Spanish by Grama editors, under the title *Sueños y despertares: Una elucidación psicoanalítica*.

Shalini Masih, PhD, is a psychoanalytic psychotherapist practicing in a low-fee clinic at Centre of Psychotherapy and Clinical Research, Ambedkar University Delhi. She is also involved in supervision and teaching of psychoanalytic psychotherapists training in MPhil Psychoanalytic Psychotherapy program of School of Human Studies, Ambedkar University Delhi. She has worked with traumatized children, adolescents, and with borderline and psychotic young adults. Her doctoral thesis was a Psychoanalytic Study on Beauty in Ugliness in Spirit Possession and Exorcism. She has a particular interest in states that do not render themselves easily to representability, body in psychoanalysis, cultural processes, and the kind of psychoanalysis feasible to a given cultural soil. She has presented papers in National and International Psychoanalytic Conferences and contributed her writing in volumes like *Psychoanalysis from the Indian Terroir: Emerging Themes in Culture, Family, and Childhood* and*Counterdreamers: Analysts Reading Themselves*.

Mario Orozco Guzmán is a research professor at the faculty of psychology of the Universidad Michoacana de San Nicolás de Hidalgo (UMSNH), México. He directed this faculty during two different periods: 2003–2007 and 2007–2011. He has a PhD in psychology from the Universidad de Valencia. Psychoanalyst, part of Espacio Analítico Mexicano. He coordinates and belongs to the academic group on Studies on Psychoanalytic Theory and Clinic, currently in the Consolidated level. He coordinates the master's program on Psychoanalytic Studies at the faculty of psychology of the UMSNH. His line of research is oriented toward studies on epistemology of the psychoanalytic clinic. He is currently working on the research project "Figuras de la alteridad. Exploración psicoanalítica de sus implicaciones clínicas y sociales." He has published in several journals and book collaborations.

Angélica Toro Cardona is a psychologist from the University of Antioquia (Colombia), research master in psychoanalysis at Paris VIII University, PhD candidate in psychopathology at Rennes 2 University. Clinical psychologist at the Psychiatric Sanitary Unit in the prison of Evreux (France), and teacher in psychopathology and criminology of the institute of continuing education AFAR. Having started her professional practice at the Medellín Women's Prison, she specialized in the prison clinic. Her research focuses on the feminine question and the passage to the act. She has participated in various scientific disclosure events in Europe and Latin America.

www.ingramcontent.com/pod-product-compliance
Ingram Content Group UK Ltd.
Pitfield, Milton Keynes, MK11 3LW, UK
UKHW041101150926
475561UK00002BA/41

9 781793 605818